In his 1946 work, "Who were the Shu
the silhouette of his philosophical me
call "paleontology." This breathtaking, r
by Jalalul Haq returns to the moral and political challenge of
Ambedkar's paleontological demand, cutting across epochs of
amnesia and textual subterfuge, as he tracks down the most
obdurate residues of India's elementary violence. Stunning in
its interpretive breadth and exegetical precision, Haq's work is
not simply a philosophical history of a civilisation's liturgical
opulence, which, as he painstakingly shows, has never been
wholly separate from the country's vicious lawlessness and
mean inequalities. His work is also a bearer of audacious
hope.—**Aishwary Kumar**, author of *Radical Equality: Ambedkar,
Gandhi, and the Risk of Democracy*

The Shudra is an original and inspired philosophical reading
of early India traditions. Though the details of its interpretations can be debated, the force of its central line of analysis is
always interesting, always stimulating. Its final pages take us to
the essential truth of early Indian history—the marginalisation
of Shudras and Ati-Shudras, who are omitted from the grand
narratives of Brahmans and Shramans, however philosophically
rich their ideas may have been.—**Uma Chakravarti**, historian

Haq speculates a philosophical trajectory in Indic culture of the
severance of materialist dialectics between finitude and infinity,
the concrete and the universal, history and truth, immanence
and transcendence. A severance which blocked the thinkability
of the human-subject, especially the Subject of Politics, which
laid the metaphysical groundwork for what Ambedkar forceful-
ly names 'the Brahminical counter-revolution'. Haq provokes us
to think that to annihilate the notion of caste is to annihilate its
metaphysical foundation, which he masterfully names as Superhumanism.—**Vaibhav Abnave**, Prabuddha Collective

Jalalul Haq taught philosophy at Aligarh Muslim University for over four decades. His books include *Nation and Nation-Worship in India* (1991), *Power, Sexuality and the Gods* (1994), and *Postmodernity, Paganism and Islam* (1999), *Hindu Tolerance Myth And Truth* (2014). He lives in Aligarh.

THE SHUDRA

A PHILOSOPHICAL NARRATIVE OF INDIAN SUPERHUMANISM

JALALUL HAQ

navayana

The Shudra: A Philosophical Narrative of Indian Superhumanism

© Jalalul Haq

ISBN 9788194865483

Published 6 December 2021

10 9 8 7 6 5 4 3 2

This is a revised edition of the title published in 1997 by Institute of Objective Studies, Delhi.

Navayana Publishing Pvt Ltd
155 2nd Floor
Shahpur Jat, New Delhi 110049
Phone: +91-11-26494795
navayana.org

Typeset at Inosoft Systems, Noida

Printed by Sanjiv Palliwal, New Delhi

Distributed in South Asia by HarperCollins India

Subscribe to updates at navayana.org/subscribe
Follow on facebook.com/Navayana

Contents

Preface

The civilisational history of India—in its variety and diversity, its ever-changing mosaics and patterns, its geographic and temporal extent—never ceases to fascinate even an amateur student of history, especially one who is interested in the history of ideas and institutions that prevailed in this blessed (or cursed, depending on your views) country. This includes the ritualism and physiolatry of the Vedas, the high philosophy of the Upanishads and Vedanta, the two grand epics, the magnificent *Gita*, even the Puranas with their fantastical stories and mythography, along with accomplishments in the fields of art, architecture, music, science, medicine—the list can be endless—all of which lend Indian culture not only a certain richness but also an unparalleled singularity.

Whether one takes a God's eye view or a worm's eye view, whether one looks at it as an outsider or an insider, every tiny element of this history presents itself to a scholar as a complex and versatile field of study that can take a lifetime to understand and analyse. Admittedly, Indian culture has had a long life and it has seen unity and diversity, continuity and change. It is also more or less true that the essentials of the Indian value system have survived many assaults, not to mention its own internal evolutionary processes. The present work is not a work of Indian historiography nor does it write a history of Indian philosophy. All it does—that too in a modest way—is philosophically gaze at the essential parts of this history, those parts that have endured the historical evolution of humanity.

What we then attempt here is a philosophical metanarrative of the conceptual category called 'man' in India. More precisely, we will examine why this latter is a largely missing category, shrunk and suppressed between the categories of superhuman and subhuman, both of which happened to be more identifiable and more real. Historical progress has not been a result of the dialectical unfolding of reason, as Hegel said, or of material forces of society and economy, as Marx believed. There is a dialectic, to be sure, but not of the thesis–antithesis–synthesis variety, and rather of the excesses and deficiencies that produce the idea of an ideal middle, that is real even in its elusiveness. The construction of India's historical anthropology requires a methodical understanding of the excesses of the doctrines of self-denial, which in turn generated an opposite excess of self-indulgence. Both these excessive tendencies were accompanied by their natural deficiencies. The march of Indian history, and of history itself, is controlled and directed by the progressive unfolding of this dialectic and the search for the ever elusive but by no means illusory middle.

The categories of superhuman and subhuman came to life right at the beginning of our story, in the death of Purusha, the creator–God. In the subsequent tradition, his successor, Brahma, was perpetually a subject of ridicule and rejection. In stature and importance, the latter was completely overshadowed by the mystical forces of the *brahman* (the absolute) and Shiva, or by the more anthropomorphic gods like Vishnu and his avatars. The question then arises if there is any intrinsic connection between the death of the personal and creative God (and the corresponding dominance of absolute and anthropomorphic gods) on the one hand and the disappearance of man on the other.

This book attempts to explore the different interpretations of Indian Spirit that emerge from the quasi-historical knowledge of the many literary traditions that surround us. These works on different facets of Indian history and philosophy have been written by both Indian and Western scholars. Among the non-scholarly authors, some wrote ethnic romances and others hard-hitting political treatises. The virtues of survival, syncretism, tolerance, diversity and unity are universally recognised and emphasised. It is also universally recognised that the core of Indian/Hindu culture consists in a veneration of saints, and not kings; the virtues of ascetic withdrawal, peace and non-violence are valued more than military conquest. But if spirituality is the quintessential character of Indian Spirit, and it is this very spirituality that gives birth to the bipolarity of superhuman and subhuman, the nature and content of this spirituality must then be closely examined.

To remind the readers and stress again, this book is not a historical or philosophical overview of what the Indian/ Hindu mind has thought through the centuries or what the accidents of history have made things to be. The focus is on the fact of the non-appearance of man and the philosophical and historical reasons generating this sorry fact. The author is professionally trained in the disciplines of philosophy and has had an amateur interest in history. Besides, the lack of access to original Sanskrit and Pali sources deprives the text of full authenticity. Not being an insider is also a deficiency which is sought to be partly compensated with a constant endeavour to treat the given subject matter with empathy and objectivity. Another point the author would like to highlight is the use of the term 'man', which is meant not as a gendered category, but rather a generic assignation for any subject of humanity.

Much has changed in the world and in India in the last two decades since this work was first published. What has come to be called political Hinduism, which was till recently a secondary but by no means a weak current, has now not only come to the fore but has more or less overwhelmed the political scene in the country. The forces of violence, aggression and suppression are emboldened and the weak are punished for their weakness. The ideals of moksha and nirvana are forgotten while the new (and Western) god of 'nation' is the sole object of worship. The priests of this new national god have successfully co-opted the hitherto deprived and oppressed sections to their cause by offering them illusions of power and prosperity. The subhuman now dreams of becoming superhuman, and in this pursuit everyone loses their essential humanity in which lies their true glory. It is a tale as old as this civilisation.

For bringing out this new edition of *The Shudra: A Philosophical Narrative of Indian Superhumanism*, all credit goes to S. Anand of Navayana, who not only retrieved the obscure first edition of 1997, but also took great pains in improving the original text which had many lacunae and defects.

Jalalul Haq
12 July 2021, Aligarh

From the *Mahabharata*

"Bhishma said, 'Listen, O king, to this story of the discourse between a vulture and a jackal as happened of old. Indeed, the occurrence took place in the forest of Naimisha. Once upon a time a Brahmana had, after great difficulties, obtained a son of large expansive eyes. The child died of infantile convulsions [at the crematorium] ... Summoned by their cries, a vulture came there and said these words: 'Go ye away and do not tarry, ye that have to cast but off one child. Kinsmen always go away leaving on this spot thousands of men and thousands of women brought here in course of time. Behold the whole universe is subject to weal and woe. Union and disunion may be seen in turns. They that have come to the crematorium bringing with them the dead bodies of kinsmen, and they that sit by those bodies (from affection) themselves disappear from the world in consequences of their own acts when the allotted periods of their lives run out. There is no need of your lingering in the crematorium, this horrible place, that is full of vultures and jackals...

At this time a jackal, black as a raven, issued out of his hole and addressed those departing kinsmen, saying, 'Surely, ye that are kinsmen of that deceased child have no affection. There the sun still shineth in the sky, ye fools! Indulge your feelings, without fear. Multifarious are the virtue of the hour.

This one may come back to life!

"The vulture said, ... 'Why do you mourn for that compound of five elements deserted by their presiding deities, no longer tenanted (by the soul), motionless, and stiff as a piece of wood? Why do you not grieve for your own selves?... ill-luck is born with the body. It is in consequence of that ill-luck that this boy has departed, plunging you into infinite grief. Wealth, kine, gold, precious gems, children, all have their root in penances. Penances again are the results of yoga... Cast off sorrow and cheerlessness, and abstain from parental affection. Leave the child on this exposed ground, and go ye away without delay'.

"The jackal said, 'Alas, terrible is the world of mortals! ... Ye cruel mights, how can you go away, casting off parental affection upon hearing the words of a sinful vulture of uncleansed soul? Happiness is followed by misery, and misery by happiness... It seems that ye are sure to obtain happiness. Ye that are afflicted with grief on account of the death of this child will surely have good luck today. Anticipating the probability of inconvenience and pain (if you remain here for the night) and fixing your hearts on your own comfort, whither would you, like persons of little intelligence, go, leaving this darling?'

"Bhishma continued, 'Even thus, O king, the kinsmen of the deceased child unable to decide upon what they shall do, were, for the accomplishment of his own purpose induced by that sinful jackal who uttered agreeable falsehoods, that denizens of the crematorium who wandered every night in quest of food, to stay in that place'.

"The vulture said, 'Dreadful is this spot, this wilderness, that resounds with the screech of owls and teems with spirits and Yakshas and Rakshasas. Terrible and awful, its aspect is like that of a mass of blue clouds. Casting off the dead body, finish the funeral rites. Indeed, throwing away the body, accomplish those rites before the sun sets...'

"The jackal said, 'Stay where you are! There is no fear even in this desert as long as the sun shines'.

"Bhishma continued, 'The vulture then addressed those men, saying that the sun had set. The jackal said that it was not so. Both the vulture and the jackal felt the pangs of hunger and thus addressed the kinsmen of the dead child. Both of them had girded up their loins for accomplishing their respective purposes. Exhausted with hunger and thirst, they thus disputed, having recourse to the scriptures. Moved (alternately) by these words, sweet as nectar, of those two creatures, viz., the bird and the beast, both of whom were endued with the wisdom of knowledge, the kinsmen at one time wished to go away and at another to stay there. At last, moved by grief and cheerlessness, they waited there, indulging in bitter lamentations. They did not know that the beast and the bird, skilled in accomplishing their own purposes, had only stupefied them (by their addresses).

Shanti Parva, CLIII (Ganguli 1883–1896, 335–40)

·

Prologue

Between the Vulture and the Jackal

To be a historian of India's cultural legacy is to stand before a magnificent castle in the darkness of night, eyes blinded both by the glitter of its dazzling domes and the gloom of its dark corners. But while the senses fail, reason still attempts to find an opening and, if possible, reach its inner sanctum where the actual drama unfolds.

The present work is, accordingly, an almost brave gesture to gaze at the philosophical interiority of cultural India and apprehend the spirit which has kept it alive through the vicissitudes of history.

Apart from the works of Max Weber and Albert Schweitzer, who wrote on Indian essentials from their respective Western and Christian points of view (and with attending merits), among Indians, Nehru and Savarkar (besides some other lesser luminaries) are known to have written similar broad metanarratives of Indian history. But while Savarkar's strong atheistic and anti-ritualist bias made him singularly out of tune with the nuances of Indian spirit, Nehru, though having similar outward sympathies, was able to identify himself with it in a more substantive sense. Through his articulate reaffirmation of the syncretic principle which he said underpinned the civilisational growth of India, he proved himself to be pre-eminently true to his personal and class ideas, about India's past glory and rich cultural heritage.

Although Nehru's Western upbringing gave him a class edge over many others, his writings lacked rigour, and, as he himself admitted, often relied on selective readings of books written by Europeans. In this respect at least, he differed from those who wrote with greater scholarly acumen but gave dispersed accounts of their subject. Starting with Rammohan Roy down to Aurobindo, Ambedkar and Radhakrishnan, there exists a line of authors and seers who touched on various facets of Indian thought and history with varying degrees of empathy and involvement.

The present work does not belong to either of the genres mentioned above; the author is intellectually ill-equipped for that task. Impressionistically, however, and taking into account the scholarly labours of seers and authors, both in the form of translations and commentaries, it does attempt a mini philosophical narrative with some presuppositions of the epistemic–ethical categories of rationality and humanism. We will claim that through their backward and forward movements, the hands of Indian history have weaved a pattern whose principal truth is that, like any other civilisation, India too had been subject to the pull and pressure of two opposite forces: of pity and withdrawal on the one hand, and power and indulgence on the other. As represented by ascetics and priests respectively, the twin forces, though seemingly opposite, formed an internal unity at both metaphysical and historical–existential levels. At the centre of this cultural thematic is the ascetic–priest himself embodying the tension of two contrary ideals of egoism and egolessness, culturalism and anti-culturalism, and abstinence and indulgence.

The Indian ascetic–priest is a real being, who, within the contradiction of his persona, represents both the mystique and the loss of Indian culture. As an eschatological–sociological category, he is the counter-image of the Shudra, who is the non-being, who is present but only in his absence; who is neither cultural nor anti-cultural, but acultural. As one who is deprived, dispossessed and depraved, he is not only the counter-concept of the Brahman, the ascetic–priest, but of humanity itself. He is subhuman, the demon, set against his superhuman and divine antagonist. And between this dichotomy of gods and demons, of Brahman and Shudra, there is a missing category, a fundamental omission—man.

The present work aims at telling the story of this disappearance of man from the Indian cultural scene which happened not at the end, not even in the middle, but right at the beginning. Underlying this narration is also the expectation of a kind of uncovering of the human. India now awaits the coming of an age of man, after having had successive eras of gods, god-men, messiahs and avatars, with their antonymic counterparts, the Shudras, the Untouchables, the women and so on.

To write a historical narrative, for one thing, is to swim against the philosophical currents of our times. Earlier, when, for example, Nehru was writing his *Discovery of India,* Indian historiography was still under the influence of German historical philosophy in which the idea of Spirit (Geist) occupied a central place. The spirit of a nation's history was precisely what was distinct about it and enlivened it as a cultural organism, unifying the different and divergent tendencies of its historical growth. Nehru also, therefore, frequently refers to an Indian spirit which was its exclusive possession and which gave India its geo-temporal unity, as a background to its subcultural plurality, which survived while the body itself underwent immense changes. Now, as one knows, this kind of spiritualisation of history is at a discount these days, one reason for this being its close association with the Nazi idea and its final nemesis in the Second World War. In the present post-modern approach, not only spirit but history itself is made to be a dubious concept. One hears not too infrequently people talking of the end of history and quite often of the end of man himself. (Interestingly, and ironically, even these ideas are in the process of being abandoned in favour of a hyper-provincialised, essentialised temporality.)

But as the ideas of unity and continuity of history are disparaged and replaced by those of fragmentation and rupture, one cannot help seeing in this another kind of extremism which is no less irrational and harmful than the previous approach. The spiritualist excess has reactively given birth to an opposite excess and one must steer clear of both to keep on the right track. Spirit of course is not empirically given nor can one justify its presence through rational considerations. But to conclude from this that there is absolutely no continuity and no organising principle as such in the historical experience of a people is to say too much and to fall into a reverse form of excess. Geo-linguistic factors while being accidental and not essential to a human group, are yet forces that require rational appreciation and explanation. Humanity appears in diverse forms, and if there is any sense in talking of man or the human, group histories must be considered as possessing unities, even though, again, these unities may be seen as embedded within the pluralities they subsume. Unity and plurality, continuity and rupture both are equally important as they are contingent upon each other. A sound methodology of history-writing, accordingly, must respect them in equal measure.

A nation's cultural history is often comprised of different sub-cultural ones, and conversely, one can see that different national histories are themselves parts of a larger human history. National histories while being created and enriched by the histories of their sub-national groups, in turn, create and enrich a human history, which is also by no means annulled by the different fragments that constitute it. While one can discount the presence of any telic or transcendental force spiritually ordering the course of events, one should not entirely rule out the possibility of some principle operating in a manner which lends the different histories, and history as such, a functional unity *amidst* (not over and above) their diversity and discontinuity.

In applying the above stated general principle to Indian history, it can fairly be said that any attempted narrative of it must keep both its external unity and internal plurality in the background and foreground respectively. Nehru was indeed not wrong when he spoke of an Indian unity behind its diversity, but his was an incomplete thesis: he failed to mention the manifest diversity in that unity. Besides, he also erred in spiritualising the unity-idea, identifying it further with a priestly praxis of syncretism and synthesis. His unitarian bias led him to underemphasise the inherent diversities of India and India's own position as one of the diverse elements embedded into human unity. In his political vision, all he could see was an ambiguously defined Asian unity at the politico-economic level. In Nehru's narrative, man as such is not missing but he is too much of an Indian, he is too historical and yet too ghostly: he is hard to come by in the vast Indian collectivity. Indian Spirit takes concrete shape only in rare individuals, for example in the Brahmans of ancient times, in Ashoka and Akbar, and probably also in Nehru himself, just as the German spirit was incarnated in Hitler.

In thus historicising Spirit (in identifying Spirit with history), Nehru, in a way, was reacting against a converse tendency among other authors of his times who had an ahistorical view of this Spirit. Spirit as God, as *brahman*,[1] was not only beyond history but was essentially a counter-principle of the historical view. For this view, if at all there was a history, including Indian history, it was at the level of maya or unreality. True, the *brahman* sometimes incarnated in human individuals, became historical, but finally, this too was an appearance, a delimitation imposed by the *brahman* upon itself. History was historically absent in India and whatever historiography was there was all in the form of de-historicised mythography. Savarkar, like Nehru, had a hypostatised view of history as deified time—Mahakal. But he too was an atheist and his temporal divinity was more secular than religious.

It would seem then that India's classicism and its modernity are ideologically antithetical configurations where either a de-historicised spirituality or a despiritualised history reigns. Between Buddha and Shankara on the one hand, and Nehru and Savarkar on the other, there is hardly anything in common except their respective excesses and one-dimensionality. Now, if one looks for the reason why such binaries of thinking have emerged, an explanatory hypothesis is a lack, on the part of both the parties, of a genuine humanistic outlook. As mentioned, man is not altogether absent in the secular discourse of Indian modernity and even Buddha's and Shankara's philosophies move around the notions of atman or purusha (man). But, atman at the level of humanity is a falsehood and deception, while in reality it is either nothingness or the *brahman*—this latter being itself a negative presence, characterless and contentless. Nehru and Savarkar, on the other hand, though self-professed humanists were yet, as historicists, anti-humanists. For them, history had absolute sovereignty over man; history indeed defined the nature of man. Man was a historical animal and that was that.

These two contrary ideas, which have so far been clashing and cancelling each other out, may be made to mutually correct and complete each other. To say, for example, that man is a historical animal is to radically distinguish him from the other animals and this may be seen to have psycho-spiritual implications. If other animals have no history at all, and if only man has it, then there must be in the human constitution something which is altogether lacking in the animal. This obviously is nothing other than what the philosophers have traditionally called man's 'rational soul'. Rationality, in being the constitutive principle of man's historicity, cannot be accounted for purely in bio-chemical terms. A transcendental principle is required to explain its presence. Its transcendental dimension gives this principle an empirically non-given character and the only possibility of its being comprehended remains through the extra-empirical device that is reason itself. Man's traditional status as a rational animal is reified, though there still remains a problem regarding the exact nature of this rationality.

Man's historicity is his spiritual collectivity—he lives in a society. This does not simply mean living or acting together as animals do. Man's social-cultural life is more a matter of believing than behaving, the latter being more often conditioned by the former. Among themselves, humans sometimes interact in the manner of animals, as far as the outward form of actions is concerned. But as one knows, these physiological or biological actions in their interiority are qualitatively much different. Parenting, for example, is a characteristic common among humans and animals, but to be a human parent is decidedly something more than simply being a biological parent of one's progeny. Different emotional and ethical factors are involved in as natural an activity as parenting. Being a parent to a child is different from being the same to a cub or a duckling. Human relationships are always 'value-loaded' in contrast to the 'value-free' character of purely biological relationships obtained among animals.

The complexity of human social relationships and its attendant dimension of value, which is an excess over its purely biological character, has a direct bearing on the various norms, taboos and traditions it births. These in turn become the symbolic media through which man thinks, believes and behaves. Indeed, they constitute the interiority of social life, and if man is social then the value-complexes are the real environment in which he breathes spiritually, so to speak. History, in being a human history, at the denominationalised level is the name of the collective sharing of these value-complexes. Man *values* a certain idea or ideal or institution or even a person or a god, which in turn become his guide in personal–interpersonal life. But values are never personal, as they have an inherent tendency towards universalisability. Whenever and wherever a conflict of values occurs, it is not because of their being too personal but because the person entertaining a particular value-system feels forced to expect others to follow. It is this fundamental and compulsive shareability of the experience of values and norms which generates among a people a sense of community and a communal history, and finally constitutes the historicity of man.

Two more things can be said about values here. Firstly, though, there is, for man, a kind of compulsion in regard to values such that he cannot be 'value-free', there also emerges an absolute possibility of freedom from within this situation of compulsion. For although man must have some values, there is still the option for him to choose between this or that set of values. Value does not merely mean the 'ought', as it also includes the 'ought-not' in its definition; both the good and bad, right and wrong, beautiful and ugly, are comprehended in the sense carried by the word 'value'. Values also admit diversification and gradation, universalisation and denominationalisation, personalisation and impersonalisation. Thus man is free to choose values commensurate to his nature or incommensurate to it; he can give precedence to the universal values over his geo-temporally denominationalised values or vice versa; and he also has the choice to adhere to his values as being his own, i.e. as having internalised them or as a matter of authoritatively dictated precepts. The freedom to make one's value-choices and the tuning of one's existential responses to them is an absolute condition of human living. Freedom is an existential condition and as such it is by itself an absolute value, which man does not have the power to renounce completely though he does often try to forget it, cover it or suppress it.

The second, equally important, thing about values is that they must be rational. Once one is presented with a choice between different value-complexes, one can critically compare them on their respective merits. Man indeed evaluates a possible mode of thinking or behaving and in this process invests value to it. Here again the contrast is presented by animals, who do not judge or prejudge the prospective courses of action but are entirely guided by their different biological instincts. Man's rational spirituality is his transcendence, his ability to distance himself from what presents itself as an objective idea. His acquiescence to this idea then signifies his value preference. Values are therefore nothing but rationally preferred objectivities, which is again not a matter of choice for man. Like his being free, man is also rational and this part of his nature he *cannot* wish away with. Man cannot become irrational; even his decision to be so has already gone above the domain of irrationality. It is always a rational choice for man to be irrational, that is, to suppress, cover up and forget one's rationality.

Man's rationality does not refer only to his ability to form concepts or formulate theories and arguments. As an evaluative faculty, it also operates in the conative and aesthetic domains, where it seeks to realise the values of the good and the beautiful respectively, in a dynamic and creative manner. Man cognitively comprehends his universe, his social environment and his own individual self. But he also tries to find suitable ways to live harmoniously within this social and natural environment and, wherever possible, enjoy the pleasurable aspects of his life. The cognitive, ethical and aesthetic faculties together form his personality, which, in its dynamic external manifestation, brings about his cultural universe. Thus, over and above his status as a socio-historical animal, man is a cultural being. Culture signifies his spirituality, which makes him transcendentally creative, as against animals, who are absolutely 'unimaginative' and non-innovative in their lives.

It is only through spirituality that man has come to have philosophy, science, technology, art, and above all, language. The resultant culture, moreover, is not a static but a dynamic reality. And it is this reality, which, in its geo-temporal delimitation, is characterised as the native or the national-historical culture. Spirituality cannot be divorced from culture, nor can cultural histories come into existence without spirituality. Spirit manifests itself through culture and through the culturally conscious and creative man for its own self-authentication. Therefore, both spiritualists like Buddha and Shankara on the one hand, and historicists like Nehru and Savarkar on the other, committed the fallacy of univocity, by not recognising the integral nature of man's concrete life as being both spiritually historical and historically spiritual.

A concrete, complete man was never allowed to exist in India's philosophical-cultural history. While the heterodox Buddha and the orthodox Shankara disbelieved the human self, Samkhya philosophy, which fell somewhere in between these two positions, held purusha (man) to be a weak and mutilated form. For Samkhya, man was the knower and enjoyer but entirely non-active, with all activity and power belonging to the opposite principle of prakriti or nature. The *Bhagavad Gita* too begins with an actionistic (karma marga) promise but then relapses into the same Brahmanistic quietism against what it seeks to revolt. The same applies to the subsequent Bhakti sects which made self-surrender to a man-God or to a teacher (guru) or to the *brahman* the cardinal idea of their doctrine. For all of these, the ego was a nullity, a falsehood or a maya, born of false consciousness, deserving of obliteration. So, the possibility of a psychology or sociology or, for that matter, a science of man was foreclosed. The only legitimate science was eschatology—the science of the end or death of man's soul, of man himself.

This eschatological theme of man's death is internally bound up with the idea of the death of God: a permanent motif in India's religious-philosophical history. The death of man is indeed contingent on the death of God, since God is nothing but the whole, of which man is a micro-image or expression. The attributes of creativity, knowledge, nobility and beauty that are possessed by man's soul are also possessed by God, though without the former's finitude. This homology between man and God was given full recognition by Indian seers who had the same word, purusha, for both man and God. In the *Rig Veda*, Purusha is a creator-God and he is also present and held in similar esteem in later Vedantic literature, though with different names like Prajapati and Brahma. He is recognised even in the supposedly atheistic sects such as Jainism, Buddhism or Samkhya. Yet, everywhere his presence is an anathema, a superfluity, that is quickly dispensed with. The Vedas themselves make a decisive start in this direction by speaking of his being sacrificed by the gods and the priests. In the Upanishads, a different strategy is adopted: he is rendered impotent, deprived of creative power. Thus emerges the *brahman* as a neutered purusha, an entity that does not create but only *thinks* the world. Neither does it have the power to intervene in worldly affairs. The power principle is transferred to Indra (besides other gods and goddesses), and in later theology to Shiva or Vishnu (and his different incarnations). In Samkhya, prakriti (nature) is the real repository of power (shakti) as personified in different mother goddesses. Brahma is constantly an object of ridicule and denigration. In the Vedas, he is eclipsed by Indra, and the Puranas make him surrender to Shiva. In Shramanic literature, he is made to wash the feet of a Buddha or a Jina (enlightened beings).

Notice that the existence of a creator-God is generally not denied; he is however disparaged or disregarded or killed straight away, and his worship universally forbidden. To be sure, God is not an ordinary object to be used, disused or abused in such manner; nor is he someone sitting on a throne in the skies who can be ignored. Philosophically, God can be defined as the principle of presence, of consciousness and of activity and enjoyment. In the world, there are trees, plants, a varied mix of species, and also a community of selves, conscious and creative, always in the pursuit of the ideals of truth, good and beauty. All this needs to be philosophically accounted for; a rationally universalised unitary presence is required, which combines in it characteristics of knowledge, creativity, love and goodness and beauty. God or Purusha or Allah is only a name given to this universal unitary presence and as such cannot be denied, seeing as how all these categories are present and present beyond doubt.

Philosophically speaking there can be no denial of God as such, if God is conceived of in its proper character, as being a principle of existence, consciousness, creative activity and beauty. Such a unitary principle of God is not altogether dispensed with, even in the atheological and pagan schemes. Here, instead of rationally realising the unity of this principle, his different aspects are given a sort of autonomy and identity of their own. In the Vedas, for example, the Purusha still creates, but at the expense of his own life; Indra is powerful; but he is not good (he is destructive, manipulative and immoral). The good belongs to Varuna, who in turn is weak before Indra. So on and so forth. In the Upanishads and the Vedanta, the need of rational unification is recognised but rationality is itself deprived of its creative, positive aspects. God is thus existence (sat), consciousness (chit) and enjoyment (ananda) but he is not creatively active. He contemplates and enjoys but has no will to create or act in love or anger. This same idea of an actionless but conscious and blissful divinity is present in all the other systems whether orthodox Vedic or heterodox non-Vedic. Mahavira and Buddha have all the characteristics of a god, except of creatorship, thus becoming not much different from Sachchidananda of Vedanta. One can even say that if Shankara was a quasi-Buddhist in his metaphysics and eschatology, then the Buddha himself was proto-Vedantist in the same respect.

In fact, the Brahmanic contentless, characterless negative divinity and Shramanic nihilism were two seemingly opposite negative formulations that also constituted an identity at one end of the religious-ideological spectrum whose opposite was a promiscuous theological pluralism. In the absence of a positive God, the negative was occupied by a non-God or no-God and, at the same time, a whole multiplicity of gods and goddesses. Thus, neither in the 'monistic' Vedanta nor in the atheistic Jainism and Buddhism are these multiple divinities denied. The more emphatic the denial of God, the greater is the need and number of gods. There may have been thirty-three gods in the Vedas but their number swelled to at least thirty-three thousand by the time of later Jainism and Buddhism. These gods, though sometimes benign and indulgent in the affairs of the world, were mostly demons and demonesses who prowled around seeking human victims for their wrath and terror.

But who were these gods and goddesses, demons and demonesses, and wherefrom had they come? Most, as can easily be guessed, were forces either of nature (the earth, the sun, the diseases) or of human nature (knowledge, greed, sexuality, power) which were invested with absolute value, and deified. Behind the worship of these powers, behind the act of deification, a force of human psyche and a social economy of power was operative. Psychologically, man needs a god (any god) to love and fear. In his weaker moments, it satisfies him easily to find this god in the concrete forces of nature or in the hypostatisation of his physical desires and emotional demands. This weakness of common human psyche intersects with the forces of greed and the quest for domination which is the possession of a few. The will to self-disempowerment or 'will to pity' (karuna) meets the 'will to power' (shakti) and through this intermingling of two forces the idea of the pagan worship of gods and demons emerges. These serve as the main tools in the hands of priests to satisfy their urge to dominate the common folk; the latter also get a semblance of satisfaction in their very act of servitude and slavery. The commoners surrender their humanity, not before the gods (for they do not exist) but before the superhuman ambitions of a few individuals—priests.

A priest is by definition a man of high ambitions. In practising the salesmanship of gods and goddesses, he aspires for his own deification. Aided by the gullibility of the 'people', he develops an eschatological philosophy which justifies in his own eyes the avarice of his ambition and hubris. The idea is that through the practice of ascetic renunciation and self-mortification (tapas), man can acquire superhuman powers of spiritual knowledge and physical strength, raising his status to divinity and securing him thereby a place in the heavens. Indra leading his Aryan army to conquer the native Indian kings became a god (a devarishi) through this tapas, as the Upanishadic and later Brahmanic books say. His example was later emulated by so many of the Kshatriya princes, even as most of them fell by the wayside. While a Mahavira or a Siddhartha Gautama could become all-knowing, all-powerful divine entities, Krishna and Rama came close to nearly perfecting the ideal of a hero-god; many less accomplished figures like Vishwamitra or Janaka could only achieve the position of saint-king (rajarishi). In Buddhism, and Jainism especially, not only princes, but ordinary men and women (even animals and birds) could join the august company of gods by their acts of renunciation and sacrifice. They became divine spirits by rising above their human discrepancies, which, in turn, was possible only by suppressing the human urges of love and creation and of positive involvement with world, society and one's own self in general. Man must dispossess himself of his humanity in order to become a god. Only in the death of God and man could gods take birth.

In the sacrifice of Purusha at the hands of gods and priests, both God and man were killed. Hence, the ceremony took the form of actual human sacrifice, the purusha-medha, to commemorate and symbolise the sacrifice of God. Other sacrifices, like the horse-sacrifice (ashwa-medha), were only imitative replacements or imperfect approximations of this its ultimate form. Gods and priests sacrificed man as a representative of God and they sacrificed God as the representative of man; only through this twin death could they live. In Christianity also, incidentally, 'Christ', the god, is born as man and killed on the cross as God's own self-sacrifice; this ceremony too is conducted by the priest during the Eucharist. When God was thus killed, and man along with him, caste was born. With the death of man, the 'caste-man' is born, who is not man at all. The caste-man is either higher, superior or lower, inferior. There are some who are superhumans: who are gods or priests or Brahmans. And there are those who are subhumans, the commoners, the Visha, the Shudra. The Brahman is superhuman because he has raised his existence beyond the human level and the Shudra is subhuman because he is by birth unfit to come to the level of humanity.

The 'caste-man' (the Brahman, the Shudra) is not a sociological but an eschatological-existential category: the sociological only follows and is contingent on the latter. The soul, although non-existent (in the case of Buddhism and Brahmanism), takes birth with specific potentials and self-nature (swa-bhava), which it strives to realise while in the world and attached to a body. The ones with higher self-nature are born in nobler families and are supposed to pursue nobler goals. Correspondingly, the souls with lower potential, born in lower caste families, must pursue the lower occupations. The highest and noblest goal in life is the realisation of *brahman*, while the lowest and the meanest is manual and menial work. The former is a condition of knowledge, enlightenment, power, privilege, enjoyment and emancipation, and the latter is a state of ignorance, disempowerment, deprivation, misery and bondage. The Shudra must realise the potential of his soul by doing the appropriate karma (swa-dharma) and the Brahman also must do the works commensurate to his noble status. Any confusion in this regard, any mixing up of occupations is perilous for society and for the self.

As an ideal type, a Brahman is a free man, having attained the state of liberation and self-realisation. From the point of his initiation into the ascetic path up to his final realisation of the *brahman* or Buddhahood, he undertakes a long journey and overcomes many obstacles of temptations and seductions, defeats many ghosts and demons and conquers his bodily demands of passion and lust. He is now a man of prajna (Buddhism) or sthit-prajna (*Gita*)—the one who has acquired a stable intellect which does not waver by any intrusion of sceptical thoughts or gets distracted by any appearance of lustful object. He is free from desires, demands, and distractions. He is neither happy nor sorrowful, neither good nor bad, neither loving nor hateful, neither angry nor pleased. He has acquired the *brahman's* own character of being not this, not this (neti neti); he has become a *brahman*, a Buddha, a nothing.

A *brahman*, a Buddha is nothing and yet everything and yet nothing. Nothing is everything and everything is nothing (Brahmanism is Buddhism and Buddhism is Brahmanism).

As one who is completely detached from his human self, he has ceased to exist. He has let the man in himself die; he has become unhuman or subhuman. For, the superhuman is also subhuman. The superhuman is not a complete man, not a historical man; he is not a man at all (he is a god or a man-god, or a god-man). He is conscious but conscious of nothing, he is blissful but enjoys nothing and he acts but acts for nothing. He is stable; he does not move, does not think, does not love (or hate). He is liberated and yet he is in bondage. His soul is the prison of his body. His soul is indeed the tomb of his own humanity. He has attained the state of samadhi; he has died.

But while the *brahman* oscillates between the opposite but identical conditions of superhumanism and subhumanity, the Shudra is subhuman all the way. The Shudra also has a mind but he does not think; he has a will to act but he never acts. From purusha he has become prakriti, nature, which does not act but is always acted upon, manipulated, manhandled, mistreated and exploited. He has surrendered himself to his fate, to his gods. He submits to the very same gods who oppress him, who bring to him miseries and sorrow. The Shudra worships gods faithfully, in the hope that they will be pleased with him; he does not realise that gods cannot be gods unless there are Shudras to worship and propitiate them. Gods, as supra-human beings, survive and thrive as the counter-concept of the subhumanity of the Shudra. They live on the Shudra's blood; they survive on human flesh. The god, the *brahman* and the Buddha live together with the Shudra. They are not enemies but intimate friends. The Shudra is supposed to be afraid of gods, but, in fact, they are afraid of their own humanity. They have killed the man in themselves; they have made themselves subhuman.

But there is also the sociological dimension to this Brahman–Shudra dialectic. The *brahman*, in a philosophical sense, is a category of knowledge, and knowledge always entails power. If not as yet a god, he is at the threshold of becoming one. In his spiritual journey, he has reached the stage where he enjoys the company of gods, and in this same journey he subjugates minor deities, demons, spirits, goblins and other such occult forces. This proximity to gods is a privilege with a lot of implications in terms of power and social status. Power comes to the would-be ascetic naturally; he is naturally inhered to become a priest. The axiology of ascetic disempowerment automatically gives birth to the economy of priestly power. Moreover, since the ascetic–priest is disinterested, he can play the game of power more indulgently and without inviting any blemish or risk to his soul's purity. As a motiveless and all-wise person, his advice is binding on kings, on the nobility and on the people at large.

But the logic of power works at two ends. The concentration of power in the hands of the few, directly implies the proportionate disempowerment of the many. The masses must be deprived of any aspiration of a share in power if the privileges of the elite have to be preserved. And the best way to get this task done is to popularise the idea of the worthlessness of power itself. The priest, having brought himself up in an environment of renunciation, understands very well the internal psychological dynamics of this ascetic theory. The Shudras are enticed into the net of slavery by the sweet talk of heavenly bliss and godhood. The clever fox lays a trap, the sheep allow themselves to be led into it.

The trap is that of renunciation and monkhood. The priest presents himself as an ascetic, which he is, and the ascetic thus becomes a priest. The two, the priest and the ascetic, become interchangeable. *Brahman* and Buddha, the jackal and the vulture are the same, as Bhishma, the grand old man of *Mahabharata* said. They both want to feed on man's corpse.

Asceticism as the principle of withdrawal, and priesthood as the practice of indulgence, are the extremities of social-personal behaviour and belief. But quite naturally, these tendencies come to operate on collective and cultural levels too. The ascetic is not simply a particular man deserving of pity (karuna) but, more generally, the embodiment of society's anti-progress, anti-science and anti-art ideology. Similarly, the priest is not a particular person prone to the weaknesses of greed and hubris, he represents the predominance, in a given society, of the forces of excessive pursuit of power and promiscuity. These two diverse tendencies, of pity and withdrawal on the one hand and of power and indulgence on the other, though seemingly acting against each other, are complementary. An excess always generates an opposite excess. But more importantly, no society can survive on the single diet of just pity or just power alone. Collective survival and equilibrium require both; and the two appear on the scene to oppose and at the same time sustain each other. Pity and power, Buddha and *brahman*, together constitute the statics and dynamics of culture. The ascetic is anti-culture and the priest is the civiliser. The latter promotes secular knowledge (for and of his own class), patronises art, architecture and also a bit of literature and science. The Brahman is the epitome of culture, the ascetic, the very opposite of it. But both cohabit as enemies and friends.

The Brahman is the worshipper of power (shakti) which
resides in the female consorts of different male divinities.
The shaktis, in truth, make the gods what they are. They
are even said to precede the gods in terms of the antiquity
of their worship. The pre-Vedic people are said to have had
a pagan religious culture with mother goddesses and priests
as its indispensable institutional accessories. There is some
ambiguity about the religious–racial affinities of the ancient
clans of rishi–priests, but it is inconceivable that no priests
existed before the Aryans arrived on the scene. Priesthood
is part of the religious package in which gods or goddesses
are propitiated through sacrifices, as happened to be the case
in India in those times. Aryans came as a band of invaders
and were for that matter mainly Kshatriya. They were
recognised as such by the native religious leaders who were
to be later known as Brahmans. Being the protagonists of
their native religion, they fought against the aliens, though,
for a while, not quite successfully. Brahmanic power was set
against Kshatriya power, and in the long run the former were
victorious as kings came under the tutelage of their Brahman
chaplains. The relevant point here is that in the Brahmanic
victory over Kshatriyas, it was the power of occultism,
coupled with secular civic knowledge, that won, rather than
the power of the sword. Brahmans presided over big sacrificial
ceremonies (where all kinds of vices like gambling, drinking
and sex were habitual); they instituted laws and gave advice
to kings on matters of state. In this way they fulfilled the
needs of society, and corrected the imbalance that the ascetics
created with their doctrine of renunciation. The priest, as a
representative of shakti, reactively complemented the forces
of karuna, represented by the ascetic, in their very negation

of it. Not rejecting asceticism as such but still insisting that withdrawal should be postponed to a later stage of life, they acted as a positive force in saving society from disorder and annihilation, which was the logical outcome of a full adherence to the ascetic theory.

But if a full realisation of the ascetic ideal by the collective meant the death of collectivity itself, the priestly practice of the naked pursuit of power was no less perilous. A community given to the excessive pursuit of physical pleasure and unrestrained power soon sets the ground for its nemesis within its own structure. Different centres of power emerge within its body politic to clash with each other and cause its final ruin. If India was repeatedly invaded and subjugated, the priests were as much responsible for it as the ascetics. The ascetics and the priests, the ascetic–priests, pulled society in opposite directions, and even if society attained a semblance of coherence in this tension, the day of doom was never far away. By acting and reacting against each other, the ascetic and the priest achieve a negative combination of pity and power, which allowed culture to survive but without the harmony and health of a positive spiritual life. This spiritual positivity can only be realised through a positive affirmation of the self and God, which is resisted by the ascetic's monasticism on the one hand and by the priest's hubris and lust on the other. The gods conspire against God, who, as an integrated principle of love, justice and beauty could ensure such a life of harmonious positivity. They kill Purusha, the God, and thereby kill purusha, the spiritual–cultural man.

*

Although in a philosophical sense both the Brahman and the Shudra are the human victims of divine conspiracy, and for that reason, a redemptive theology must take both of them to be its rightful audience, it is nevertheless not likely that the entrenched class-psychology of the Brahman would allow him to hear the voice of reason, especially as it involves him losing the privileges of power. The Shudras, on the other hand, are numerous and through their positive struggle, they stand to lose nothing except their chains. They have waged this struggle before without success, for the gods, against whom they pretended to fight, still held them spellbound or otherwise defeated them through treachery or stratagems. In an old story it is said that once when the war between the gods (Aryan Kshatriyas with their native Brahman patrons) and demons (Shudras) was still raging, the leader of the latter, who happened also to be an ascetic, withdrew and went up to the mountains in his occult pursuits. This considerably weakened the demons and gave Indra, the leader of the gods, an opportunity to mount a decisive assault. But the demons made the departed rishi's wife their leader, fought bravely, and thanks to their numerical strength, were on the brink of victory. Indra, thus frustrated in his designs, begged Vishnu for help, who assumed a disguise and killed the lady in command, ensuring the defeat of the anti-god party. The Shudra were defeated in spite of their strong position because of the treachery of the gods and also because of the betrayal by their own ascetic leader.

Even in our times, there is some talk of Shudras regaining their position vis-à-vis their Brahman oppressors. But towards this end the same old strategies, of either withdrawing ascetically from the world or playing the game of power more indulgently, and relentlessly, are adopted. These prescriptions, however, are bound to fail now as they have failed before. The two forces of pity and power, as already said, are enemies and yet friends. One doesn't exist without the other. The ascetic is not an enemy but an ally of the priest—he is himself a priest in disguise. Vishnu came in the guise of Buddha to deceive the Kshatriyas (when they rose in revolt against Brahman domination) by showing them the path of renunciation and the world's worthlessness. The thrall of such machinations ensnares the Shudras and no one knows what new trick Vishnu has up his sleeve. In the present work, in any case, there is no intention to add voice to the rhetoric of Shudra revival. The endeavour here, is to make a case for the uncovering of a spiritually positive life in Indian humanity. To seek emancipation through sheer political activism or through renunciation is to fall into the same Vishnuite trap in which man's spirituality is torn apart by the two contrary forces of pity and power, as represented by the ascetic and the priest, the vulture and the jackal.

1

Death of Purusha

Our immediate concern is the source of the spiritual–ascetic culture elaborated earlier, and the speculation of its most original form(s). There is now a fair degree of unanimity among scholars that the antecedents of India's spiritual culture are very old, older than what is known as the Vedic age. Possibly because Vedic culture proper was nurtured by Brahman priests opposed to the ideology of Shramanism, original scriptures do not mention the latter. However, the few stray references that do occur are suggestive and are further illumined by descriptions in allied texts like the Brahmanas and Upanishads. Scholars have also established a connection between these references and some of the materials found in Indus Valley excavations. The picture of the Vedic times gleaned from these studies reveals the prevalence of a cult of wandering ascetics, called munis, who distinguished themselves from the common populace: the munis had a peculiar style of living even if they shared beliefs with common folk. The *Rig Veda* describes these men calling them 'conquering Maruts':[1]

Who are these radiant men in serried rank, Rudra's young heroes borne by noble steeds? / Verily, no one knoweth whence they sprang: they, and they only, know each other's birth. / They strew each other with their blasts, these Hawks, they strove together, roaring like the wind (Griffith 1896; VII, 56).

In Mandala X, these munis are referred to as Kesin, literally the long-haired:

He with the long loose locks supports Agni, and moisture, heaven, and earth: He is all sky to look upon: he with long hair is called this light./ The Munis, girdled with the wind, wear garments soiled of yellow hue. They, following the wind's swift course go where the Gods have gone before. / Transported with our Munihood we have pressed on into the winds: You therefore, mortal men, behold our natural bodies and more. / The Muni, made associate in the holy work of every God. Looking upon all varied forms flies through the region of the air. / The steed of Vata, Vayu's friend, the Muni, by the Gods impelled, In both the oceans hath his home, in eastern and in western sea (Griffith 1896; X, 136).

While these verses confirm the presence of a sect of munis, who were predecessors to the later Parivrajaka phenomenon, they eschew any inferences about their specific views, their problems of life and world. Much of the philosophy and cultic ideas that are associated with these sects are later constructions, which, at the present stage of our discussion, we may ignore. If at all there is a continuity of tradition from the Vedic muni sects to its later manifestations, it has not found sufficient expression in literature. Although munis have been mentioned in the Upanishads, representing vigorous mysticism and asceticism, theirs was a mysticism which was of a decidedly different nature and order compared to what followed.

The Vedic figure of Rishabh, the supposed founder of this ascetic ideology, is often brought up in this regard. Jainas recognise him as their first tirthankara or Jina. But again, most of the stories about him are later Jaina creations which, though similar to Puranic accounts, are not mentioned anywhere in earlier authoritative texts. Besides, the other characteristics and features that attend to the Rishabh idea in the *Rig Veda* do not exactly fit with his image as an old-king-turned-saint as the Jainas claim. Though a kind of literary interruption makes the relationship between the older Vedic sect of munis and the later Shramanic movement tenuous, there is another mystical current which claims an equal antiquity for itself. In its original form this movement seemed opposed to Vedic Brahmanism, but it later became a part of it, and was even elevated to the position of orthodoxy itself. This is the movement centred around the cultic figure of Shiva, who, though absent by that particular moniker in the *Rig Veda*, is justifiably recognised as a development of the Vedic 'Rudra'. That Shiva is an ascetic par excellence (mahayogi) is clear from his description in the Brahmanas, Upanishads and subsequent literary works. What entitles him to a claim for Vedic or even pre-Vedic anteriority is precisely his substantial resemblance to Rudra, a non-Aryan native god, at first rejected and reviled by the Aryanised priesthood of India, only to be later admitted into its fold, seemingly under duress. That Rudra became the god of terror, death and destruction is indicative of this—recall the famous story of Daksha's sacrifice, which was disturbed by Shiva and the former was then forced to recognise the supremacy of latter.

These two ancient ascetic movements had obviously their points of divergence even as they converged, both equally important in that they help understand the origins, evolution and general character of Indian spiritualism. For one thing, while Shiva is a dreaded figure, identified with death and destruction (his calamitous dances, his wearing of a garland of skulls, his residing in cremation grounds), munis were supposed to be the epitome of compassion and non-violence. More importantly, their atheistic beliefs, it is supposed, made them directly opposed to Shiva, who, while already being a quasi-theistic character, never aspires to assume a full-fledged theistic-pantheistic form (as for example in *Svetashvatara Upanishad*) at the civilising hands of Brahman priests. In this regard, his character seems to suffer great stress. Despite being an ascetic, and thus forbidden from sexual activity, he is asked to pro-create the world, thereby usurping the privileges of Brahma Prajapati who was originally assigned this job.

But there are also pertinent similarities that prevent the two currents from completely falling apart. The most obvious one is their combined opposition to the institution of sacrifice. Shiva creates Virbhadra, who leads an army of ghosts (bhutas) to destroy the sacrificial ceremony arranged by Daksha; the *Rig Veda* contains descriptions of the enemy tribes of Dasyus (to whom the munis belonged) as non-performers of sacrifices. In addition, the Vedic verses cited earlier suggest that going into ecstatic and trance-like states were the most characteristic features of munis. Shiva is also known for his ecstatic dances which were often induced by intoxicants. The factions also share the symbol of a bull, though it must be admitted that its meanings in the two cases are diametrically opposed. While in Shiva's case the bull stands for unrestrained sexual prowess, in the other, it symbolises the mastery of the ascetic over his passions. Being naked and sitting cross-legged in the yogic posture are common images for both sects. Related to this is their common association with the worship of the phallus and the cult of promiscuity. One of the reasons why Vedic Brahmans despised the munis was their phallus-worship (Shishna Deva). It is no surprise then that the famous Pashupati seal discovered in Indus Valley excavations, which depicts a cross-legged seated figure with an exposed phallus, surrounded by different animals, has been regarded as the prototype of Shiva and Rishabh by the two rival schools of thought. Incidentally, the site where the seal was discovered, in Dholavira (in present-day Kutch, Gujarat), also has clear evidence of attempts to destroy images with phallic symbology (Joseph 2018, 188–91).

But these similarities, though important, appear incidental when compared to two essential features which unite not only the two schools of our present concern but also other religious–cultural streams that emerged in the course of history, either as offshoots of these two or independently. The first is that all of them are steeped in what has been termed as animism. So, while Shiva is Pashupati, the lord of animals, in the Vedas, he is also described in the same texts as Bhutapati, the lord of spirits, meaning he presided over an army of ghosts, demons and other evil phenomena. In later literature, he is the consort of the dreaded demoness, Kali, and father to Virbhadra, Kartikeya and Ganesha, all of whom are malevolent spirits. He is a friend of Kubera's, who, though the lord of wealth, is a demon of some antiquity. Shiva is also accompanied by yakshas and yakshinis and vidyadharas (goblins). Most of these beings also figure prominently in later Shramanic literature as deities of reverence and as beholden to the Buddha or the tirthankaras.

Related to animistic beliefs is the concept of tapas, a technique to bring the earlier mentioned supernatural beings under control. Shiva was not merely one among these supernatural beings; he lorded over them by virtue of being a tapasvin, a self-mortifier, of the highest order. Many of the godly feats he performed came from this. It is also believed that it pleased him when a devotee involved himself in penances and austere practices; through such acts of tapas, gods and demons could be subdued and coerced into fulfilling the desire of a devotee. Shaivite literature, both Puranic and Agamic, is filled with stories of people bringing a rakshasa or a yaksha or some other such being under their control through this method. The same holds for Jaina, Buddhist, yogic and Tantric schools as well. Tapasic technique, in various forms and of varying intensities, was resorted to by all of them to acquire occult powers over supranatural beings, enabling devotees to perform strange feats. The miraculous exploits of the muni–Shramanic cult, like flying, are already evident in the verses of the *Rig Veda* quoted earlier.

What we have described until now fits pretty well with the conception of man present in the *Atharva Veda*. It is also not altogether different from the notions of the *Rig Veda* either. Back then, Early Indians, still living and believing through their animistic modes of thought, naturally had a more fanciful understanding of the various forces and phenomena comprising nature. Their world was full of roaming 'spirits', some of whom were benevolent, but most were evil, out to harm man. With the ordinary man in constant fear of them, a class emerged which sought to subdue them and bring them under their control through occult practices, including tapas. This phenomenon, in Western scholarly parlance, is well known as Shamanism and the term's phonetic resemblance with the Indian Shramanism seems to be due to more than accidental reasons.

It follows then that at least a part of what is known as Indian spiritualism was actually, to use a little used term, 'spiritism', whose practitioners were muni–Shramans or Shamans. It was not spiritualism, in the sense of being a philosophy that elevated human souls morally and spiritually, as the two terms are commonly understood. In hindsight, such occultism may even be regarded as morally and spiritually not only unedifying, but also a sign of great depravity and degradation. The idea, nevertheless, that, through self-mortification one can enjoy control over the dark and occult forces of nature, was a persistent theme of the Indian spiritual tradition. It was, by all means, a theme of negation which, rooted in India's earliest cultural beliefs, continued to bedevil the tradition through to its anti-cultural consequences.

A negative theme of this kind is bound to permeate the different layers of social and psychological life, and affect and alter them profoundly in direct and indirect ways. The early pre-civilised man, not as yet technologically equipped to cope with the threatening forces of nature, became an even more insecure being, surrounded by what he considered hostile powers of supranatural character. More importantly, it gave rise to cultural tendencies which not only defied the rules of negative prescription but ran parallel to them, moving by their own logic of psycho-social dynamics. For, the non-recognition, suppression or denial of a fact does not imply its extinction. Reality is divvied up into unreal compartments, each independently pursuing its course and harnessing man onto its journey towards its unnatural demands. The dialectic of social movement does not occur in a neat and chronological succession, even as it folds and unfolds within a single timeframe.

It may be because of this early excessive emphasis on the spiritual that, instead of suppressing the ideologies of matter, it uplifted them, resulting in the emergence of a highly developed civilisation, relatively speaking. As the current opinion among archaeologists and historians goes, the Indus–Harappan culture was precisely such a civilisation that the Early Indians of pre-Vedic times enjoyed, which, we can say, came to an end with the destruction wrought by Aryan invaders led by Indra. Though these invasions appear narratively compressed in the ancient texts we consult, historians argue that it was a long-drawn process that lasted a few centuries (Joseph 2018, 161–201). Consequently, even within Vedic texts, the signs of a well-developed civilisation among the native populace are unmistakably present. The sequences described in Vedic mantras suggest the presence of a quasi-urban mode of living among Early Indians, which they sought to protect, albeit unsuccessfully, from the marauding band of Aryans.

In this connection, the first thing historians point to is the frequent mention of forts and other smaller fortifications of Dasa and Dasyu chiefs, which Indra usually destroyed through treachery. Thus, the god came to be called 'Purbhid' or 'Purandra'—the destroyer of castles. The Rig Veda describes how he shattered the forts of Susna (Griffith 1896; I, 51.11),

Pipru (Griffith 1896; I, 51.5 and VI, 20.), and even a moving fort (Griffith 1896; VIII, 1.28). But his greatest feat was his conquest of Sambara's estate which comprised ninety-nine (Griffith 1896; I, 30.7 and II, 19.6) or a hundred (Griffith 1896; XV, 16.6) forts. Besides, these Dasyu chiefs seem to have had large armies at their disposal. In the war of ten kings, for example, the army of the anti-Aryan alliance is described to have consisted of sixty-six thousand, six hundred and sixty-six men. Now, disregarding the element of alliterative exaggeration, we can still assume that armies deployed for different kinds of warfare were quite large in number. So, when Sarama, the canine messenger of Indra, tells the Panis to lie low, the latter retort that 'our weapons are also sharp' (Griffith 1896; X, 108.4). In fact, Indra's most effective weapon in securing crucial victories over his enemies—the Vajra or thunderbolt—was given to him by none other than a native priest named Kavya Usana.

Other than the *Rig Veda*, Brahmana literature also reveals that Aryan victory over the natives was neither an easy nor a short-lived affair. The natives not only put up a prolonged resistance, but until the final stages, when the situation changed dramatically, they were the dominant side. This is clear from the accounts of the war given in the Brahmanas and also in Puranic books. The following passages from the *Satapatha Brahmana* are illustrative:

> The gods and Asuras, both of them sprung from Prajapati, were once contending for superiority. With staves and bows neither party were able to overcome the other. Neither of them having gained the victory, they (the Asuras) said, 'Well then, let us try to overcome one another by speech, by sacred writ (brahman)!

He who cannot follow up our uttered speech by (making up) a pair, shall be defeated and lose everything, and the other party will win everything!' The gods replied, 'So be it'.... Thereupon the Asuras were defeated and lost everything, and the gods won everything from the Asuras, and stripped their rivals, the Asuras, of everything (Eggeling 1882, 153–4).

As is obvious, the second and more decisive stage was that of magical warfare, but it was clearly preceded by an active armed conflict in which the Asuras/Dasyus were, in material terms, quite strong and powerful. In fact, if the personalities and events described in the Vedas are not merely mythological and if the historical approach to Vedic exegesis is, in general, correct, then the conclusion is inescapable that the civilisational remains discovered in Indus–Harappan excavations are those of pre-Vedic indigenous tribes who enjoyed an organised political life with the attendant paraphernalia of armies, forts, weapons... with which they were able to hold up against external aggression, until they weren't.

The question naturally arises: what eventually brought them down? The common approach is to say that it was the 'brute' force represented by Indra, his superior mobility, which proved decisive. But considering the fact that the Dasyus far outnumbered the Aryans, had well-fortified defences and were by no means logistically or militarily deficient, the above explanation can only be partly valid. The whole truth must lie elsewhere. Since they were materially strong and superior, only 'non-material' factors can account for their defeat. From the point of view of the philosophy of history, they seem to have suffered at the hands of the same laws which proved to be the undoing of so many other civilisations. Material strength, in the absence of moral and spiritual force, necessarily declines; such civilisations may even suffer complete extinction. This clearly appears to have happened in early India too.

The force of matter unrestrained by the force of spirit, either by virtue of the latter's self-withdrawal or its inability to exert effective resistance, makes the former a centre of power in itself with its own logic and its own dynamics. Disregarding the values of compassion and co-existence, a materialistic culture seeks to expand itself excessively, being governed by the motives of greed and megalomania. This process of self-enlargement cannot go on indefinitely because of the presence of other expansive centres of power which also have the same motivating forces guiding them. The conflicts that result out of their encounter lead to either the extinction of one power centre or the other, or both. This is the inner limit that nature has imposed upon power, so it does not see itself as 'natural' law supreme for a very long time. In the Vedic times, Sambara with his hundred castles was formidable, but he had an enemy, Divodasa, who finding himself weak, sought the helping hand of the alien Indra. This paved the way for Indra's easy entry into the land of the Dasyus. Divodasa was victorious and so was his grandson Sudasa who, again, with the help of the priests of the new Aryan religion, humbled the allied power of ten kings.

Exploiting the disunity among enemies, and setting one against the other, have been techniques used by imperialists in all times and all places. Indra too employed them to the hilt in besting his native foes. More significantly, he won the support of community leaders, the priests, which proved decisive in tilting the scales in his favour. Usana Kavi, the most intelligent priest of the Asuras, became a turncoat thanks to the intervention of Kutsa, Indra's cohort and aide, who acted as a go-between for him and Indra. The incident is related in various Brahmanas in greater detail but a brief mention is also found in the *Rig Veda*. The verse V, 29.9 describes Indra's visit to Usana's house, along with Kutsa: 'What time ye came with strong steeds swiftly speeding, O Usana and Indra, to the dwelling, Thou camest thither conquering together with Kutsa and the Gods: thou slewest Susna.' Usana enquires about the object of their visit (Griffith 1896; X, 22.6), a deal is struck, and Indra returns happy and satisfied: 'When Indra hath rejoiced with Kavya Usana, he mounts his steeds who swerve wider and wider yet...' (Griffith 1896; I, 51.11). Usana even helps Indra by giving him the mighty weapon, Vajra: 'The might which Usana hath formed for thee with might rends in its greatness and with strength both worlds apart' (Griffith 1896; I, 51.10). It meant the end of the fight against Susna (Griffith 1896; I, 121.12). In return, of course Indra fulfilled all of Usana's wishes (Griffith 1896; VI, 20.11).

Usana was not alone in deserting his former comrades. As we will see, Angirases, Bhrigu, Vamadeva, Gotama, Atri, all belonged at one time to the Asura side but crossed over for personal and/or ideological reasons.

Such desertions on the part of leaders must be taken as symptoms and not as the cause for the actual defeat of the native people. They may be taken as signs of a general weakening of public spirit, to which several other related factors may have contributed. One such factor was obviously their general superstitious nature. A people haunted by spirits, ghosts, demons and goblins are bound to be superstitious and thus weak in a certain material–political sense. The non-hieratic *Atharva Veda*, which is said to represent more faithfully the beliefs of the ordinary man, is full of references to evil spirits out to harm him and the various spells and charms supplied by the priest that can act as deterrents. Even the *Rig Veda* is not utterly devoid of such references to magic and its use to secure victory over enemies. This Samhita calls the Asuras by the general name of Mayains—believers or practitioners of magic. But this magic apparently failed them when faced with the intelligent handling of warfare by their Aryan foes or when a superior magical force was used by the latter. Later Brahmanas and epic texts even described the war between these two parties as a contest between two parties of magicians.

Occultism, the cult of religious magic, has always been related to sex rites, which, on one level at least, does not regard licentiousness as morally reprehensible behaviour. The idea of spiritual realisation through rituals involving sex is not uncommon historically speaking and whenever these have been put into practice, prostitution, or at least religious prostitution, has flourished. Apart from the earlier mentioned Pasupati seal depicting a naked yogin with an erect phallus, Indus excavations also include a number of other seals on which figures of nude mother goddesses are depicted. Also found are figures of nude women standing in erotic postures, clad in necklaces and bangles. About such figures the general surmise is that they represent a class of prostitutes, perhaps in employ for religious purposes under priests or priest-kings (the accuracy of such interpretations notwithstanding, a certain level of sexuality can indeed be attributed to such artefacts).

The *Rig Veda* mentions the worship of the phallus god (Sishna Deva) in two places.[2] Sayana, a famous interpreter of the *Rig*, reads these references to mean, those who indulge in amorous practices. The worship of the phallus and deviant sexual behaviour in the upper classes of society go together. So, an entire section in the *Rig* on the Dasyus' worship of the phallus suggests the presence of a culture of religious promiscuity. In fact, famous apsaras like Urvashi, Tilottama and Rambha cannot but be taken to belong to this class of women. They were Indra's women often sent down to earth to entertain kings or to seduce rishis, distracting them from their endeavours to threaten Indra's mighty status as a super-god. While the apsaras sang and danced before their patrons, their male counterparts, the Gandharvas, played music and served them wine (soma), which they brought from the Meru mountains, where they are said to have lived. As if to make the picture of a corrupt culture complete, these same Gandharvas are also said to be experts in games of dice, with which they amused the Devas.

Among the stories suggesting some kind of perverted behaviour by the upper classes in general, and the priestly class in particular, some can be considered as later inventions of epic or Puranic story tellers, while others can be traced to older sources. There is, for example, the story of a blind rishi Dirghatamas, the author of the "Nasadiya Sutra" of the *Rig Veda*. Sayana reports that he was born blind because of a curse. While he was still in his mother's womb, she was propositioned by a rishi who happened to be her brother-in-law. The foetus fearing injury to itself entreated his uncle to desist from such an act. These pleas, however, did not pacify the rishi's passions, and although he couldnt satisfy his desire in the end, he lay a curse on the foetus and Dirghatamas was born blind. The same woman, incidentally, was consorted by her husband's younger brother, Brahaspati, out of which relationship was born the famous rishi, Bharadwaja.

Sexual permissiveness was only one part of the depravity that characterised the native communities. In their urban mode of living, not unexpectedly, the trading classes indulged in vices that seemed to be related to their professions. The Panis, for example, are described by the Vedas as faithless, non-sacrificing, greedy niggards and usurers:

> The foolish, faithless, rudely-speaking niggards, without belief or sacrifice or worship,— Far far sway hath Agni chased those Dasyus, and, in the cast, hath turned the godless westward (Griffith 1896; VII, 6. 3).

> He gathers up for plunder all the niggard's gear: excellent wealth he gives to him who offers gifts (Griffith 1896; V, 34. 7).

> Destroy the greedy Pani, for a wolf is he (Griffith 1896; VI, 51. 14).

These allusions to economic exploitation in addition to promiscuity, superstitions and spiritual decay seem to indicate, at least in part, what enabled a foreign invader like Indra, with his 'brute' force and unrestrained methods of warfare, to secure victory over them. The natives did resist for a time but were gradually demoralised. The goddess of fortune, Lakshmi, first deserted them and then came the final defeat.

> ...The gods and the Asuras, both of them sprung from Prajapati, entered upon their father Prajapati's inheritance, to wit, speech—

truth and untruth, both truth and untruth: they, both of them, spake the truth, and they both spake untruth; and, indeed, speaking alike, they were alike. / The gods relinquished untruth, and held fast to truth, and the Asuras relinquished truth, and held fast to untruth. / The truth which was in the Asuras beheld this, and said, 'Verily, the gods have relinquished untruth, and held fast to truth: well, then, I will go thither!' Thus it went over to the gods. / And the untruth which was in the gods beheld this, and said, 'Verily, the Asuras have relinquished truth, and held fast to untruth: well, then, I will go thither!' Thus it went over to the Asuras. / The gods spake nothing but truth, and the Asuras nothing but untruth. And the gods, speaking the truth diligently, were very contemptible, and very poor: whence he who speaks the truth diligently, becomes indeed very contemptible, and very poor; but in the end he assuredly prospers, for the gods indeed prospered. / And the Asuras, speaking untruth diligently, throve even as salt soil, and were very prosperous: whence he who speaks untruth diligently, thrives indeed, even as salt soil, and becomes very prosperous; but in the end he assuredly comes to naught, for the Asuras indeed came to naught (Eggeling 1897; IX, 5.1.12–17).

To represent the Deva–Asura fight as a war between truth and untruth may well be a retrospective rationalisation of events. All the more so when it is known that such interpretations were made by the party directly involved in the dispute—the victors no less. Leaving, however, for the present the question of truth and untruth open, attention here may be focused on the different socio-religious forces that built what is still for many the mainstream tradition of Indian spiritualism. The tradition is of course the orthodox Vedic one, as created by rishis and sustained by Brahmans—the rishis' spiritual descendants.

The all-important question then is who were the rishis? It is futile to go into the etymology of the word because there is a great deal of difference of opinion among scholars about its literal roots. But generally, the word has been interpreted keeping in view the suppositions one has about the status and function of the figures marked by the term. It is sufficient for our purposes to accept its rendering in English as 'seers', though it would still be a matter of disagreement and speculation what the seers really saw, and the manner of their seeing whatever they saw. For, while this seeing has been taken to mean as sublime an event as the revelation of the divine secret, as understood in the Judeo–Islamic theology, it is also interpreted as simply a poet's manner of versifying 'war songs'. The two interpretations need not be mutually exclusive though. Much depends on one's idea of divinity itself, and 'war' can be both for a righteous cause or for worldly purposes. If Indra was really a god of truth and justice, a war on his behalf hardly invites moral or rational censure.

About Vedic lore, it is not controversial to state that it represents a counter-culture to the cult of munis who followed the philosophy of renunciation and other-worldliness. In contrast, the Vedic rishis were not only family men, indulging in marital as well as extra-marital sexual relationships, having children and dabbling most actively in politics, they were also seen asking their gods to give them wealth, public honour and power, and even revelling in these when attained. This, despite their status as spiritual leaders of their communities, performing religious rites and formulating religious–philosophical ideas. Their position as advisers to kings, and their right in performing big sacrificial ceremonies for the benefit of royal patrons, made them a class apart from the sects of wandering ascetics, Shaivite or Shramanic.

In Vedic and post-Vedic texts, though rishis were human beings, they were also described as possessing the divinity of stars and constellations. Perhaps an outcome of the general tendency among writers to combine the mundane with the sublime, the historic with the mythic. Confining ourselves to the discussion of rishis as members of the this-worldly community, there are seven clans (gotras) to which they could usually be aligned; sometimes an eighth name is added to this list. These are Vishwamitra, Jamadagni, Bharadwaja, Gotama, Atri, Vasishtha and Kashyapa; Agastya is the eighth one. This is the standard list, but in some places one or two names are swapped for different ones. Some sources claim that originally there were only four clans of rishis—Angirases, Kashyapas, Vasishthas and Atris. Some traditions even claim that the most ancient and original rishi clan was that of the Angirases, and other clans were branches and sub-branches of it. Since the Angirases (sometimes accompanied by or identified with the clan 'Bhrigu') are taken to be the oldest family of rishis, it would be fruitful to begin our study of the religion of rishis with them, both as individuals and as social beings.

From the accounts given in various texts, Angirases were the first sages to establish the cult of sacrifice in India. 'Angirases, holding the rank of sages, first honoured sacrifice's holy statute', the Rig reads (Griffith 1896; X, 67.2). They also discovered fire: 'O Agni, the Angirases discovered thee what time thou layest hidden, fleeing back from wood to wood' (Griffith 1896; V, 11.6). They possessed special powers which they employed to support Indra in his fight against the native Dasyus.

> The mountain, for thy glory, cleft itself apart when, Angiras!
> thou openedst the stall of kine. Thou, O Brhaspati, with Indra for
> ally didst hurl down water-floods which gloom had compassed
> round (Griffith 1896; II, 23.18).
> First the Angirases won themselves vital power, whose
> fires were kindled through good deeds and sacrifice. The men
> together found the Pani's hoarded wealth, the cattle, and the
> wealth in horses and in kine (Griffith 1896; I, 83.4).

At the disposal of Angirases are of course the powers of magic and witchcraft; in *Atharva Veda* particularly, they are described as being the masters of these crafts. The Dasyus were great practitioners of sorcery, but apparently, in this they were outsmarted by the Angirases. That the latter are the chief allies of Indra, in his campaign of plunder and conquest, is clear from the verses quoted earlier. But apart from this, their association with the god of death, Yama, also makes them a dreaded people, ruthless and unsparing in their dealings with their enemies. This, along with their description in Zendic texts (where they are referred to as 'Angara') as heretics from Ahura's cult of Zarathustra, and patrons of demon/Daeva-worship, suggests that they were a condemned people who were probably driven out from their place of origin for their unorthodox beliefs and undesirable activities.

The close association of Angirases with Indra/Devas, in both the Iranian and Indian contexts, probably explains their conspicuous lack of connection with Varuna, at the time considered the chief rival of Indra. But this does not hold true with the other two ancient clans of the Bhrigus and the Atharvans, who though equally associated with Indra and Agni, are at the same time found to have a certain kind of allegiance to Varuna. Bhrigu, like the Angirases, is described to have brought fire from heaven (Griffith 1896; III, 2.13) or from waters (Griffith 1896; X, 46.2), and often sides with Indra in warfare. But he is also referred to as Varuni Bhrigu, implying a religious and/or physical kinship with the god. Besides, the word Bhrigu literally means 'to burn' or 'to shine', and in the *Mahabharata* he is said to have been born of fire, at a sacrifice performed by Varuna. Brahma, who was present at the ceremony, was unable to check his passion at the sight of beautiful damsels present there, and his semen fell into the fire, birthing Bhrigus, Angirases and Kavis.

Atharvans are also helpers of Indra and propagators of the cult of sacrifice and fire-worship. And from the *Atharva Veda*,[3] we can glean their connection to Varuna. The god is supposed to have given them a speckled cow as a gift, which he then demanded back, for an obscure reason. It was a cow that performed miracles and the rishi naturally refused to return it. This may simply suggest that the earlier allegiance of the rishi to Varuna was forsaken in favour of a new deity (Indra?), but which heresy he refuses to acknowledge.

From all this it appears that some of the oldest families of rishis were associated with the fire cult and had Varuna as their chief deity. But, as is known, in the Vedas, Varuna is called an Asur; we must remember, too, that Ahura was the god worshipped by Iranian Zoroastrians. It would follow then that these families of rishi priests were originally Iranians who worshipped Ahura–Varuna through fire ceremonies.

They migrated to India in the remote past, indicated by the Vedic allusion to their having brought fire from a far-off place. On the other hand, it may very well be possible that these were indigenous people who were converted to the fire cult of the Iranians after coming in contact with them. They could also have belonged to some intermediate regions between Iran and India, like present-day Afghanistan or Kashmir: the Devas' close relationship with apsaras of the Gandhara region seems to suggest this. Moreover, these clans of rishis, particularly Bhrigus, are later described to be closely associated with the Early Indian Asuras: they even fight wars against Indra and his allies. This makes them seem like indigenous clans, instead of being Aryan in the sense of being foreign migrants.

It is important to recall that the native Indians, before being conquered by the Aryans, had an animistic religion: the worship of mother goddesses was quite prominent. Such a situation requires the presence of priests to administer rituals and perform related duties, like exorcising spirits, providing religious guidance and attending to ceremonial occasions of marriage and mourning, among other things. It naturally follows that the rishis of the Vedic variety were none other than the native ascetics (or their descendants) who converted to the Aryan religion in different phases of their priestly development.

While this makes their racial origin a matter of dispute, it clarifies that the early Vedic rishis were in some way associated with the monotheistic religion of Ahura–Varuna worship, which they seemed to have forsaken in favour of the worship of fire. Having associated themselves with Daevas in Iran, where they were the enemies of Ahura (Daeva/Deva is a demon in some of the later Iranian books), as well as in India, they would have been considered as heretics and possibly even discarded by the orthodoxy, thus forcing them to migrate eastward. Whatever the historical facts, which will remain a matter of conjecture, one thing which is clear is that a visible tension of orthodoxy and heresy, as represented by pure Varuna-worship and the worship of Daeva-Deva Indra respectively, haunted some rishis. Vasishtha, for example, probably the most important and the most colourful personality in the entire Vedic corpus, is among the most enthusiastic promoters of the Indra cult. At the same time, he is closely connected with Varuna worship. For one thing, he is the spiritual/physical progeny of Varuna–Mitra, born of their combined insemination of Urvashi, the heavenly nymph. Varuna is also said to have gifted him access to the mysteries of the universe (Griffith 1896; VII, 88.4). But like other rishis, he too goes over to Indra's side and indeed becomes his favourite, as stated in hymn VII, 33.2 of the *Rig*. In the same verse, it is said that he brought Indra to this land from somewhere far away, and in a Brahmana text he is again said to have first seen Indra. But despite such a close relationship, he is also the one who never forgets his original self and his past communion with Varuna. In moments of intense spiritual crisis, he laments his heresy, resents it, and asks his God for forgiveness. In the "Varuna sukta", which is regarded as the pearl of Vedic hymns, the pathos of Vasishtha's emotion and angst flows through:

> Present to Varuna thine hymn, Vasistha, bright, most delightful to the Bounteous Giver, Who bringeth on to us the Bull, the lofty, the Holy, laden with a thousand treasures. / And now,

as I am come before his presence, I take the face of Varuna for Agni's. So might he bring-Lord also of the darkness-the light in heaven that I may see its beauty! / When Varuna and I embark together and urge our boat into the midst of ocean, We, when we ride o'er ridges of the waters, will swing within that swing and there be happy. / Varuna placed Vasistha in the vessel, and deftly with his night made him a Rsi. When days shone bright the Sage made him a singer, while the heavens broadened and the Dawns were lengthened. / What hath become of those our ancient friendships, when without enmity we walked together? I, Varuna, thou glorious Lord, have entered thy lofty home, thine house with thousand portals. / If he, thy true ally, hath sinned against thee, still, Varuna, he is the friend thou lovedst. Let us not, Living One, as sinners I know thee: give shelter, as a Sage, to him who lauds thee. / While we abide in these fixed habitations, and from the lap of Aditi win favour, May Varuna untie the bond that binds us. Preserve us evermore, ye Gods, with blessings (Griffith 1896; VII, 88).

Vasishtha was not alone in facing such an existential crisis. There were others who hesitated as well, before finally giving up. Kavya Usana was blackmailed into switching to the side of Indra with the promise of the release of his grandson who was captured by the god. In the *Rig* (IV, 18.2), conversations between Indra and his mother, and between him and Vamadeva, the author of the fourth mandala, have been recorded, where the rishi is similarly persuaded to come over to Indra's side. But the rishi raises certain moral objections, pointing to Indra's drinking habit and killing of Tvashtra, when he was visiting the latter at home. Aditi defends her son, not by refuting the charge or giving an explanation of the incident, but by simply pointing out the greatness of Indra. Vamadeva is unable to resist the psychological pressure and succumbs. The *Brihaddevata*, an allied text, also refers to the rishi's fight with Indra as soon as he was born (Griffith 1896; IV, 131–139). He engages the latter for ten days and nights, overpowers him and then tries to 'sell' him in an assembly of seers.[4] This may simply mean that he accepted Indra's supremacy and became a sponsor of his religion on his own terms.

Other than receiving wealth and honour, the rishis also took to Indra for other reasons. Their religion was different from local cults, and relations with indigenous people were shaky. They were often harassed and persecuted, and they looked to Indra for succour and support. Atri, for example, was thrown in a dark dungeon by Asuras[5] and secured his release only with the timely intervention of the Asvins, allies of Indra. The Asvins also rescued the rishi Kanva, whom the Asuras threw into a dark cell in order to test his Brahmanhood.

The native kingdoms had already passed their heyday and were on the decline. The rishis were therefore wise not to stick to old allegiances. Indra and Divodasa had already demolished the main strongholds of Dasyu power. The rishis scrambled to join their side. Originally, Bharadwaja was the chaplain of the Divodasa family but during the times of Sudasa, Vishwamitra replaced him. When Sudasa decided to confront the allied forces of ten kings, he first invited Vasishtha, who was at the time associated with the Tritsus, a rival tribe of the Bharatas, to take up the position of royal priest. Vishwamitra was infuriated and what followed was the famous clash between these two rishi clans which continued for many epochs. While thus humiliated, Vishwamitra went over to the Dasyus' side, Vasishtha formed an alliance between Sudasa and Tritsus and secured victory for them over the allied power of ten kings, a battle first referenced in the seventh mandala of the *Rig*.

Apart from these clans, others like Kanvas, Atris and Bhrigus, who had come to the subcontinent earlier and therefore had lived in the native surroundings for a longer period of time (if they were not already native, that is), took their time to move to the side of the conquerors. But they too were ultimately won over.

The advantages of being on the right side of the struggle are obvious. It ensures the continuance of privileges that one enjoyed in the previous establishment. Vedic rishis, in any case, never pretended to be unworldly monks like the munis or Shaivites; they enunciated a 'positivistic' outlook on matters of life and world. They desired and prayed for wives, healthy progeny, wealth and power—and in these desires they were hardly ever disappointed. To take the example of Vasishtha himself, we find him to have had several wives (the most famous being the native Arundhati) and enjoyed, all through his life, the patronage of kings and related benefits. In fact, the word Vasishtha literally signifies richness, 'the greatest'. Vishwamitra, his rival, was also no stranger to extramarital relationships. His royal lineage suggests that he must have already been a prosperous and powerful man, and, as chaplain to several kings, he would have hardly suffered any want. Yet, he was ever jealous of Vasishtha and could never reconcile himself Vasishtha's successes.

Besides, there are several mentions in Vedic literature of rishis getting extravagant gifts from their royal patrons. In *Brihaddevata* (5, 28–36), Atri is said to have received 10,320 cows and a gold wagon with two oxen from king Trayyuna;

Aiksavaka got a hundred oxen from king Asvamedha and much wealth from king Trasadasyu. The *Rig Veda* (Griffith 1896; VIII, 49.10) tells us that Kanva received cows and gold from the Asvins. One of the reasons the Panis, and for that matter the Dasyus in general, were disliked by the rishis was their reluctance to oblige in financial and other remunerative respects. They were generally described as misers, but if one of them (such as Brhu) was generous and obliging, he was instantly praised. Moreover, the whole institution of sacrifices, which was at the centre of the Vedic religion, was a means of obtaining precious gifts from kings and other sections of the people.

All in all, the rishis seem to have a great sense of honour and self-righteousness, differentiating themselves from the rest of the populace in terms of language, race(?) and religion, looking down on them as inferior and degraded. They too were of course largely natives who had partly adopted foreign ways of life and faith, keeping themselves aloof from their brethren, for which reason they were hated and opposed.

The native culture was decadent and declining due to its intellectual and moral bankruptcy and a new force represented by Indra was emerging on the horizon, with which the priestly class had religious–racial affinity. After initial hesitation and doubt about the lasting capacity of this new dispensation, they eventually went over and supported it with all their skill and power. In return, they were not only saved from daily harassment by their native detractors, they were also able to re-establish their authority as leaders of the community, acquiring worldly luxuries in the form of women, wine and wealth.

This does not exhaust a full description of the 'positivism' of the Vedic religion. There are other aspects which are in need of unpacking to understand the whole complex of culture represented by rishis or rishi-priests. For one thing the rishis were great synthesisers. An endeavour towards synthesis and reconciliation of antagonistic ideologies was to become the hallmark of Brahmanist methodology in later epochs of Indian history. In the Vedic age, this meant simply upholding both sets of ideals together without attempting to weld them into a single whole.

The early periods of Vedic history suggest the subcontinent to be a welter of races and creeds. There was no unified vision of the world; the beliefs of different groups were tinged by different levels of acculturation, as they co-existed while also vying for supremacy. The rishis themselves were divided by their affinities and allegiances to different segments of society. For instance, when Indra mounted his religious and political assault, they were at first puzzled but soon recovered, and a compromise was worked out in which they acquiesced to Indra's supremacy. But the older allegiances were not forgotten. To be sure, their new faith was not spontaneous or an outcome of rational consideration. Instead, they were forced by the exigencies of the situation and a reflexive instinct for survival. To be sure, much of the pluralistic theology, characteristic of the Vedas, is due to this priestly trait to let all the gods and goddesses, of different sections of people, co-exist happily with each other, so long as they did not come in the way of their acquiring material benefits.

Taking, once again, Vasishtha as an example, we have seen that he was originally a Varunite but had later converted to the Indra cult. But even after this conversion, he did not altogether renounce his earlier faith, and tried to be on both sides. Vasishtha's rival, Vishwamitra, on the other hand, after being pushed out from the Aryan fold, became a sworn enemy of Indra, and under Bhriguite influence, adopted many traits of native belief systems, though the evidence for it comes not from the *Rig* but mostly from the *Atharva Veda* and later Puranic texts. This is also generally true of Atri, Kanva and Bhriguites, who were all affiliated with indigenous tribes. Among other rishis, Gritsamada (to whom the second mandala of the *Rig* is ascribed) was the first to adopt the non-Aryan god, Rudra, into his roster, a trend which was continued by the Agastya, Vasishtha's twin brother. Similarly, the rishi Bharadwaja had brought about a reconciliation between Pusana, believed to be the most ancient pastoral god in India, and the new Indra cult (Griffith 1896; III, 57.7 and VI, 57). If the previously discussed myth of Brahma casting his semen into the fire, and thereby giving birth to various rishi clans, is examined, it would appear that rishis were, in some sense, products of some kind of a synthesis between an already existing Brahma-based religion and a new Varunite faith (which was itself, in turn, renounced in favour of a religion of Indra and other Aryan gods). On the other hand, the famous myth, of Vasishtha being born of a combined insemination of Urvashi by Varuna and Mitra, also suggests the fertilisation of native faith by the Varunite–Aryan ideas, through which at least one clan of rishis became the chief protagonists.

Synthesis, it seems, was the lifeblood of the rishi-priests. But aside from being synthesisers, these rishis were also great civilisers, so to speak. Naturally, they were accomplished men, excelling in worldly wisdom and spiritual refinement. They were, like the Shamans of the west, medicine men, magicians, philosophers and scientists. Angiras' discovery of fire in the forest may be taken both as a religious revolution and a technological breakthrough. Kavya Usana fashioned the Vajra, which proved to be decisive for Indra in his fight against the Dasyus. The *Atharva Veda* (Whitney 1905; VI, 13 7.1) narrates how Jamadagni dug out an herb called kesavardhanim for curing her daughter. Kavya Usana is also described as a good poet and a fine speaker. Rishis often dabbled in magic, even if some of them sometimes disapproved. Vasishtha, who cast a sleep spell on some men so he could enter Varuna's house and commit robbery, later fiercely denies the charge of being a sorcerer or a yatudhani (Whitney 1905; VII, 104. 15-16). Jamadagni restores Vishwamitra's speech with magic, after he is confounded by Vasishtha's son, Shakti, during a religious debate. The Bhriguites too liberally practised magic, and Atri and Kanva were so adept in sorcery that in the *Atharva Veda*, they are even called goblins.

This dabbling in magic and sorcery by rishis, incidentally, gives us important clues about the origins and essential characteristics of Vedic spirituality. Most rishis, of differing allegiences, seem to share the same (or similar) background in asceticism and occultism, which they otherwise pretended to disapprove of. Of course, there is little evidence of this in the Vedas, though the epics and Puranas abound with legends of their indulgence in austere practices aimed at acquiring mastery over cosmic forces. Even the Brahmanas, which immediately followed the Vedas and are attached to them liturgically, frequently mention these practices with reference to rishis.

Given the fact that these stories were generally built on traditions handed down from Vedic times, it would not be altogether unreasonable to assume that the rishis underwent some kind of training in occult mysticism before embarking on a career of priesthood. Even otherwise, it does not seem entirely plausible that the great power and prestige they enjoyed in society, especially their proximity to kings, was just because of their intellectual abilities, and had nothing to do with their 'spiritual' powers. In the *Rig*, rishi Agastya's wife, Lopamudra, once became tired of her husband's abstinence and requested for intercourse, which the considerate rishi consented to after some hesitation (Griffith 1896; I, 179; I, 25. 7-8).[6] Later, he expiated this indulgence, which suggests that sexual activity was regarded as obstructive to the spiritual path, even in Vedic times. It seems that although rishis found the lifestyle of munis unpalatable to their finer tastes, there was no feeling of enmity as such against them. Indra is even said to be a friend of munis.[7] Their hostility was more directed against the yatis, practitioners of witchcraft and sorcery. Indra, again, is said to have thrown the yatis to the wolves (Griffith 1896; X, 8.80).

It would then appear that the disagreement which existed between rishis and munis was not in their basic philosophical outlook, but in their respective styles of living. The latter were of course atheistic (Griffith 1896; VII, 6.3), but only in the sense that they did not believe in Aryan gods like Indra, Varuna, and Agni. They rightly regarded them as alien deities. But then they had their own gods to worship— the phallus, yakshas and yakshis, apsaras and other such goddesses and gods (anti-gods, even). That they were described as foolish, niggardly and foul-mouthed, indicates that it was their mannerism and general style of living which was disliked by the rishis, who themselves lived a pompous and extravagant life befitting their status in the society. While the munis continued to pursue their spiritual quest in forests and mountains all through their lives, the rishis returned to the world in order to make use of whatever powers they had acquired from their ascetic occupation. If there is any historical substance to the Vasishtha–Vishwamitra clash, it seems like even their spiritual pursuits were made for egoistic reasons and not out of any urge for moral elevation.

The rishis, and their native foes in pre-Aryan India, both had their respective sets of deities and were generally polytheistic in their religious outlook. But this does not mean that the idea of a single, supreme creator of the universe was altogether absent. There are strong reasons to consider the Tvashtra–Vishvakarma duo, described in several of the Vedic verses and later Brahmana texts, as an indigenous name for such a supreme God whom Indra killed. The Vedic pantheon as such can be divided into two parts. One part consists of gods who are creations of nature in being Adityas, sons of Aditi, 'the unbounded nature'. The other part comprises not exactly of several gods but probably a single God called variously as Brahmanaspati, Brahaspati, Prajapati, Hiranyagarbha, Purusha, Vishvakarman, and so on. These were all Vedic names of the God Brahma, after whom the rishis, and more importantly their spiritual descendants, came to be called Brahmans.

It is quite clear that with its polytheistic beliefs, the *Rig Veda* also has a view of God that is monotheistic in its purest and most precise sense. The Prajapati Brahma, as described in this text, is the lord of the universe, its creator and preserver, similar in sense to Judaism or Islam. This is made evident from the following hymns which are taken from the *Rig Veda* (verses with similar import can be found in other Vedic texts too). The famous "Purusha Sukta" (Griffith 1896; X, 90) describes God and his creatorship thus:

> A thousand heads hath Purusa, a thousand eyes, a thousand feet. On every side pervading earth he fills a space ten fingers wide. / This Purusa is all that yet hath been and all that is to be; The Lord of Immortality which waxes greater still by food. / So mighty is his greatness; yea, greater than this is Purusa. All creatures are one-fourth of him, three-fourths eternal life in heaven. / With three-fourths Purusa went up: one-fourth of him again was here. Thence he strode out to every side over what eats not and what eats (Griffith 1896; X, 90.1–4).

> He formed the creatures of the air, and animals both wild and tame (Griffith 1896; X, 90.8).

> When they divided Purusa how many portions did they make? What do they call his mouth, his arms? What do they call his thighs and feet? / The Brahman was his mouth, of both his arms was the Rajanya made. His thighs became the Vaisya, from his feet the Sudra was produced. / The Moon was gendered from his mind, and from his eye the Sun had birth; Indra and Agni from his mouth were born, and Vayu from his breath. / Forth from his navel came mid-air the sky was fashioned from his head, Earth from his feet, and from his car the regions. Thus they formed the worlds (Griffith 1896; X, 90.11–14).

X. 81 and 82 similarly describe the Vishvakarman:

He who sate down as Hotar-priest, the Rsi, our Father, offering up all things existing,— He, seeking through his wish a great possession, came among men on earth as archetypal. / What was the place whereon he took his station? What was it that supported him? How was it? Whence Visvakarman, seeing all, producing the earth, with mighty power disclosed the heavens. / He who hath eyes on all sides round about him, a mouth on all sides, arms and feet on all sides, He, the Sole God, producing earth and heaven, weildeth them, with his arms as wings, together (Griffith 1896; X, 81.1–3).

The Father of the eye, the Wise in spirit, created both these worlds submerged in fatness. Then when the eastern ends were firmly fastened, the heavens and the earth were far extended. / Mighty in mind and power is Visvakarman, Maker, Disposer, and most lofty Presence. Their offerings joy in rich juice where they value One, only One, beyond the Seven Rsis. / Father who made us, he who, as Disposer, knoweth all races and all things existing, Even he alone, the Deities' name-giver, him other beings seek for information (Griffith 1896; X, 82.1–3).

That which is earlier than this earth and heaven, before the Asuras and Gods had being,— What was the germ primeval which the waters received where all the Gods were seen together? / The waters, they received that germ primeval wherein the Gods were gathered all together. It rested set upon the Unborn's navel, that One wherein abide all things existing (Griffith 1896; X, 82.5–6).

The same hymn in the sequel, throws further light on the mystery surrounding this God:

Then was not non-existent nor existent: there was no realm of air, no sky beyond it. What covered in, and where? and what gave shelter? Was water there, unfathomed depth of water? / Death was not then, nor was there aught immortal: no sign was there, the day's and night's divider. That One Thing, breathless, breathed by its own nature: apart from it was nothing whatsoever. / Darkness there was: at first concealed in darkness this All was indiscriminated chaos. All that existed then was void and form less: by the great power of Warmth was born that Unit (Griffith 1896; X, 129.1–3).

Who verily knows and who can here declare it, whence it was born and whence comes this creation? The Gods are later than this world's production. Who knows then whence it first came into being? / He, the first origin of this creation, whether he formed it all or did not form it, Whose eye controls this world in highest heaven, he verily knows it, or perhaps he knows not (Griffith 1896; X, 129.6–7).

Once the lordship of the real God is recognised, the rishi has no hesitation in worshipping him and him alone:

In the beginning rose Hiranyagarbha, born Only Lord of all created beings. He fixed and holdeth up this earth and heaven. What God shall we adore with our oblation? / Giver of vital breath, of power and vigour, he whose commandments all the Gods acknowledge. The Lord of death, whose shade is life immortal. What God shall we adore with our oblation? / Who by his grandeur hath become Sole Ruler of all the moving world that breathes and slumbers; He who is Lord of men and Lord of cattle. What God shall we adore with our oblation? / His, through his might, are these snow-covered mountains, and men call sea and Rasa his possession: His arms are these, his are these heavenly regions. What God shall we adore with our oblation?

/ By him the heavens are strong and earth is steadfast, by him light's realm and sky-vault are supported: By him the regions in mid-air were measured. What God shall we adore with our oblation? ... / What time the mighty waters came, containing the universal germ, producing Agni, Thence sprang the Gods' one spirit into being. What God shall we adore with our oblation? / He in his might surveyed the floods containing productive force and generating Worship. He is the God of gods, and none beside him. What God shall we adore with our oblation (Griffith 1896; X, 121.1–8)?

The final pronouncement, that Purusha is the God of gods and there is none beside him, was a strong monotheistic current, which, however, became weaker and weaker with time. The earlier story about Brahma's inability to hold his semen at the sight of Aryan beauties was a clear indication of his weakening hold over popular imagination. Priests were born out of this decline, and in these priests, God met his final nemesis. In later literature, he is made to surrender to the gods of occult, allowing thereby the culture of mysticism and magic to flourish.

It is also somewhat curious to note here that in the hymns quoted above, while the lordship and creatorship of Purusha or Prajapati is emphasised, no indication is given about the moral component of his being. One reason for this may be that the priests who wrote these hymns wanted to project his image primarily as a deity of sacrifice, which, at least partly, was an immoral exercise. It was not that God had no moral side, as we will see later, he did create dharma—the moral order of society. But in the Vedas, Prajapati is ethically neutral while Varuna is made to be the upholder of morality, who, despite Indra's eventual triumph, had his own moments of glory.

I am the royal Ruler, mine is empire, as mine who sway all life are all Immortals. Varuna's will the Gods obey and follow. I am the King of men's most lofty cover. / I am King Varuna. To me were given these first existing high celestial powers. Varuna's will the Gods obey and follow. I am the King of men's most lofty cover. / I Varuna am Indra: in their greatness, these the two wide deep fairly-fashioned regions, These the two world-halves have I, even as Tvastar knowing all beings, joined and held together. / I made to flow the moisture-shedding waters, and set the heaven firm in the scat of Order. By Law the Son of Aditi, Law Observer, hath spread abroad the world in threefold measure (Griffith 1896; IV, 42.1–4).

Whatever law of thine, O God, O Varuna, as we are men, Day after day we violate. / give us not as a prey to death, to be destroyed by thee in wrath, To thy fierce anger when displeased. / To gain thy mercy, Varuna, with hymns we bind thy heart, as binds, The charioteer his tethered horse. / They flee from me dispirited, bent only on obtaining wealth, As to their nests the birds of air. / When shall we bring, to be appeased, the Hero, Lord of warrior might, Him, the far-seeing Varuna? / This, this with joy they both accept in common: never do they fail The ever-faithful worshipper. / He knows the path of birds that fly through heaven, and, Sovran of the sea, He knows the ships that are thereon. / True to his holy law, he knows the twelve moons with their progeny: He knows the moon of later birth. / He knows the pathway of the wind, the spreading, high, and mighty wind: He knows the Gods who dwell above. / Varuna, true to holy law, sits down among his people; he, Most wise, sits there to govern all. / From thence perceiving he beholds all wondrous things, both what hath been, And what hereafter will be done. / May that Aditya, very wise, make fair paths for us all our days: May he prolong our lives for us. / Varuna, wearing golden mail, hath clad him in a shining robe. His spies are seated found about. / The God whom enemies threaten not, nor those who tyrannise o'er men, Nor those whose minds are bent on wrong. / He who gives glory to mankind, not glory that is incomplete, To our own bodies giving it. / Yearning for the wide-seeing One, my thoughts move onward unto him, As kine unto their pastures move (Griffith 1896; I, 25.1–16).

Varuna, King, of hallowed might, sustaineth erect the Tree's stem in the baseless region. Its rays, whose root is high above, stream downward. Deep may they sink within us, and be hidden. / King Varuna hath made a spacious pathway, a pathway for the Sun wherein to travel. Where no way was he made him set his footstep, and warned afar whate'er afflicts the spirit. / A hundred balms are thine, O King, a thousand; deep and wide-reaching also be thy favours. Far from us, far away drive thou Destruction. Put from us e'en the sin we have committed. / Whither by day depart the constellations that shine at night, set high in heaven above us? Varuna's holy laws remain unweakened, and through the night the Moon moves on in splendor (Griffith 1896; I, 24.7–10).

So then, despite the presence of such a God, who was God of all beings including the Devas, why did the rishis opt to worship the latter? The answer to this question is of course simple but nevertheless of great significance. To begin with, the idea of a Prajapati or a Varuna being the lord creator of all human beings, necessarily entailed at least a notional equality of all human beings irrespective of their being born as gentry or as rabble. This obviously wasn't very appealing to the people who had a disposition to look at themselves as different and superior. More importantly, a God who was the creator of all human beings would also be a lord over them. As against this, gods that are creations of the same forces that created the priest are more tolerable, they are easier to control. After all, they are gods created by the priests themselves. Natural forces are intrinsically in the service of man, never demanding prostration or worship. But a priest makes them into gods because he thinks that through worship, they can be appeased, persuaded and even coerced to perform certain tasks. It is an illusion he creates, not for himself, but for others—his clientele.

But before the priests could create gods, it was necessary to first remove God from the scene. This was accomplished without much ado when the priests invented the idea of his self-sacrifice for the purpose of the world's creation. In the "Purusha Sukta", God's death at the hands of gods and priests is central:

> When Gods prepared the sacrifice with Purusa as their offering,
> Its oil was spring, the holy gift was autumn; summer was the
> wood. / They balmed as victim on the grass Purusa born in
> earliest time. With him the Deities and all Sadhyas and Rsis
> sacrificed (Griffith 1896; X, 90.6–7).

With Purusha's death, gods and priests became formidable. In this sacrificial ceremony, the gods' presence was invoked to fulfil the desires of the sacrificer. But as it happened (or was arranged), this invocation could be done only through priests, who would recite hymns and perform the rites: pouring ghee, butter, cereals, among other things, into the fire. It was the hymns and not the gods which were instrumental in fulfilling the desire of the sacrificer. Mantras, with their mysterious power, enabled priests to make instant contact with the addressed deity, persuade it to assume the site of the ceremony and grant the sacrificer's prayers. Mantras were not magic, but neither were they simply prayers, as the concept is understood in Semitic religions.

This was the essence of what is called the Veda's sacrificial mysticism. Although Prajapati was the lord of sacrifices, prayers were seldom directed at him nor did he receive oblations. This is understandable: as a creator and master in his own right, he was unmanipulable, while the other gods could be easily willed to do any job the priest had in mind. Moreover, most of the prayers were for the fulfilment of innocuous worldly desires, like having a healthy offspring, a faithful wife, longevity, physical powers, victory in war, and so on. Bigger ceremonies, like one to celebrate the victory of a king over his enemies, were occasions for such indulgences which by ordinary ethical norms would be immoral. The atmosphere of festivity that marked such occasions, invariably became an orgy of the most permissive kind of drinking, gambling and sex.

Importantly, the immorality of these ceremonies implies that no ethical norms or guidance can be derived from a religion which is exclusively based on such sacrifices as happened in Vedic religion. It is not that the entire Vedic culture was bereft of morality, for no society or civilisation can survive without adhering to certain ethical principles that prevent it from falling into chaos and anarchy. But that, in such cases, morality rests more on the conscience of individuals, while the conventions of society are by nature weak and unreliable. For a robust moral culture, a Varuna is needed—Varuna as a supreme God in his own right, the lord of 'rta', who can command and compel man to behave, chastise and punish him for misdemeanour and defiance. This is, to be sure, a different Varuna when compared to his Vedic caricature as just one of the gods, a creation of nature, an Aditya.

The greater difficulty arises when the object of sacrifice is not an animate or inanimate power of the universe, but instead, the prototype of an indulgent king, like Indra. It is necessary in such a case that morality suffer an eclipse, paving the way for immoral forces to take the upper hand.[8]

Unfortunately for India, it was precisely Indra who was favoured, at the expense of all other gods. It is not that Prajapati Brahma and Varuna were entirely forgotten; they were retained, but only as one among the numerous gods and goddesses, with only lip service paid to them. Even later, when the native population recovered from its mental slavery and the Aryan gods were forgotten, Indra was allowed to continue.

Before proceeding, a little digression to understand the profound significance that the above fact carries. For, behind it is a story of a revolution which was both political and religious in nature. The last phase of the Vedic era and the early Brahmanical age, traditionally called by old-school historians as the period of Aryan expansion, marked a gradual eclipse of Aryan political domination and religion, excepting the rampancy and intensification of the cult of big sacrifices. As evidence, Vasishtha and Vishwamitra, earlier the most ardent champions of the Aryan cause, lose their prominence in this period, only surviving in the

stories about the previous era. Vasishtha's hundred sons
were killed by Saudasa, a descendent of the earlier Sudasa,
who had patronised the rishi. Vishwamitra, on the other
hand, himself cursed and disowned fifty of his sons for their
disobedience, while the remaining fifty (obedient) sons were
placed under the leadership of Sunhasepa, his adopted son.
Thus, two prominent clans of rishis suffered ignominy and
were almost forgotten, until they were once again revived by
the Brahmans in the age of epics.

In contrast, rishis with stronger connections to native
religion and culture were more active during the final phase
of the Vedic era. This is especially true of the Bhrigus, who
were suddenly in centre stage. These Bhrigus, or Bhargava
rishis as they are alternatively known, did side with Indra
in his campaign of plunder and destruction, but their hearts
were still set on the 'demons' with whom they shared a
fidelity more antique. There does seems to be some latent
animosity between them and the rulers of Aryan dynasties;
take for example how the Aryan prince, Krtvirya, destroyed
the ashram of Jamadagni on the pretext of his non-compliance
with some demand the prince made. Jamadagni's son, the
famous Parashurama, himself a rishi, then sought revenge
by exterminating the entire Aryan–Kshatriya race from the
face of the earth.

By this time, the scene of action had shifted from the
Sapta–Sindhava region to Kuru–Panchal areas—in present-
day North India, near western Uttar Pradesh. The native
population was recovering, and not just politically: the old
religious cults with their attendant magical practices were
also revived. It was so that Parashurama, like his father,
was steeped in occult lore, which was probably how he

performed incredible feats against his Kshatriya enemies.

A related development was that of the coming into prominence of Rudra, who in the *Rig Veda* was a malevolent deity, a source of affliction and disease. This character of the deity is preserved in later literature too, but it is supplemented by his association with some benevolent qualities, making him 'Shiva'—auspicious. In the *Vajsaneyi Samhita* (16.21), while he is described as the lord of forests and the protector of hunters, highway robbers, thieves, cheats, outcastes and such (16.22), he is also at the same time, hailed as the lord of medicinal herbs and described as the heavenly physician (16.5). While he is the lord of demons and outcastes, he is also one who can kill venomous demons, night rangers and female demons (16.5).

Shiva's rise as the chief deity of the occult presages Indian religious tradition's relapse into the very cultic mysticism and sorcery from which many Vedic seers tried to rescue it. Nevertheless, the counter movement representing the principle of positivity and power also gained momentum. As before, from among the groups of wandering ascetics (munis), a section emerged which pursued worldly ends in the name of preserving the purity of their religion. This time though, they were far more numerous, even as their religious integrity and credibility was subject to question and doubt. They were priest–Brahmans, who, unlike the rishis, settled themselves in towns, and performed religious rites on occasions of celebration or mourning, directly involving themselves in the lives of people. Unlike the rishis, they were not an alienated lot, keeping themselves aloof from the hurly burly of workaday life. Yet, they maintained a sense of superiority over the common folk, demanding the right to be treated as the most distinguished members of society. Since the basic ingredient of a culture of priesthood is a belief in multiple deities, allied with sacrificial liturgy to propitiate them, these elements were preserved with utmost care in the newly emergent religion. The gods, earlier at the beck and call of the mantras recited by priests, now became entirely governed by these linguistic devices with the consequence that they became even more powerless. The gods were no longer cajoled or propitiated to get a job done; the utterance of a hymn, with purity of accent and literal integrity, was enough to force the gods to do whatever was desired. Power did not and could not belong to the god. It now rested in the mantras, and since only the priest knew and had the authority to recite them, ultimately, he was the one who enjoyed power, and thus, authority.

So, the importance of sacrifice was highlighted by associating it with various kinds of religious–philosophical ideas and by weaving various myths around it. With the rise in importance of mantras, and thereby of priests, the gods became subject not only to the words uttered during sacrificial ceremony but also to the techniques employed in it. They even could be punished for errors committed by them in the performance of a sacrifice. Such a mistake was what led to the god Bhaga's eyes being burnt; Pusana's teeth were knocked out, and Savitra lost one of his arms similarly. In the *Rig Veda*, Tvashtra's son, who was sent to kill Indra, ended up dying when a spell rebounded due to a wrongly uttered syllable.

It goes without saying that the power gained from mantras had political as well as economic implications. It helped the priestly class to develop an intimacy with the Kshatriya establishment, and enabled them to extract enormous wealth, in all its forms, by way of dana and dakshina (gifts and fees). The sacrificial lore was directly responsible not only for the concentration of socio-politico-economic power in the hands of a few priests, but also for the emergence of a graded society with well-defined class–caste distinctions. The "Purusha Sukta's" significance in spelling out God's sacrifice for the purpose of creating the world (from which the justification for sacrificial liturgy was drawn) cannot be understated: it is here that we see, for the first time, the emergence of four classes of people from God (Purusha). The verse itself may be a matter-of-fact description of the division of work that any society would inevitably require and the consequent social gradation that such division would entail. But in the form of its institutionalised praxis, it meant that all rights were enjoyed by the few at the cost of total deprivation for the rest of the masses. What is more, it was also a source of the complete spiritual and existential mutilation of the people. As the *Aitareya Brahmana* says it,[9] ordinary masses could be oppressed, enslaved, and in the case of Shudras, even killed by the two upper classes at their sweet will. The Vaishyas of course were entitled to partake in sacrifices and oblations, a right absolutely denied to the Shudras, but they too were incomplete beings: only the Brahmans and Kshatriyas were complete (Eggeling 1882; 6.6-3-12). Though the Vaishyas had a right to partake in sacrificial ceremonies, there were marked differences. In the Rajsuya sacrifice, for instance, Vaishyas were given a cup of honey by the priest, whereby 'he [smote] them with untruth, misery and darkness'. As against this, while holding the same cup for Kshatriyas, the priest '[imbued] them with truth, prosperity and light'.[10]

Also in the *Aitareya Brahmana*, one can find descriptions of the duties of the Brahmans: 'to receive gifts, drinking soma and roaming at will', these in addition to their optional submission to the king. The roaming at will, in principle, meant free access to all women, not the least to the women of a king's harem. For bigger sacrifices, like Rajsuya, Vajpeya and Ashwamedha, priests and kings, along with the entourage of queens and wives of other sections of the nobility, indulged in drinking, gambling, and licentious sexual activities. In the Ashwamedha sacrifice, for example, the chief queen was made to lie down with the slaughtered horse in a posture of sexual intimacy, the horse's genitals were placed in the queen's hands, as the coterie priests recited sexually explicit dialogue with the corresponding sections of women present there.[11] In the Mahavrata sacrifice, the student priest actually indulged in sexual intercourse with a woman especially employed for the purpose. This extremely permissive trend reached its crescendo in the Gosava ceremony, where a sacrificial ox was praised for its ability to fertilise multiple partners, which was followed by the performers of the sacrifice actually imitating the bull by committing incest with their mothers, sisters, or other female relations, as described in the *Jaiminiya Brahmana* (2.1).

The question that naturally arises is whether this extreme immorality of a certain class can be explained away in terms of a 'fall' from some original ideal, or if it was due to extraneous influence, like that of the cults of magic and sorcery characteristic of the Rudra–Shiva religion, which involved such vices as part of its system. The latter possibility is undoubtedly there, but the Vedic religion was a product of a synthesis, a blending together of the nature worship of the

Aryans and native mysticism; a majority of rishis had their roots in the latter, with only a superficial and opportunistic sympathy for the former. Vasishtha and Vishwamitra, who were comparatively more averse to the indigenous religion and tried to checkmate its influence, also succumbed to their egotistic temptations and brought each other down through their reckless quarrels, thereby paving the way for decadent local tendencies to reassert themselves and take over religious bureaucracy under the pretext of perpetuating and preserving the legacy of the Vedic seers. Besides, within the Aryan system, Varuna lost his ascendancy, while Indra, who was far from being a paragon of virtue and moral rectitude, gained in stature.

If at all it was a fall, it was so, not from the Vedic ethos, but from pre-Vedic ideals, about which only a few certainties have survived, like the rishis' original faith in Prajapati–Brahma and Varuna. As a god of 'rta' and also a 'spy', Varuna could have been an effective check against the decadence and depravity that flourished. But in the mainstream of the tradition he was made to come to Indra's side, who was in the past his enemy and moral counter-image. In the later tradition, a systematic campaign of character assassination was launched against him to further eliminate his influence. This is evident, for example, in the story of king Harishchandra of Kashi, who was asked by Varuna to sacrifice his first son for him; the god tortured and tormented the king when he did not comply to the demand on time.

What the priests did with Varuna openly, they did with Brahma with greater sophistication and subtlety. Varuna's moral authority was eroded and he was emasculated of his power. With regard to Brahma, this was done through philosophy. Philosophy, as per its natural function, was deployed to save an idea from falling prey to raised fingers and intellectual objections. Given the fact that sacrifices were the primary source of class domination, class exploitation and immorality, it would have been unnatural for any rational community to tolerate them without protest. The society of the time, though enslaved and brainwashed, still had a flicker of rebellion left. Thus, in the *Satapatha Brahmana*, people are seen to be full of doubts and questions.

> Now those who made offerings in former times, touched (the altar and oblation) at this particular time, while they were sacrificing. They became more sinful. Those who washed (their hands) became righteous. Then unbelief took hold of men: 'Those who sacrifice become more sinful, and those who sacrifice not become righteous', they said. No sacrificial food then came to the gods from this world: for the gods subsist on what is offered up from this world. / The gods thereupon said to Brahaspati Angirasa, 'verily, unbelief has come upon men!' Brihaspati Angirasa then went and said, 'How comes it that you do not sacrifice?' They replied, 'From a desire for what should we sacrifice, since those who sacrifice become more sinful, and those who sacrifice not become righteous' (Eggeling 1882; 1, 2.5)?

The *Chhandogya Upanishad* also says the same: 'Therefore they call even now a man who does not give alms here, who has no faith, and offers no sacrifices, an Asura, for this is the doctrine (upanishad) of the Asuras' (Müller 1879, 137; VIII, 8.5). Now the fact that the authors of the Brahmanas condescended to mention such protests would suggest that the sceptics were by no means few in number, and that they seemed to have outgrown their earlier primitivist superstition that entertaining heretical thoughts or acts of defiance would cause them to be harmed (cursed). Other factors also led to the philosophical elaboration of the idea of Brahma. One was the impact of Shaivism; the other, the growing acculturation of society resulting in its being more articulate and self-reflective. The Vedas had already incorporated Rudra-worship as part of its religious system; but now, as a result of native rishis dominating the scene, the religious establishment was almost completely Rudra-ised. In practice, this meant that mystical and occult elements were mixed with simple Brahma worship. The old yati spiritism was a system of acquiring magical power by gaining access to the dark and evil forces of the universe. It was a religion of 'knowledge', and when applied upon the Brahma idea, the result was a speculative philosophy which pretended to be a religion of knowledge (gyana) and not of action (karma). Brahma was transformed into the *brahman*, which was not an object of worship but of knowledge and realisation. Brahma was of course not entirely abandoned; instead, he was subordinated to the *brahman*, and made into a mere chimerical manifestation of the latter.

Before we elaborate the cosmological and ethical aspects of the 'new' atman–*brahman* doctrine of the Upanishads, it is necessary to clarify that such ideas, though often perceived as an outcome of some higher kind of mystical knowledge, were not in any manner opposed or implied harm to the institution of priesthood. The priests were primarily an intellectual class, and it was expected of them to set the agenda of a given historical moment commensurate to the intellectual development of humanity. As part of their civilising function, they had to work upon and develop the ideas already present in nebulous and inarticulate form. A cosmology centred around the conception of Brahma and an eschatology of personal chastisement or redemption were part of the Vedic religious system. These were accepted as given, though recognising their implications for the practical life of man was dreaded. The cry of the rishi Dirghatamas that reality is one (ekam sat) was clearly an outburst of some rational kernel of his thought, which had in its psychological background the weariness with the multiplicity of gods and goddesses who could disrupt a rational-synthetic understanding of the cosmic reality around him.

But the avarice of senses affects the functioning of the mind. The priests, with all the limitations of their character, first made Brahma the lord of sacrifice (by sacrificing him) and when the institution began to teeter under its own weight, they devised a new way to make God non-interfering in their professional predilections. The Brahmanas, especially the later ones like *Satapatha* and *Taittiriya*, are not devoid of references to the idea of atman–*brahman*. In fact, a discussion of these issues was part of sacrificial ceremonies and was known by the technical name, Brahmodaya. This is sufficient enough to prove that these new ideas represented the internal, organic growth of the speculative minds of intellectual priests which could by no means have been designed to be detrimental to their professional or other interests. Besides, had they been a product of some higher spiritual experience, they could hardly be a matter of discussion, like the many other issues that find mention in the various Upanishads. The stillness and equipoise attained through this realisation did not lead to quietude of mental faculties, on the contrary, it caused a great stirring of recondite verbosity and incomprehensible jargon. Brahmans debated the issues of God and soul among themselves and when, at times, they couldn't resolve matters, they took it to kings. Yajnavalkya, the court priest of king Janaka of Videha, organised a grand debate over this very issue. He even managed to win the debate and get a pretty sum as reward. Not only this, his vanquished intellectual rival was even beheaded, as per the conditions of the debate. Ajatasatru of Kashi, another adept thinker of the mysteries of atman, assisted the king of Kaikeya in getting his father, Bindusara, killed, to succeed on the throne. Clearly, such an atmosphere of violence and egoism is more in keeping with an atmosphere of priestly intrigue than a culture of mystical experience or spiritual realisation.

The great saintly king, Janaka, is also recorded to have celebrated a horse sacrifice presided over by Yajnavalkya, confirming that sacrificial practices were not entirely abandoned with the rise of mystical speculation. However, there is no doubt that they were on the decline. The stature of Brahmans was diminishing at a popular level, and new challengers to the status quo were on the rise, with the emergent power-structure of eastern kings and chieftains. With growing urbanisation and political organisation of society, these new chiefs must have accumulated enough power to reject priestly supremacy, which undermined their honour and authority, and acted as a law unto itself. Part of the realisation that sacrifices were 'leaky boats', unable to take man to emancipation might have been due to the reluctance on the part of the new political authorities to go along with the priests on their greatly wasteful and abominable exercises in the name of religion.

Even though the diminished importance of sacrifices was a blow to the priestly institution, the new mysticism came to its rescue in a different way. After all, these new developments were also centred around the notion of knowledge, of cosmic mysteries rather than gods and mantras of yore. Yet, these cosmic mysteries were only accessible to Brahmans; all other classes were completely denied the privilege thanks to their births at a lower status. It is true that Kshatriyas were also experts in the discussion of mystical issues, but theirs was a theoretical knowledge. Actual realisation was only the possession of the Brahman caste. The stories of some Brahmans taking intellectual matters to kings for elucidation, if not an exercise in flattery, could at best be an indication of the fact that the lower order of this class had suffered a decline on the front of knowledge and learning. As far as the upper echelons were concerned, perfect realisation was still their prerogative. Vasishtha was a Brahmarishi by natural right; and no amount of tapas or austerities could help Vishwamitra, a blue blood Kshatriya, to elevate him to that status. That Vasishtha was a role model, a Brahmarishi, calls into question all this talk of realisation and emancipation as an otherworldly exercise; the sage, in this new milieu, still showed the same human weaknesses which were characteristic of him in the earlier phase of his spiritual career.

By now Vasishtha was very much a mythical figure, and not much historically relevant information can be deduced from the stories about him from this later period. What is certain is that a new culture of renunciation and self-mortification replaced the earlier (Vedic) culture of sacrifices. The divine mysteries that were revealed from the practices of self-mortification were subtle and profound, and could not be shared with all and sundry. Only a Brahman initiate, by virtue of his inborn nobility, could possess it; and that too under the guidance of a teacher of equally noble birth. It was an esoteric knowledge par excellence, which the teacher transferred to a selected disciple through the rigorous training of his mind and spirit—a teacher–disciple or guru–sishya system of spiritual education. Such an arrangement was crucial for the survival of the institution of priesthood. Faith in the idea that the teacher was a repository of all knowledge, led pupils, and through them the ordinary public, to pay him reverence, often even elevating him to the status of a god. The teacher was not only a 'knowing' person, but also all-powerful, and could make or break the fortunes of the common folk.

The new Brahmans clinched the matter in their favour when they adopted and popularised the doctrine of metempsychosis. As is agreed by scholars, neither the Vedic collections nor the subsequent Brahmana literature had any trace of this doctrine. The eschatology found in these books is a simple belief in the birth of the soul in another world after one's death in this world, with the attendant notions of heaven and hell derived from the merit of man's actions. This was for the most part quite similar to Islamic belief. However, it was suddenly abandoned in favour of the doctrine of cyclical rebirths. This probably originated in the spiritistic milieu of old native preculture, now with respectability and reformulation at the hands of Brahmans. The original linear theory was not entirely abandoned though; it was retained and supplemented by the claim that only a Brahman was entitled to final emancipation, all others having to suffer repeated deaths before being born as Brahman and thereby attaining salvation. An individual's birth in a certain varna was a result of his actions (karma) in previous births, and so, being born in a Brahman or a non-Brahman family was no accident of birth: it was the individual himself who was responsible for his success or failure in achieving his goal of liberation. Brahmans were therefore entitled to the claim of spiritual realisation as a birth right, and all others were denied it for the very same reason.

To highlight the fundamentally Brahmanical origin and character of Upanishadic mysticism, however, does not mean that it was the sole factor responsible for its emergence in Indian social history. Philosophical creativity cannot be said to always and, in all its aspects, be rooted in class consciousness. There is a factor of human ingenuity working in the background which comes forth whenever a certain ideological situation becomes unbearable and unsatisfactory. The gradual rise of the new system does indicate that the sacrificial religion of the Vedas failed to solve social problems and the multiple gods were no succour to alleviate the spiritual agony of the Indian. Hence the quest for a new system of ideas.

The essence of Upanishadic philosophy is a rational search for a unitary principle behind the multiplex of physical reality. Dirghatamas had set the tone for this but his approach was confined to dissolving the plurality of gods and replacing it with the idea of a single, supreme God. It was a genuine rational endeavour of a mind seemingly tired of unviable and self-contradictory metaphysics. But Upanishadic philosophy is human imagination run riot. The seers here are trying to comprehend what is avowedly incomprehensible and tend to speak a lot about what they have already declared to be unspeakable. Instead of confining themselves to a reasonable frame of what was given to them, as an idea of a single, supreme Brahma, creator and preserver of the world, they began to imagine what was for human reason a big void or emptiness. The new substance, *brahman*, insofar as it was absolute and without attributes, was also *intellectually* non-existent. For, logically, existence is what is knowable, and what is unknowable is ipso facto non-existence. To say that though it is rationally unknowable, the absolute can be comprehended through some supra-rational mode of experience may be an acceptable proposition, but in the case of Upanishadic seers, it was clearly based on an afterthought. No record of observations by mystics about their supposed spiritual realisation is available: the Upanishads were more works of pure philosophy. Yajnavalkya of course gave a long lecture to his mystically inclined wife on the nature of atman and *brahman,* before leaving for his spiritual quest. But what he actually realised at the end of his mystical journey is not recorded in history.

The Upanishads, however, do not contain a uniform or unified system of doctrines and are to a great extent heterogeneous in character. Although at places, there is a pretence of novel elements being offered, large parts of it are a continuation of ideas which were already present in the Brahmanas. The theory of metempsychosis was of course novel, as is evident from the surprise (*Chhandogya Upanishad;* 5.3) which Shwetketu and his teacher, king Pravahana Jaivali, express at the mention of it. This is true for the idea of salvation and the related pronouncement, that not sacrifices but a mystic gnosis could help man achieve emancipation, mentioned in the same passage of the *Chhandogya Upanishad.*

As for the idea of the *brahman*, in the early stages, it was not in any way radically different from the earlier notion of Brahma or Prajapati. Vedic Brahmanic cosmogony was largely retained, but now it was systematic and more elaborate. A few quotations from the *Brhadaranyaka* and *Chhandogya Upanishads*, for example, will show this to be the case.

The *Brhadaranyaka Upanishad* describes the process of creation of the world by the *brahman*, here called atman (self), and Purusha in the following manner:

> In the beginning this world was Self alone, in the shape of a person (purusha). He looking round saw nothing but his Self. He first said 'This is I;' therefore he became I by name. ... / He feared, and therefore any one who is lonely fears. He thought, 'As there is nothing but myself, why should I fear?' Thence his fear passed away. For what should he have feared? Verily fear arises from a second only. / But he felt no delight. Therefore a man who is lonely feels no delight. He wished for a second. He was so as large as man and wife together. He then made this his Self to fall in two (pat), and thence arose husband (pati) and wife (patni) ... He embraced her, and men were born. / She thought, 'How can he embrace me after having produced me from himself? I shall hide myself.' She then became a cow, the other became a bull and embraced her, and hence cows were born. The one became a mare, the other a stallion; the one a male ass, the other a female ass. He embraced her, and hence hence one-hoofed animals were born. ... / He knew, 'I indeed, am this creation, for I created all this.' Hence he became the creation, and he knows this lives in this his creation of (Hume 1877, 81; 1.4.1–5).

It is clear that, though crudely put, the doctrine presented here *is* monotheistic and, in a manner, resembles the

Biblical account of creation. There is another section (2.1) in the same Upanishad where the one supreme God is arrived at by transcending the idea of him being the sun, moon, lightning... much like the description in the Quran of prophet Abraham reaching the same conclusion through a similar process. Here the learned Brahman, Gargya Balaki, comes to king Ajatasatru of Benaras and offers him instruction about the *brahman*. The king gladly accepts the offer and then starts the following dialogue:

> Gargya said: 'The person that is the sun, that I adore as Brahman!' Ajatasatru said to him: 'No, no! Do not speak to me on this. I adore him verily as the supreme, the head of all beings, the king. Whoso adores him thus becomes supreme, the head of all beings, the king.' / Gargya said: 'The person that is in the moon (and in the mind), that I adore as Brahman.' Ajatasatru said to him: 'No, no! Do not speak to me on this. I adore him verily as the great, clad in white raiment, as Soma, the king. Whoso adores him thus, Soma is poured out and poured forth for him day by day, and his food does not fail.' / Gargya said: 'The person that is in the lightning (and in the heart), that I adore as Brahman.' Ajatasatru said to him: 'No, no! Do not speak to me on this. I adore him verily as the luminous. Whoso adores him thus, becomes luminous, and his offspring becomes luminous' (Hume 1877, 93; 2.1.2–5).

> Gargya said: 'The person that is in space, that I adore as Brahman' (Hume 1877, 94; 2.1.11).

> [Ajatasatru said:] As the spider comes out with its thread, or as small sparks come forth from fire, thus do all senses, all worlds, all Devas, all beings come forth from that Self. The Upanisad

(the true name and doctrine) of that Self is 'the True of the True.'
Verily the senses are the true, and he is the true of the true
(Hume 1877, 95; 2.1.20).

This apart, the Upanishads also retain the Vedic notion of
water being the primeval matter from which the golden
egg (hiranyagarbha) arose and which, in turn, became the
source of all created phenomena. This too is in agreement
with the Quranic account that Allah first ruled over the
waters. The *Brhadaranyaka Upanishad* (Hume 1877, 93; 3.6)
states that though physically the original substance is water,
ultimately, all has come from the *brahman*. At another place
in the same work, the order is reversed but the idea is same.
'In the beginning this (world) was water. Water produced the
true, and the true is *brahman*. *Brahman* produced Prajapati,
Prajapati the Devas. ...' (Hume 1877, 151; 5.5.1).

Similarly, *Chhandogya* (Hume 1877, 256; 7.10.1) says: 'It is
just water solidified that is this earth, that is the atmosphere,
that is the sky, that is gods and men.... all these are just water
solidified.'

The idea of the *brahman* in the Upanishads as the
ultimate ground of the world, as a soul or breath, was
not in essence different from the one presented in Vedas
and Brahmanas: it was only a further development of the
same. It was a movement in the right direction insofar as
the transcendental and immanent character of God, of the
universal—being *mysterium tremendum*, there will always be
some aspects of God which will not be comprehended by
man, at least through ordinary noetic faculties of rational
experience. It could even be said that such an emphasis had
become necessary since the original Prajapati or Brahma

had been reduced from his exalted status to just one among the many gods. By speaking of a transcendent *brahman*, the qualities of Brahma were transferred to the *brahman* and the earlier monotheistic idea was restored.

But the Upanishadic idea of God was not monotheism in its pristine originality and purity. While the *brahman* as transcendental and immanent was overemphasised, with the meanings of these concepts overstretched, there was no attempt to do away with the older pantheon consisting of multiple nature gods. Just as sacrifices continued to enjoy acceptance, the pagan outlook surrounding it also held its sway, albeit with reduced importance. The gods were still at the call of priests, and sacrifices were still a means of achieving worldly ends and heaven. The Vedic priestly ethos was supplemented by new ideas of gnosis and deliverance. The way of action (karma) was not decried nor the occult knowledge of mantras rejected. People were, however, exhorted to go beyond them. The path of the Vedas was, as the *Mundaka Upanishad* says, baser, compared to the superior path of knowledge. Thus while exhorting the 'Movers of truth' to follow scrupulously the sacred sayings of the Vedas, they are at the same time warned (Hume 1877, 366; 1.1):

> He said to him: 'Two kinds of knowledge must be known, this is what all who know Brahman tell us, the higher and the lower knowledge.' / 'The lower knowledge is the Rig-Veda, Yagur-Veda, Sama-Veda, the Atharva-Veda... but the higher knowledge is that by which the Indestructible (Brahman) is apprehended' (Hume 1877, 366–7; 1.1.4–5).

In the same Upanishad, while rewards of ceremonial

observations are promised in the form of 'Brahma world, gained by good works' (Hume 1877, 368; 1.2.6), one is reminded in the same breath that these are no help in achieving final deliverance: 'But frail, in truth, are those boats, the sacrifices, the eighteen, in which this lower ceremonial has been told. Fools who praise this as the highest good, are subject again and again to old age and death' (Hume 1877, 368; 1.2.7).

There are passages where the tone against sacrifices is more stringent but, on balance, the attitude seems to be that of keeping the two ideologies together. Thus it is said in the *Chhandogya Upanishad* that: 'if one offers the Agnihotra sacrifice without knowing this—that would be just as if he were to remove the live coals and pouring the offering on ashes. But if one offers the Agnihotra sacrifice knowing it thus, his offering is made in all worlds, in all beings, in all selves' (Hume 1877, 239; 5.24.1–2). In the *Brhadaranyaka Upanishad*, similarly, it is said: 'This that people say, "by offering with milk for a year one escapes repeated death." One should know that this is not so, since on the very day that he makes the offering he who knows escapes repeated death' (Hume 1877, 87; 1.5.2).

This strategy of supplementing rather than replacing older ideas was the basic stand taken by the mainstream of Upanishadic sages. It was motivated partly by the realisation on their part of the vulnerability of the older practice, that it was against human reason and needs, and partly by the genuine urge to philosophise about the phenomena of the world. The overemphasis on the immanence of God in the world, however, reinforced physiolatry. At the same time, by overstretching the meaning of transcendence, God was made too detached to have any significance in man's day-to-day life. Polytheism and pantheism, which are mutually exclusive doctrines, came here to co-exist without feeling antagonistic to each other.

Upanishadic metaphysics is a movement of thought in the realm of void. After having declared the indescribability of the *brahman*, 'it is not this, it is not that' (neti neti), seers persisted in speculating and theorising it. The more they did, the more they became incoherent and illogical—the whole discourse was reduced to a jumble of statements grounded neither in experience nor in discursive reason. After the *brahman* was theorised as without predicate, they were faced with the problem of explaining how the world, whatever its ontological status, arose from this *brahman*. The need of a demiurge, of Prajapati, was immediately felt, and resolution was sought by declaring the latter to be an immediate (first) creation of *brahman*. Not only this, but much in the fashion of later Neoplatonists, a series of spiritual entities were conceived to serve as intermediaries between creator and creation. This is shown in the following citation from the *Brhadaranyaka Upanishad*:

Then Gargi Vachaknavi asked, 'Yagnavalkya,' she said, 'everything is woven, like warp and woof, in water. What then is that in which water is woven, like warp and woof?'

'In air, O Gargi,' he replied.

'In what then is air woven, like warp and woof?'

'In the worlds of the sky, O Gargi,' he replied.

'In what then are the worlds of the sky woven, like warp and woof?'

'In the worlds of the Gandharvas, O Gargi,' he replied.

'In what then are the worlds of the Gandharvas woven, like warp and woof?'

'In the worlds of Adityas (sun), O Gargi,' he replied. ... [&c.] (Hume 1877, 113; 3.6.1).

Through regression, the seer moves from the sun to the moon, then to the world of stars, then to gods, to Indra, to Prajapati and finally to the world of *brahman*. Once this stage is reached, further questioning becomes irrelevant and Yajnavalkya asks his inquisitive wife to stop speaking: 'Gargi, do not question too much, lest your head falls off. In truth, you are questioning too much about a divinity about which further questions cannot be asked. Gargi, do not over-question.' Thereupon Gargi, of course, holds her peace.

With variations, the same scheme has been presented elsewhere also. It is reminiscent of Plotinian theory in its principle of 'vac' or speech, which Brahma created before he created creation itself, just as in the Greek system. Here, Logos was the first being which came out of the absolute being and led to the creation the world. Vac or Saraswati is described as the daughter of Brahma with whom he consorted incestuously. This primordial incest has been described several times in the Puranas, but the idea with some variation is found in earlier literature as well. In the *Rig Veda* the goddess is described like this:

I travel with the Rudras and the Vasus, with the Adityas and All-Gods I wander. I hold aloft both Varuna and Mitra, Indra and Agni, and the Pair of Asvins. / I cherish and sustain high-swelling Soma, and Tvashtar I support, Pusan, and Bhaga. I load with wealth the zealous sacrifice who pours the juice and offers his oblation / I am the Queen, the gatherer-up of treasures, most thoughtful, first of those who merit worship. Thus Gods have stablished me in many places with many homes to enter and abide in. / Through me alone all eat the food that feeds them,— each man who sees, breathes, hears the word outspoken They know it not, but yet they dwell beside me. Hear, one and all, the truth as I declare it. / I, verily, myself announce and utter the word that Gods and men alike shall welcome. I make the man I love exceeding mighty, make him a sage, a Rsi, and a Brahman. / I bend the bow for Rudra that his arrow may strike and slay the hater of devotion. I rouse and order battle for the people, and I have penetrated Earth and Heaven. / On the world's summit I bring forth the Father: my home is in the waters, in the ocean. Thence I extend o'er all existing creatures, and touch even yonder heaven with my forehead. / I breathe a strong breath like the wind and tempest, the while I hold together all existence. Beyond this wide earth and beyond the heavens I have become so mighty in my grandeur (Griffith 1896; X, 125.1–8).

In Puranic accounts, the same Saraswati (who is the daughter of Brahma in the Upanishads) is the wife of Kashyap (Vision), himself a grandson of Brahma, who by his other two wives, Diti and Aditi, fathers the anti-gods (Daityas) and gods (Devas). Being the water goddess, Saraswati is the source of all creation, including the rishis, in whom she enters to endow them with the sacred knowledge of mantras.

The denial of creative activity to Brahma, and his ascription to the lower level of reality, resulted in a static and immobile conception of God. It was, then, futile for man to worship him or praise him or seek his favours in this world or in the other world. To this idea, of the irrelevance of God in man's practical life, corresponded the idea of the world being unreal or only nominally real in comparison with the reality of God. Insofar as the Upanishads preach a pantheistic metaphysics, the problem of determining the ontological status of the world was palpable—so the world itself was retained as a lower form of the *brahman* and, contrarily, all physical forms were declared as names devoid of content. God was said to be hidden behind the veil of physical forms or, alternatively, the latter were nothing but ideal, as opposed to material, manifestations of God.

In either case, man's objective was to remove the veil and apprehend reality. But if the sensual world did not reflect the correct nature of reality, and the *brahman* itself was concealed behind phenomenal experience, how then could one approach it and communise with it? While the whole world, including the human body, was illusory, the soul (atman) of man was declared as the seat of the *brahman*, which man could approach and realise. The soul was not a creation of the *brahman;* it was rather an abode of the *brahman,* the *brahman* itself. The realisation of atman was therefore the realisation of the *brahman*—hence in the *Brhadaranyaka Upanishad,* the declaration of the realised, aham brahmasmi: 'I am *brahman'* (Hume 1877, 83; 1, 4.10).

Once the purpose of man's life was declared as the realisation of God and not his worship, it logically followed that the path to this goal was through knowledge and not through action. And since the knowledge of God was the knowledge of one's true self, it implied that knowledge did not consist in the possible cognition of something which one could learn, something one was unaware of. For, one's self was not something other than or external to him: it was his own essential personality. But this essential self is not immediately revealed to man because it is hidden behind the exterior of the body, just as the *brahman* is hidden behind the world. Self-knowledge was then a discovery, a removal of ignorance, and seeing and breaking the veil.

But the 'ignorance' pertaining to physical reality was not just *about* it but also *because* of it. Man's vision of true reality was blurred not because of any inherent defect in human nature but because of his immersion in physical reality. Man takes the phenomenal world to be real, acting in it and acting for it. Engagement with nature makes him forgetful of what is really real: his own essential atman. The more one is involved in the world, the more he is ignorant of, and distant from, true knowledge. Salvation then lies in the conscious decision to reverse this process and expunge ignorance by gradually disengaging from the world. This mysticism makes such a theory of knowledge a philosophy of renunciation and asceticism par excellence. To quote the *Brhadaranyaka Upanishad*:

> He who overcomes hunger and thirst, sorrow, passion, old age and death. When Brahmanas know that Self, and have risen above the desire for sons, wealth, and (new) worlds, they wander about as mendicants. For a desire for sons is desire for wealth is desire for worlds. Both these are indeed desires. Therefore let a Brahmana, after he has done learning, wish to stand by real strength; after he has done with that strength and learnig he becomes a Muni (a Yogin); and after he has done with what is not the knowledge of a Muni, and with what is the knowledge of a Muni, he is a Brahmana. By whatever means he has become a Brahmana, he is such indeed (Hume 1877, 112–3; 3.5.1).

The *Mundaka Upanishad* similarly says:

They who practice austerity (*tapas*) and faith (*sraddha*) in the forest, / The peaceful (*santa*) knowers who live on alms / Depart passionless (*vi-raga*) through the door of the sun, / To where is that immortal person (Purusha) e'en the imperishable spirit (*atman*) (Hume 1877, 369; 1.2.11).

The importance of these passages cannot be understated—they are the first recorded proclamations in support of the practice of quietude and mendicancy in Indian literary history. The culture of munis that prevailed in the most ancient times in India, in all probability, produced this new iteration of Vedic rishis. But we know precious little about the general philosophy of the seers of old; earlier literature contains only a few references of their ascetic character. But the Upanishads hold a well-articulated system of onto-cosmological theories which background the mystic–ascetic practice. In this system, Spirit does not comprehend matter but stands in opposition to it. A spiritual life therefore demands the suppression of the urges of the body as also a control over the proclivities of mind.

Apart from the serious psychological and social dislocations that this idea implied, it also gave rise to a dual system of ethical conduct—one set of values for an ordinary life and another for ascetics and those who have realised the absolute. The ordinary scheme of moral conduct was of course: 'The doer of good becomes good. The doer of evil becomes evil' (Hume 1877, 149; 4.4.5). But the ethics of the ascetic entailed the transcending of distinctions between good and evil, since the *brahman* itself was beyond such distinctions. The idea was that, to attain liberation, not only evil actions, but also good actions were to be avoided;

the latter too was, after all, an action performed for some worldly purpose and therefore equally motivated by desire. And desire, according to this theory, led to involvement and ignorance. Good acts of course carried rewards, but in the end, they were futile and perishable, even perhaps harmful.

> Considering sacrifice and good works as the best, these fools know no higher good, and have enjoyed (their reward) on the height of heaven gained by good works, they enter again this world or a lower one. (Hume 1877, 369; 1.2.10)

Though the ascetic is expected to be ever pure and free of the taints of sin and evil, ultimately these do not make any sense in his life. Once the atman is known, all the effects of the evil he might perform are washed away at once. '...and if people pile even what seems much (wood) on the fire, it consumes it all. And thus a man who knows this, even if he commits what seems much evil, consumes it all and becomes pure, clean, and free from decay and death' (Hume 1877, 156–7; 5.14.8). For such a person, the thought of what is right and what is wrong hardly matters. 'He does not distress himself with the thought, Why did I not do what is good? Why did I do what is bad? He who thus knows these two (good and bad), frees himself. He who knows both, frees himself' (Hume 1877, 289; 2.9).

The role model here is, of course, none other than Indra himself; Indra who, as the *Kaushitaki Upanishad* says (Hume 1877, 320–1; 3.1), 'departed not from the truth, for Indra is truth':

> To him then Indra said 'Understand me, myself. This indeed

I deem most beneficent to men—namely, that one should understand me. I slew the three-headed son of Tvashtri. I delivered the Arunmukhas, ascetics, to the wild dogs. Transgressing my compacts, I transfixed the people of Prahlada in the sky, the Paulomas in the atmosphere, the Kalakangas on earth. Of me, such as one as I was then..., not a single hair was injured; So he who understands me—by no deeds whatsoever of his would he be injured, not by stealing, not by killing embryo, not by the murder of his mother, not by the murder of his father: if he has done any evil (*papa*), the dark colour departs not from his face; (i.e., he does not become pale').

Now it is unlikely that such blatant amorality could have been practised on a wide scale by sages without putting in jeopardy the social existence of man. The Upanishads in themselves do not give much historical information about the actual state of man's life. However, the two epics of *Ramayana* and *Mahabharata*, though basically fictional in content and character, are accepted by scholars to represent the value system of society roughly during the same period. In these texts, one finds abundant information suggesting a relaxed moral code in the upper echelons of society. It is an irony that while at the level of common people, a strong code of personal and public ethics prevailed, as we reach at the level of those who were supposed to be the most ardent adherents and preservers of said morality, things are far more lenient. In both the epics, particularly in *Mahabharata*, on critical occasions the rishis and the gods violate the rules under one pretext or other. To take only a few famous examples, when sage Parashara invites Satyavati, the fisher woman, for intercourse, the latter is shocked at the proposal but she eventually consents on the assurance that the rishi would use his powers to ensure that she would not lose her virginity. In a similar incident, Kunti, the mother of the Pandavas, had to succumb to the advances of the god, Surya, even though she was not convinced of the desirability of the act. Indra seduced many women including the wife of sage Gautama by appearing in disguise. Brihaspati pressed his brother's wife for sex even though she was already carrying a child in her womb. Later he begot a son, the famous sage Bharadwaja, by the same woman. The king of Panchala was dismayed when he heard of the polyandrous marriage of his daughter with the five Pandava brothers at the behest of lord Krishna. Despite an advanced code of war ethics, the heroes of *Mahabharata*, on both sides, break every rule during the course of war. On the Pandava's side, the exhortation to do so comes from none other than lord Krishna. In the *Ramayana* too, Rama kills Vali, the monkey king, in defiance of all moral conventions.

As is known, the comprehensive word to denote the whole gamut of ethical activity was 'dharma'—a development of the earlier 'rta' of Varunite origins. This dharma, to a very large extent, ensured a harmonious collective life, even though its dispensation by the priestly system meant that its purity was considerably lost. That this concept flourished was necessitated thanks to the Upanishadic promulgation of a philosophy, which was not only amoral but highly asocial. Its goal was the liberation of the individual at the cost of society; society itself was a manifestation of physical bonds which fettered the soul and prevented its access to the truth. But though in essence highly individualistic, these Upanishads could not totally turn away from the necessity of having rules to maintain social order—the survival of the individual depended on this as well. Though rare, references to social consciousness do occur in these texts, even if encumbered by the Vedic idea of Purusha being the source of the four classes of society. The *Brhadaranyaka Upanishad* (Hume 1877, 84–5; 1.4.14) says:

> He was not strong enough. He created still further the most excellent Law (dharma). Law is the Kshatra (power) of the Kshatra, therefore there is nothing higher than the Law. Thenceforth even a weak man rules a stronger with the help of the Law, as with the help of a king. Thus the Law is what is called the true. And if a man declares what is true, they say he declares the Law; and if he declares the Law, they say he declares what is true. Thus both are the same.

Adherence to dharma on a personal level, then, was a source of a virtuous life which had its reward in the enjoyment of heaven. But for the renunciate, who was beyond the distinctions of virtue and vice, pleasure and pain, there was a still greater reward in the form of omniscience and omnipotence. Having realised the *brahman,* he had the whole world at his feet. All his desires could be fulfilled and no harm could be done to him; he was made invincible. The *Brhadaranyaka Upanishad* thus says: 'That Udgatri priest who knows this—whatever desire he desires, either for himself or for the sacrifice, that he obtains by singing. This, indeed, is world conquering' (Hume 1877, 80; 1.3.28) ... 'this whole world, whatever there is, is five-fold. He obtains this world who knows this' (Hume 1877, 85–6; 1.4.17). 'He who knows this becomes eater of every thing; everything becomes his food' (Hume 1877, 96; 2.2.2). 'He (Indra) is without a rival—He who knows this has no rival' (Hume 1877, 88; 1.5.12). 'Whoever strives with one who knows this dries up and finally dies' (Hume 1877, 151; 5.4). In the *Chhandogya Upanishad*: 'As a lump of clay would fall to pieces in striking against a solid stone, so falls to pieces he who wishes evil to one who knows this, and he, too, who injures him. Such a one is a solid stone' (Hume 1877, 179; 1.2.8). The *Taittiriya Upanishad* (Hume 1877, 291; 3.7) similarly: 'He who knows that food which is established upon the food, becomes established. He becomes an eater of food, possessing food. He becomes great in offspring, in cattle, in the splendour of sacred knowledge, great in fame'. The *Kaushitaki Upanishad* (Hume 1877, 316–7; 2.13): 'Verily, indeed, if upon one who knows this both mountains should roll themselves forth—both the southern and the northern—desiring to lay him low, indeed they would not lay him low. But those who hate him and those whom he himself hates—these all die around him.'

It goes without saying that such great prosperity and power that accrues from one's knowledge of the *brahman* was conceived to serve as a means, by later rishis, to reacquire the authority they had lost in the wake of rising Kshatriya assertion. This 'knowledge' was obviously not exactly magic as the word is ordinarily taken to mean these days. The Upanishads themselves are almost free of references to magic. But it should also not be forgotten that in the epics, the knowledge of the *brahman* (Brahmavidya) was always depicted as something which engendered miracles, which the rishis possessed and which they used to the hilt to perpetrate their hegemony over the Kshatriyas and the lower sections of society.

The first time the word *brahman* is used as a neuter God is in the *Atharva Veda*—the book of magical spells and charms.

The first chapter of the *Mudanka Upanishad* also describes this form of knowledge to have been first received by the Atharvans, who, again, are known to have been especially connected with the cultus of magic.[12] In the *Brhadaranyaka Upanishad* (Hume 1877, 148–9; 4.6) a long list of teachers who especially propagated this doctrine can be found: Gautama, Tvashtri and Asuri and Asurayana, all known to belong to the older non-Aryan cults of spiritism and asceticism. This is again confirmed by a casual reference in the *Baudhayana Sutra* (Bühler 1882, 260; 2.6.28) that it was Kapila, the son of Prahlada, who out of rivalry with the gods made a division of life into four stages, of which the sanyasa or complete renunciation is the last. Indra's opposition to this culture of renunciation, as depicted in the epics and Puranas, can also be seen in the same light.

The clear association of the concept of the *brahman* with the Asuras and the Asuric way of life and knowledge is somewhat mystifying to a modern historian of India. Yet, it appears that what was originally a philosophical search for a unitary principle behind cosmic diversity, was soon appropriated by priests and changed into an ideology of power. Whatever be the historical substance of the great epics, it is clear that they represent this ideology in full swing at a certain period of Indian history. It should also be clear in this context that with the Upanishads, we enter into the twilight zone of Indian history. Many of the kings mentioned in this kind of literature—Janaka of Videha, Kaikeya, Pravahana Jaivali—have dubious historicity. But such kings as Bimbisara, Ajatasatru and Prasenjit are surely historical figures as their names frequently occur in contemporaneous Jaina and Buddhist literature. They are found to propound a doctrine which has strong affinities with another set of ideas which were later to be called heretical but whose roots nevertheless lie in the orthodox legacy of the Vedas themselves.

2

Sangham Sharanam

By the end of the fifth century BCE, the religious mainstream in India was divided into the orthodox and the so-called heterodox streams of thought. Even in this, the two shared a commonality at their cores. The division is also, though loosely, based on geographical lines. One brand of Brahmanism, with a strong influence of Shaivite ideas, was popular in the upper central regions of the subcontinent, stretching down to the southern provinces. The semi-organised cults of Shramanic ideology, meanwhile, were popular in the eastern reaches of India. Upanishadic doctrines were restricted to the small region between these two major groupings. It is interesting that while having similarities (as also differences), the Brahmanic and Shramanic ideologies did not interact much except in socio-political contexts.

The commitment of Brahman priests to Upanishadic mystical ideas, that downgraded the notion of sacrifices, was at best half-hearted and may have been the result of a compromise with the ruling class, with whom they wanted to maintain a cordial relationship. The rulers themselves had no reason to persist with the practice insofar as it undermined their authority and family honour. The Kshatriyas of the Gangetic plains (Janaka, for example) still practised it, but those further east had their own ethnic pride and native religious beliefs, and were not at all obliging or submissive. The eastern heterodoxy was, therefore, at once, an assertion of Kshatriya superiority over Brahmans and also a philosophical rearticulation of native beliefs.

Around the same time that the Upanishadic Brahmans were consolidating their philosophy in cities like Kaikeya, Videha and Kashi, further east, in what is now Bihar, a great number of sects with more or less uniform ascetic ideas flourished. Of these, only three—Ajivikas, Jainism and Buddhism—survived. Later, even Ajivikas waned, leaving only the latter two to struggle it out. Buddhism and Jainism, in fact, did not just survive, they flourished. This was because they originated among the Kshatriyas, thus ensuring instant royal support wherever their message reached. The only possible opposition could come from the Brahmans, but in the eastern regions, Brahmans were already a degraded lot, bereft of knowledge and culture, dependent on charity and dole. In influence and authority, they were a pale shadow of their counterparts out west, who looked down upon them and contemptuously called them 'Brahman bandhu', literally meaning 'Brahman brother', with tongue-in-cheek connotations.

The original teachings of Shramanism are lost to history. Much of what is attributed to their religion is a later construction; even the attendant philosophy is a rationalisation of practices which the followers of these sects came to adopt. But, assuming that later thinkers must have built on nebulous elementary ideas handed to them by teachers, who may have been part of an original tradition, certain obvious conclusions can be drawn—first, during this period, the ruling class showed a strong inclination towards renunciation and withdrawal from the world. In the Upanishads we come across kings who taught mystical ideas to Brahmans, some of them even taking to a life of asceticism. The same is true about the founders of Jainism and Buddhism, who abandoned family life in their prime, and opted for a life of self-mortification and renunciation.

Second is that, even in sharing certain values with Brahmanic mysticism, they were not enamoured by the grandiose philosophy of atman–*brahman*, which was still associated with the institution of sacrifices. In order to effect a clean break with the Brahmanic system, they made their opposition to this philosophical motif the main plank of their religious movements. Gautama Buddha is of course known to have shunned metaphysical speculation, but in Jainism, the tendency to philosophise was strong. They preferred a naturalistic cosmology, which was akin to Samkhya, another school that preached mysticism and asceticism, though still nominally showing faith in the Vedas. Both Jaina and Samkhya, then, believed in eternal and differentiated individual souls, and ascribed to a more active ontology of matter, where material forces determined the forms and destinies of human beings and the universe.

Interestingly, all three systems—Samkhya, Jainism and Buddhism—profess their association with Kapila, the illustrious Asuri Brahman muni of pre-Vedic anteriority. This suggests not only their common origin, but also their shared concerns about humanity. But there were crucial differences in their ontological and cosmological views. This meant that they differed on questions about the destiny of the soul and the precise nature of the world. In spite of this, their similarities are consequential.

The two supposedly rival schools of Brahmanism and Shramanism had a common geo-traditional genealogy in the munis of the pre-Vedic era and their predecessors, the Vedic rishis. Indra, first as a political and military figure, and then as an Aryan arch deity, eclipsed the worship of primitive gods and goddesses. But the Aryan conquest of the Early Indian mind and body was not an altogether one-sided affair, as the sages recovered their ground and a compromise was reached where all other alien deities were to be forgotten except for Indra. The priests found Indra to be an ally insofar as he fought against Varuna, who was not favourable to them, being ethically censorious. After being the bane of munis, Indra not only became their 'friend', but was elevated to the status of an amoral sage, as is described in the Upanishads. Moreover, as a Kshatriya, he was a patron of sacrifices and an exponent of an actionist worldview.

In this last aspect, he even replaced Prajapati, who was only retained at the philosophical level of priestly theology, as the creator of the world. It is quite remarkable that Indra, in all his multifarious aspects, makes regular appearance in Buddhist and Jaina texts, though of course he is subordinate to the Buddha or Jina. The latter two attained a more exalted status in the spiritual hierarchy compared to Indra, whose abode was a quasi-materialist heaven (Indraloka). Like the Shramanists considered Indra to represent a lower level of religiosity, the more ritualistic Brahmans also considered his saintly postures as pretentious, fit only for the consumption of the more degraded munis. At most, he was to be accepted as Rajarishi—one who did not and could not attain the higher status of a Brahmarishi. In a later Puranic story, Indra steals a sacrificial horse from a king and while fleeing to avoid the wrath of the priest, he abandons his mantle which is acquired by the native Kshatriyas and their degraded saints.

This complicated mosaic, in a way, reflects the convoluted ways in which the Shraman and Brahman ideologies interacted with each other. There were, to be sure, fundamental divergences, both at doctrinal and institutional–ethical levels, but culturally the strains were so interfused that neither can be fully disentangled. While the Buddhists and Jainas accepted Indra as the king of his subordinate deities, they also, at a certain level, recognised Brahma and his heavenly kingdom (Brahmaloka). The Vedic theory of heaven and hell, and an action-based ethics of piety, were also accepted even if emphasis was paid to transcending this binary, again, reminiscent of the Brahmanistic ideal. In fact, as scholars have argued, the Buddha's 'discovery' of truths— human existence was necessarily a miserable condition, the root cause of this misery was the soul's ignorance and so on—were all hardly novel or original. These ideas were a common Brahman–Shraman legacy, and exerted common ethical and institutional practice and lifestyle. There were, of course, important doctrinal differences which gave birth to diverse eschatologies and differences in practical attitudes, including the attitude towards sacrifices.

Doctrinal considerations aside, there were also personal and historical reasons why Shramans were hostile towards sacrifice. The Buddhists, who did not fully subscribe to the theory of nonviolence, in rejecting it, do not go beyond polemics, saying that if the sacrifice was a means of sending the sacrificial animal to heaven, why not the priest or the sacrificer himself be slain to meet a similar, desirable end. The virtue of 'non killing' as part of ascetic discipline was emphasised, but it was not a general moral requirement binding on the non-monkish laity. The historical reason for this was that, apart from involving an enormous waste and being a symbol of Brahman supremacy, sacrifices had adverse implications on the perception of a king's personal honour and the health of his public treasury. During that time, there was already a section of Brahman ascetics opposed to sacrifice, though the reason in their case might have been more practical than theoretical. Seeing that not all kings were equally amenable to priestly manipulations, some of them, especially those belonging to the more eastern parts, being openly hostile, ascetic–priests might have found it prudent to at least partly do away with sacrifices, if only to retain the residual authority and respect of their Kshatriya patrons.

This aside, Buddhism and Jainism (and also Samkhya) differed on a more contentious issue—the nature of the human soul. Buddhists subscribed to the doctrine of non-soul or anatmatta (anatta, in Pali) as their point of departure, not only from the orthodoxy but also from fellow heterodox opinions. It is well known that the Buddha observed a calculated silence about this doctrine. But it is not altogether improbable that he, through his silence, wanted to avoid a discussion on the issue, thinking it to be philosophically recondite, which can be illuminated only through mystical insight. Additionally, he may also have disliked the contentiousness and philosophical hair-splitting which could result as a consequence of indulging in such discussions. Indeed, he prohibited his monk followers from dabbling in such exercises. Moreover, the atman doctrine was seen as a part of Vedic theistic ideology, and the Buddha, through his silence, might have sought to preserve the future identity of his creed, a task about which he was so conscious.

These are, however, conjectures, or, at most, secondary reasons for the Buddha's non-committal approach. What is more certain is his settled view that the different scholastic positions taken by different sectarians over the question of the soul—or even metaphysical issues in general—insofar as they are based on philosophical reasoning and speculation, are by their very nature suspect. These metaphysical issues were for him 'profound, difficult to realise, hard to understand, tranquilising, sweet' which were 'not to be grasped by mere logic'. They were subtle, 'comprehensible only by the wise', which the Tathagata alone, 'having himself realised and seen face to face', could set forth. Such things could only be spoken of by the ones who could 'rightly praise Tathagata in accordance with truth' (Rhys Davids 1899, 37). The scholar was essentially no different from ordinary mortals as far as the status of his being and thought were concerned, and so was subject to his own physical limitations, thus being incapable of accessing truths. It is therefore that only 'when a brother understands as they really are, the origin and the end, the attraction, the danger, and the way of escape from the six realms of (sense-) contact, that he gets to know what is above, beyond, them all' (Rhys Davids 1899, 54).

Now, for a mystic like the Buddha, taking such a position was quite understandable. For one thing, his denial of the soul was not a definitive but more of a relative one, i.e. in relation to a positive affirmation of it. Even so, historically Buddhism was decidedly identified with a soul-rejecting atheology, its philosophical development being entirely in line with nihilism and negation. Where the Buddha kept a stubborn silence, his followers indulged in verbal euphoria to explain, interpret and even celebrate the rejection of the soul. This denial stemmed from the view that the soul suffered a radical misconception about itself. It was precisely this ignorance that led the soul to assert its own existence. This extraordinary hypothesis was ripe for speculative minds to interpret and build upon. But there was a problem. How could the soul be ignorant about itself if it did not exist? Ignorance is not a (material or spiritual) 'thing', that could cause delusion or misapprehension. It is a state of mind, a disposition, and the very fact that the soul was stated to suffer from this disposition proved that it existed.

Even before philosophers and logicians like Dharmakirti and Chandrakirti (both from the seventh century CE) began examining this problem, there were intense debates about it, like the one between the Buddhist sage, Nagasena, and Milinda, the Bactrian Indo-Greek king of second century BCE. The king, known in Greek as Menander, asked how the identity of a person could be established by its specific name and qualities, if the self was identical with the body, and the body itself was in a constant state of flux. That is, if the self was not there, or if it also changed and died with the body, how could it be recognised by its name or its qualities. Nagasena's reply is philosophically familiar. He takes a nominalist position, saying that the personal identity emerges through the configuration of subtle physical and psychical elements which, though finally unreal, can persist as long as ignorance is not fully removed. A 'chariot' is no more than, and not apart from or independent of the various parts of which it is comprised. 'Just as it is by the condition precedent of the co-existence of its various parts that the word 'chariot' is used, just so is it that when the Skandhas are there we talk of a 'being" (Rhys Davids 1890, 45; II, 1, 1).

This is obviously a familiar fallacy: a category mistake. It is not very sensible to apply the same logical framework on two levels of existence which are radically distinct from each other. A 'person' cannot be so easily reduced to the level of a 'chariot', and while it is controvertible that a 'chariot' is nothing more than the sum total of its parts, it is still doubtful that a soul or a self can emerge by combining its constituent physical or psychical elements. A 'person' carries any number of qualities and abilities (such as rational thinking, transcendental volition, emotions of love and belonging, and so on) which are not found even among animals, not to mention simpler material objects. The 'soul' of a person is therefore a different kind of presence and not reducible to material elements. It cannot be claimed that it is born of, affected by or even destroyed by the latter. Besides, the soul's perceived invisibility is not an argument against its self-presence, but against its absence. For, if visible, it would be contingent on the body, and hence, as the Buddha himself said, subject to death and decay. But because the soul does not vanish like material objects do, its 'presence' becomes all the more palpable.

This difficulty is further compounded by its eschatological component, even as this aspect was a clear advantage for Buddhism. The Buddha believed in the doctrine of karma which made his teachings consanguineous with the contemporary Brahmanism in important respects. But while in the case of Brahmanism, belief in the substantiality of the soul gave rise to the idea of its repeated births, in Buddhism the question naturally arose as to how a non-substantial soul could still be born and reborn successively until the end comes? If the self disappeared when its constituent elements perished, then how could it reappear in a different incarnation? Perhaps, some invisible law forced the scattered elements to reunite again, ensuring a kind of continuity and identity to the self-same self through its repeated births. Though this is not exactly a rationally unimaginable proposition, it was obviously too far-fetched, and some uncertainty persisted even among Buddhist scholars about its unambiguous acceptability.

The self in consecutive births must in some respects be identical to itself, while in other respects it had to be different. If the same self did not persist across births then the basic idea of a person suffering the consequences of his or her actions in different births would be lost. And since these consequences materialise in higher or lower forms of birth, a *different* identity has to be created to enable the person to go either higher up or go down to a lower level of existence. Nagasena explains the situation with the analogy of a lamp that is lit every night. It remains the same lamp but the flame is different each night. The continuity of a person or even a thing is maintained thus: 'One comes into being, another passes away; and the rebirth is, as it were, simultaneous' (Rhys Davids 1890, 64; II, 2, 1).

Such analogies, while illuminating in some respects, are also deceptive. The idea of the persistence of the self through successive births, if conceived mechanically, as in the case of lamp, may lead to dangerous consequences while also being philosophically unsubstantiated through experience and reason. Its logical conclusion is absolute karmic determination, as was believed by the Ajivikas, a view which the Buddha categorically rejected. According to him, while the present and the past may have determinate responsibilities, the future was open to contingencies. Taking a middle position between absolute determinism and absolute free will, he stressed that though the self was a creation of the dark forces of ignorance and lust, it still had the freedom and power of will to dispel ignorance and attain nibbana (popularly known as 'nirvana'). But the difficulty was that even if freedom was partially admitted, its locus had to be found in a self which was declared as immaterial. The four skandhas (which can be translated as 'groupings') in Buddhist theology, that described the make-up of an individual, constituted, at most, the physiology of the human self, not its essential psycho-spiritual personality. As a total being, man thinks and wills and enjoys transcendentally. This specific and human way of cognising and willing and enjoying suggests the presence of a transcendental self, which the Buddha was not prepared to admit, though he steered clear of any nihilism or determinism or materialism which denied in clear terms the essentiality of the human.

In Buddhist texts, one scarcely finds a full-fledged discussion of man's rationality or his aesthetic creativity. The emphasis is mostly on karma and its implications. In their tradition, the world, just like the self, emerges, or more precisely, is the name of the process, the becoming, of the dissolution and re-emergence of elementary physical particles, creating an illusion of the persistence and permanence of reality. The question of what brought these elements into existence, and for what purpose, is met with a deafening silence. Karma perhaps is the process which excludes from itself the idea of meaning or design. The question of origin is presumed to be unanswerable. What is known is the simultaneous emergence and dissolution of matter. The chicken and the egg in a circular dance of cosmic generation and destruction. That, says Nagasena, 'which has not been becomes; as soon as it has begun to become it dissolves away again. In reference to that the ultimate beginning is unknown.' (Rhys Davids 1890, 81; II, 3, 3).

In Buddhist cosmogony, the entire universe has its repeated phases of destruction and re-emergence. Once destroyed, the cosmic elements remain in a state of hibernation, in an ideal world, until they reunite to cause the appearance of the material world. Creation is gradual, in steps and stages—first, all being water, then the earth emerging out of it and then the rest. In the "Aggañña Suttanta" of *Digha Nikaya*, a water cosmogony, not unlike that of Vedic–Upanishadic (or even that of Biblical–Quranic), is propounded:

> Now at that time, all had become one world of water, dark, and of darkness that maketh blind. No moon or sun appeared, no stars were seen, nor constellations, neither was night manifest nor day, neither months nor half-months, neither years nor seasons, neither female nor male. Beings were reckoned just as beings only. And to those beings, Vasettha, sooner or later after a long time, earth with its savour was spread out in its waters. Even as a scum forms on the surface of boiled milky rice that is cooling, so did the earth appear. It became endowed with colour, with odour, and with taste.
>
> ...
>
> Then, Vasettha, some being of greedy disposition, said: Lo now! what will this be? and tasted the savoury earth with his finger... And from the doing thereof the self-luminance of those beings

faded away. As their self-luminance faded away, the moon and sun became manifest. Thereupon star-shapes and constellations became manifest. Thereupon night and day became manifest, [...] Thus far then, Vasettha, did the world evolve again (Rhys Davids 1921, 82–3).

Through this process of progressive decline, mushrooms, plants and trees emerged. Now the point is that though the scheme presented here is superficially creationistic, and even some mysterious (and mischievous) beings are shown to be at work in bringing out this descent towards multiplicity, the creator himself is conspicuous in his absence. In another sutta of the same text, though in a different context, Brahma does make an appearance.

3. 'Now there comes also a time, brethren, when, sooner or later, this world-system begins to re-evolve. When this happens the Palace of Brahma appears, but it is empty. And some being or other, either because his span of years has passed or his merit is exhausted, falls from that World of Radiance, and comes to life in the Palace of Brahma. And there also he lives made of mind, feeding on joy, radiating light from himself, traversing the air, continuing in glory; and thus does he remain for a long long period of time.

4. 'Now there arises in him, from his dwelling there so long alone, a dissatisfaction and a longing: "O! would that other beings might come to join me in this place!" And just then, either because their span of years had passed or their merit was exhausted, other beings fall from the World of Radiance, and appear in the Palace of Brahma as companions to him, and in all respects like him.

5. 'On this, brethren, the one who was first reborn thinks thus

to himself: "I am Brahma, the Great Brahma, the Supreme One, the Mighty, the All-seeing, the Ruler, the Lord of all, the Maker, the Creator, the Chief of all, appointing to each his place, the Ancient of days, the Father of all that are and are to be. These other beings are of my creation. And why is that so? A while ago I thought, 'Would that they might come!' And on my mental aspiration, behold the beings came" (Rhys Davids 1890, 30–1).

The above passage appears in a discussion of the beliefs of the semi-eternalists—for whom the world may have been created by the creator, but not the soul. The Buddha neither accepts nor rejects this position, claiming that he alone knows the truth of this matter. This non-committal attitude is interpreted, perhaps rightly, as his non-belief in the creatorship of Brahma. But as already seen, Brahma and his world frequently appear in the Buddha's discourses, and on occasion, the former himself pronounces his faith in the Buddha and praises his doctrine. There is therefore a certain ambiguity about his position on Brahma and the question of creatorship, which is in sharp contrast to the Jainas who were clearer and more forthcoming on this issue.

Since the Buddhist denial of the creator–Brahma was made in the context of non-belief in the soul itself, it was implicit that, for them, there was an internal connection between the twin denials. The Jainas, however, accepted the existence of the soul, but they considered it more of an evanescent (though material), conscious presence rather than a concrete, creative, thinking and willing agent. The same was also the case with Samkhya and Vedic–Upanishadic speculators. For Samkhya, while all activity belonged to prakriti (nature), the purusha (creator) was a passive, powerless entity who could do nothing except watch and take delight in the play of material forms. The orthodox Vedic–Upanishadic seers derecognised the human self for all practical purposes, presenting it as only a distorted apperception of the *brahman* itself.

All these schools then were anti-creationists to a certain extent, rejecting in their respective ways the actionist–creative principle. But the denial of a cosmic creative principle entailed the denial of human creativity itself, which belief went against empirical experience and implied a gross form of anti-culturalism. Human culture, as has already been argued, is generated by the twin factors of human creativity (which covers man's cognitive, conative and aesthetic functions) and the 'sociality' of the human self. One could of course disregard culture as part of one's life-denying or world-denying schemes, an idea which would be self-legitimated. The point, however, is that a positive cultural outlook is not possible except through a positive affirmation of both the self and God, in their creative and concrete incarnations. The Indian programme of the depersonalisation of man followed the Brahmans' depersonalisation of Brahma, who sacrificed him at the altar of some other gods. The Shramans, on the other hand, distinguished themselves by derecognising God himself, while elevating their own leaders to his status.

The Buddhist theory of the emergence of civilisation finds a brief mention in the "Book of Genesis" of *Digha Nikaya*. About the emergence of male and female beings, the Buddha says: 'Then truly did woman contemplate man too closely, and man, woman. In them contemplating over much the one the other, passion arose and burning entered their body. They in consequence thereof followed their lusts. And beings seeing them so doing threw some, sand, some, ashes, some, cowdung, crying: Perish, foul one! Perish, foul one!' (Rhys Davids 1921, 85). Sexual intercourse was obviously considered a blatant act of immorality and fall, disapproved by both the 'beings' as well as the humans. The defaulters were barred from entering their village for months, and were 'set to work to make huts, to conceal just that immorality.' A similar fall was also perceived to have happened when people, instead of being content with having their daily meals, began to hoard food stock for the future. The divines again bewailed saying: 'Evil customs, sirs, have appeared among men. For, in the past, we were made of mind... We set to work to make the earth into lumps, and feast on it... But since evil and immoral customs became rife among us, the savoury earth disappeared... [They said c]ome now, let us divide off the rice fields, and set boundaries thereto! And so they divided off the rice and set up boundaries round it' (Rhys Davids 1921, 85–7).

With civilisation came corruption—in the form of stealing, lying and violence. This made it imperative 'to select a certain being, who should be wrathful when indignation is right, who should censure that which should rightly be censured and should banish him who deserves to be banished' (Rhys Davids 1921, 88). The one chosen, accordingly, was 'the handsomest, the best favoured, the most attractive [and] the most capable' (Rhys Davids 1921, 88). He was called 'raja'; he charmed others through his dhamma and those of his race, who also established the dhamma, were called Kshatriya—the foremost class. Others, who were disgusted by the evil ways of people, left society altogether and became hermits, making their dwellings in forests, where they meditated and performed penance. These were the Brahmans, who emerged during the second stage of social evolution. Those among them who could not endure the hard life of forests and mountains came to live in towns and villages where 'they ma[d]e books'. The tradesmen and Shudras followed to do their respective class professions.

The fact that Shudras came last in the social hierarchy, relegated to activities like hunting and 'suchlike trifling pursuits', may have been a simple recognition of the class situation of those times. In fact, class stratification is an inevitable part of acculturation, and in this sense even the Vedic description of Shudras being born from Brahma's feet may have simply been a description of existent social facts. However innocent the intentions of the original authors may have been, the historical development of these attitudes had a malignant spirit, which characterised the Shraman schools as much as it did the Brahman school. The two upper classes remained socially superior, though with the obvious difference that for the Shramans, Kshatriyas came first. For them, all theorisation of superiority was done to press home the point that Brahmans' claim of priority was based on conceit and ignorance. In a manner of turning the table, it is now the Brahman who is asked to admit the superiority of Kshatriyas:

> The Khattiya is the best among this folk
> Who put their trust in lineage.
> But one in wisdom and in virtue clothed,
> Is best of all 'mong spirits and men (Rhys Davids 1921, 94).

The idea of the natural superiority of Kshatriyas over

Brahmans is indeed a settled matter for Shraman ideology. While being distinguished in valour, social status and the establishment of dhamma, the nobility was also seen as ever willing to renounce the world for higher pursuits. The Shraman ideal is the same as the Brahman one—renouncing the world before or after the fulfilment of one's secular duties. The social implication of renunciation is that, once the decision is taken, the distinctions between classes vanish and all become equal in merit and status. But in order for the Kshatriyas to have an upper hand over the Brahmans, distinctions had to be maintained. The Buddha himself never let any opportunity to emphasise this point be wasted. In the *Digha Nikaya*, he argues that while a son born out of wedlock between a Brahman youth and a Kshatriya maiden would not be accorded any social respect, in the reverse situation, the child would still deserve the customary caste privileges given to a Kshatriya. In the former case, moreover, the child would be an outcast. This, in effect, meant that 'even if a Khattiya has suffered extreme humiliation, he is superior and the Brahmins inferior' (Walshe 1995, 118).

In the above sutta, the Buddha humiliates his interlocutor, Ambattha, a young, brash Brahman, by pointing out the latter's humble origins and the 'purity' of his own Sakya race. He tells the story of an ancient king, Okkaka, who, wanting to divert the succession in favour of his favourite queen's son, banished his elder children from the land. The children then took up their dwelling on the slopes of the Himalayas and to preserve the purity of their lineage they married their own sisters. From this incestuous wedlock came the Sakya clan. Now, the same Okkaka had a slave girl from whom was born a black baby, who exhibited miraculous powers as a child, and grew up to become a famous rishi. Ambattha was born from the lineage of this rishi. Hence, even in degradation, Kshatriyas were superior to Brahmans. The Buddha tells this story with characteristic modesty, in a tone free of malice. His object is to shock the Brahman youth out of his brashness. Nevertheless, the content of his argument reflected common class prejudices, even if in their milieu they may not have been considered very malignant. Such prejudices were not peculiar just to the Buddhists. Jainas too entertained the same sentiments. In their case, every tirthankara was born of Kshatriya women. In the case of the last tirthankara, when this pattern wasn't followed, as recounted in the Kalpa Sutra, the mishap was quickly corrected.[1]

So, it is not entirely unjustified to conclude that for Shramanism, even if real religious merit was not conditioned by the circumstances of one's birth, socially, one's pedigree was somewhat of a factor to be reckoned with. This class consciousness may partly have been prevalent because of the rivalry that existed between the two powerful upper classes. But philosophically, it has to be considered as stemming from the denial of the self, which in effect meant the denial of the common humanity in all men, irrespective of class or caste difference. By not recognising universal human potentialities, social subjectivity was seen to be determined by factors of lineage and profession. The existential vacuum created by this spiritual denial was then filled by psychological determinants, such as pride in race or lineage. The Kshatriya aspiration for religious leadership, which was already prevalent in the Vedic orthodoxy, and was intensified in Shramanism, was a result of the philosophical and psychological effect of their having held secular power. Now they felt that transcendental religiosity too was not out of reach, or, at least, could not just be the exclusive possession of Brahmans.

Aside from that, another decisive reason for the generation of class identity was the doctrine of karma itself. As long as the doctrine of karma was in operation, the differentiation between 'higher' and 'lower' classes was inevitable, a logical outcome of individuals' accumulation of merits in their previous births. Privileges and deprivations of different classes, then, were natural. The society at large, or the privileged classes, forsook any responsibility in this regard. Not that there was no escape from this karmic stranglehold. One could transcend it by ceasing to be caught up in karmic games—by becoming asocial and unworldly. It must be noted that neither the Buddha nor Mahavira was a believer in caste segregation, at least not in its extreme iteration, as in the theory and practices of later Hinduism. But it is still doubtful that they disapproved of class differentiation as such. All the more doubtful is the presence of any programme of social reform or revolution in their religious scheme. Not equality, but inequality was the law of nature and one could overcome inequality not by being faithful to nature but by acting against it, by denying the social or rational nature of man, by becoming asocial and irrational.

Interestingly, unlike Jaina tirthankaras, who were invariably Kshatriyas, the Buddha's previous births took place in both Brahman or Kshatriya families. Though occasionally, he incarnated in animal forms (such as in the body of a swan or an elephant or a woodpecker or even a pig), he was never born in a Shudra or an outcast family. Within the framework of karmic ideology, 'lower' births were indeed an anomaly. Hence the apology and explanation: '… it is also an impossibility that good actions should have evil as their result. But it must be the influence of small portion of (evil) karma that caused him now and then, notwithstanding his knowledge of righteousness, to be in such (low) states' (Speyer 2010, 445).

Being born as a Kshatriya or a Brahman was still noble, and as a tradesman or a Shudra, deficient. At least as far as 'the talk is of marrying, or of giving in marriage' (Rhys Davids 1899, 124), and by extension, matters of acquiring power or position, were concerned, caste mattered. But in the end, all the notions of birth, lineage, pride of social position, had to be transcended to reach a higher plane of equality. 'Do not ask about the descent, but ask about conduct,' says the Buddha categorically (Fausböll 1881, 77). Again, in the "Vasalasutta" (vasala meaning outcaste) in the *Sutta Nipata*, he says that 'not by birth does become one an outcast, not by birth does one become a Brahmana but by deeds one becomes an outcast, by deeds one becomes a Brahmana' (Fausböll 1881, 23). Matanga, the low-born, attained salvation while many Brahmans still awaited their final emancipation. At the religious level, there was absolute equality—but only when one enters the state of homelessness, and forsakes being a householder. In other words, when one switches from the social to the asocial state.

Ironically, this culture of asceticism and renunciation, which was, in principle, a harbinger of 'higher' equality, ended up creating a class of priests with exclusive privileges and power, and a laity with its inherent spiritual and mental

handicaps and deprivations. The ascetic ideal of homelessness and powerlessness backgrounded the priestly praxis of
power and privilege. A king's slave, once he has donned the
yellow robe and once he 'dwells restrained, content with
mere food and shelter delighting in solitude' (Rhys Davids
1899, 77), becomes worthy of respect and reverence from the
king himself. He also becomes deserving of free lodging,
medicine and food, and requires 'watch and ward to be kept
for him according to the law' (Rhys Davids 1899, 77), as the
Buddha says in the "Samannaphala Sutta". This certainly
should not be taken as an ordinary reward for one's labour,
or something given out of love; this was the beginning of the
emergence of the priest from what was hitherto the persona
of an ascetic saint.

The religious merits that were now accorded to the
clergy, only added to the charisma of the ascetic-becoming-
priest. In the "Samannaphala Sutta", that features in the
Digha Nikaya, the Buddha says that the recluse, for sure,
'thoroughly knows and sees, as it were, face to face this
universe—including the worlds above of the gods, the
Brahmas, and the Maras, and the world below...' (Rhys
Davids 1899, 78). Before his fulfilment in becoming an arhant,
he acquires the 'wondrous gift', the Iddhi, whereby 'being
one he becomes many, or having become many becomes
one again; he becomes visible or invisible; he goes, feeling
no obstruction, to the further side of a wall or rampart or
hill, as if through air; he penetrates up and down through
solid ground, as if through water; he walks on water without
breaking through as if on solid ground; he travels cross-
legged in the sky, like the birds on wing; even the Moon and
the Sun, so potent, so mighty though they be, does he touch

and feel with his hand; he reaches in the body even up to the heaven of Brahma' (Rhys Davids 1899, 88–9).

The attainment of miraculous powers as a by-product of one's spiritual accomplishments was an idea common to all shades of ascetic ideologies, including the Brahmanic ones. Truth is, at this level, there is hardly any substantial difference between a Buddhist/Jaina arhant or an Upanishadic sage or a Samkhya yogin or even a Tantric siddha. The Buddha never even opposed Brahmanism as such, his emphasis was on sticking to what he considered the original and essential Brahman ideal—rising above human finitude. In the "Ambattha Sutta", he chides the Brahman youth for not being true to the ideals of his rishi ancestors. The Buddha admonishes that unlike Ambattha, his peers and teachers and teachers' teachers, sages like Vasishtha, Vishwamitra, Angirasa, Bhrigu, Vamadeva, did not 'parade about well groomed, perfumed, trimmed as to their hair and beard... in the full enjoyment of the five pleasures of sense.' The Buddha was mistaken, though. All the rishis he mentions lived a worldly life, having all kinds of wealth and comfort at their disposal, and dabbling in politics and furthering their personal interests. In another instance, that figures in the *Digha Nikaya* as the "Tevijja Sutta" which deals with knowledge of the Vedas, he goes so far as to identify his own ideals of arhathood with the Brahmanic goal of achieving unity with Brahma.

'Very good, Vasettha. Then in sooth, Vasettha, that the Bhikkhu who is free from household cares should after death, when the body is dissolved, become united with Brahma, who is the same-such a condition of things is every way possible!

'And so you say, Vasettha, that the Bhikkhu is free from anger, and free from malice, pure in mind, and master of himself; and that Brahma is free from anger, and free from malice. pure in mind, and master of himself. Then in sooth, Vasettha, that the Bhikkhu who is free from anger, free from malice, pure in mind, and master of himself should after death, when the body is dissolved, become united with Brahma, who is the same-such a condition of things is every way possible!' (Rhys Davids 1899, 319).

In general, Shramanism can be said to be Brahmanism without Brahma or *brahman*. Metaphysics and rituals excluded, in most other respects—ethically, eschatologically and institutionally—the two schools have more things in common than not. While the two were different philosophically, in terms of lifestyle and cultural dynamics, they attained a certain unity of purpose and content. Brahmanism remained identified with the doctrines of soul and God on the one hand and with the Vedas and sacrifices on the other, all of which was either disapproved of or rejected or condemned by the heterodox school. But equally, the Brahmans themselves had sacrificed the Purusha–Brahma, and while sacrifices were gradually gaining disrepute, the Vedic pantheon was all but abandoned, except for a subordinated and naturalised Indra, who was mysticised and kept purely for liturgical purposes. Indra's succumbing to the charm of the muni-cult was indeed an indication of Kshatriyas becoming asceticised and then priesticised. The complex mosaic that this situation presented was that of a unity in a variety of sectarian dissemblance rather than doctrinal opposition.

Neither the Buddha nor Mahavira appear to have

borne any ill-will against the Brahmans, at least not in the sense of regarding them as the oppressors or exploiters of the masses. Brahmans too, while being suspicious of their unconventional ideas, still generally approached them with reverence and respect. This might have been partly because of the teachers' royal backgrounds and partly also for their religious accomplishments, which earned them considerable fame and following among the people. If there was any animosity, it was more visible within the different circles of Shraman sectarians rather than with the Brahmans. But this is a matter of relatively minor significance. What is more important is that, for all of them, higher life meant a life of renunciation (as symbolised through the yellow robe and the begging bowl), and the highest attainment was that of quiescence and non-action. Non-action did not mean sitting absolutely still with eyes closed and adopting a posture of serenity and ecstasy, as is often depicted in frescoes. Invariably, the pace of activity in the lives of such seers increased after their attainment of the goal. This equipoise instead meant their having completely emancipated themselves from the bondage of desire.

Their lives became 'detached', insofar as no ordinary human emotions or sentiments acted as the cause of their actions. It was a divine and superhuman life; there was left neither fear nor hope, neither love nor hate, neither pleasure nor pain. In this kind of spiritual life, all actions are considered at one level to be evil in being a source of bondage and misery. The so-called good sentiments are no longer good and any propensity to do good to others becomes a positive vice. As Mahavira says in the *Akaranga Sutra*, hate and love both are equally binding and therefore equally evil:

He who knows wrath, knows pride; he who knows pride, knows
deceit; he who knows deceit, knows greed; he who knows greed,
knows love; he who knows love, knows hate; he who knows hate,
knows delusion; he who knows delusion, knows conception;
he who knows conception, knows birth; he who knows birth,
knows death; he who knows death, knows hell; he who knows
hell, knows animal existence; he who knows animal existence,
knows pain. Therefore, a wise man should avoid wrath, pride,
deceit, greed, love, hate, delusion, conception, birth, death, hell,
animal existence, and pain (Jacobi 1884, 34).

This was, in a nutshell, the essence and outcome of what
is known as the gyana marga (the way of knowledge),
as opposed to the karma marga (the way of action) of the
sacrificial system of Vedic (a)theism. The rejection of power
led to the negation of love itself. This philosophy of two-
fold negations, as could be its logical outcome, was one of
existential vacuity in the case of Buddhism, while in Jainism
it quite quickly led to the glamorisation of death. It was not
a philosophy of a positive acceptance of life in all its myriad
manifestations, which could be joyous or painful, but of
surrender and escape—an escape unto death.

Shramanism was essentially an ideology of the
celebration of death. Death was a hard fact, while life was full
of possibilities. It was therefore ordinary, and indeed, human,
to be afraid of death and to cling to life—to embrace death at
the expense of life, on the other hand, was superhuman and
divine. Life, with its ordinary passions and emotions, could
at best be tolerated when higher sentiments aroused in man
a death wish. But to deny life its due and valorise death was

excessive, and had its own contradictions and consequences. Seen from a more positive perspective, both life and death were the 'facts', which complemented and confirmed each other. While life could not be meaningful without its final apogee in death, death also would be a senseless idea, if not contrasted by its opposite idea of life. When the Buddha insisted that all things must ultimately die, he forgot to add that before death things also live. Life, by its very definition, stands for self-preservation and self-perpetuation, and resists extinction. It is true that death as a complementary idea to life necessitates its positive acceptance, but this must be accomplished in favour of life. An individual's death, in this case, is, positively speaking, the preservation of the life of the race. The ascetic's self-willed movement towards death does not have a martyrological positivity, but the negativity of the fugitive.

In this respect, the Buddha faltered more seriously than other Shraman sectarians, like Jainas, Samkhya or orthodox saints. For, while in the case of these latter schools there was still a life beyond death, which was conceived in its emancipated form as either a state of pure bliss or of absolute knowledge, the Buddha idealised death per se, adopting it in the most literal sense of annihilation. In relation to the ultimate non-self-existence of an arhant, neither the omniscience of Jina nor the pure bliss of a Brahman was of any value. The latter were only the stages in preparation of the final goal which was that of a state of absolute non-experience. In the "Mahaparinibbana Sutta", the Buddha says:

'By passing quite beyond all idea of space being the infinite basis, he, thinking "it is all infinite reason," reaches (mentally) and remains in the state of mind to which the infinity of reason is alone present—this is the fifth stage of deliverance. / 'By passing quite beyond all idea of nothingness he reaches (mentally) and remains in the state of mind to which neither ideas nor the absence of ideas are specially present—this is the seventh stage of deliverance. / 'By passing quite beyond the state of "neither ideas nor the absence of ideas" he reaches (mentally) and remains in the state of mind in which both sensations and ideas have ceased to be—this is the eighth stage of deliverance (Rhys Davids 1881, 52).

Since its conception, an ambiguity surrounds the Buddhist notion of nibbana. Being averse to philosophical speculation, the Buddha could not have articulated the idea in precise terms. But even his later interpreters did not successfully elucidate what their teacher meant by the term. Depending on the philosophical background of the interpreter, nibbana could mean anything: the Brahmanical version of blissfulness, the Jainas' omniscience, or even the Buddhists' own absolute nescience. Going by Buddhist logic, if the assertion of the self was a product of ignorance, a state of knowledge would automatically imply the self-non-assertion. This was the fundamental paradox of any Buddhist philosophy: an experience or assertion of the absence of the self necessarily involved an experience of the presence of that self. Ignorance and knowledge are both but the states that presuppose the presence of the mind or the soul. Jainism went to the end here: because the life of the individual self was futile, after reaching a state of omniscience, the tirthankaras opted for self-immolation. This indicates another paradox at the heart of Buddhism. They explicitly forbade such extreme self-mortification, but then the question was, why should the body be nursed or nourished if it was a source of evil? Nagasena makes a commonsensical argument that the body was not entirely a negative presence. This argument can be further elaborated as saying that life in the world carried a certain positivity in being a necessary means of securing salvation.

But the Buddha's moderation was half-hearted, and he still clung to the idea that life was generally evil. The world, though not necessarily illusory, had such charm and attractiveness, that it forced the soul to get entangled in it, in a repeated cycle of rebirths. The spiritualist could see no beauty either in nature or in human artifacts; nor was there any joy in such simple human pleasures as cuddling an infant or caressing a lover. Misery and pain were hidden behind all experiences of joy, and a wise man was one who could see through the deception and not fall for worldly enjoyment. The propensity of the soul to be attached to the world was because it did not know the real character of the phenomena of the world.

In the *Buddhacharita*, Asvaghosa's poetic biography of the Buddha (second century CE), when the family priest of the Buddha's father asks young Gautama to think of his wife 'who now mourns widowed yet with her lord still alive— like a swan separated from her mate or a female elephant deserted in the forest by her companion' and 'thy only son, a child little deserving such woe, distressed with sorrow', the Buddha's refrain is:

'Since parting is inevitably fixed in the course of time for all beings, just as for travellers who have joined company on a road,—what wise man would cherish sorrow, when he loses his kindred, even though he loves them / 'Leaving his kindred in another world, he departs hither; and having stolen away from them here, he goes forth once more; "having gone thither, go thou elsewhere also,"—such is the lot of mankind,—what consideration can the yogin have for them?' (Cowell, Müller and Takakusu 1894, 97).

The Buddha was obviously on his way to attain superhuman goals and considered such tender human emotions as love and affection for his wife and child to be stumbling blocks. He could of course say that he still loved them, in a deeper sense even, since his endeavour was to finally deliver his own people from the miseries of life and the fear of death. This was precisely the explanation given by Nagasena to king Milinda, when he expressed wonder at an incident that happened to an earlier reincarnation of the Buddha—in a fulfilment of his ascetic vow, the Buddha sat still, even as his terrorised wife and children were carried away by a callous Brahman. But the presumed assumption in Nagasena's argument is that spirituality is in conflict with humanity. In the metaethics of his ascetic spirituality, it was not the cultivation but the killing of one's humanity that led to the realisation of divinity. The Buddha himself became a god by leaving his humanity behind, and so did the sages and seers of other Shraman schools.

However, one can also argue that spirituality, rather than being hostile to humanity, is a principle of its affirmation and development. From this point of view, simple human sentiments could themselves be spiritual in contrast to the baser sentiments of hate, hubris, greed, lust, and so on. As man is always confronted by the two opposite forces of good and evil, at the existential level, a struggle against the latter may itself be taken to be an affirmation of spirituality. Such ethics has a 'purity' in both psychological and social senses: it must be both internally authenticated by a subject, and externally conducive to social health. This would first require the affirmation of the psycho-social reality of man himself. Since Shraman ideologies either ignored or underemphasised this reality, humanity was undermined in their system. Man, as man, is constituted by his existential expression of love, which functions creatively at all levels—cognitive, conative and aesthetic. Ethical spirituality, then, is a constant pursuance of 'good', which harmonises in itself this trilogy. In ontological terms, it is this 'good' which is spoken of as God, or Brahma, in traditional Indian terminology.

But the Buddha was not prepared to accept any such possibility—he argued that no one had 'ever seen Brahma face to face.' Not the Brahmans who read and recite the three Vedas, not their teachers, nor even ancient rishis like Vasishtha, Vishwamitra or Bhargavas. He dismissed all talk of Brahma as a foolish (Rhys Davids 1899, 305). Now whether or not Vedic rishis or their descendants have actually seen Brahma face to face is irrelevant. The issue is of the possibility of Brahma being an ethical ideal, who combined the different goods that man by his nature pursues. Even Brahmans themselves have all but renounced this Brahma, having put their faith in nature deities on the one hand, and in a neutral *brahman* on the other. In this, they are almost allies of the Buddha. But there is something compelling about a God who is an active and creative being, whose worship leads to positive activity and creativity in the human self, in contrast to the passivity and inertia generated by the denial of Brahma by the Brahmans and Shramans.

In fact, to the extent that Brahma still had a place in the Brahmanical worldview, the householder's life was very much a part of their ethical scheme of things. They believed that living an involved life of piety and dutifulness was enough to take man to his goal of salvation. 'Religion is not wrought out only in the forests, the salvation of the ascetic can be accomplished even in a city; thought and effort are true means; the forests and the badge are only a coward's signs,' says the Brahman priest sent by his father to Gautama in the *Buddhacharita* (Cowell, Müller and Takakusu 1894, 94). After all, liberation was attained by so many of the kings, seers and sages, who married, had children and performed their duties towards family and state. Ancient rishis like Vasishtha, Vishwamitra and Parashurama, were much married men despite being recluses, and men like Indra achieved merit and final bliss even though they 'wore diadems, and carried strings of pearls suspended on their shoulders... and lay cradled in the lap of fortune.' So there was no contradiction in obtaining both royal magnificence and control over the mind. But the Buddha contemptuously dismissed these claims, and declared that he was not prepared to be satisfied with achieving what was, in his view, a much inferior goal. He would rather prefer absolute death over a life of pleasure in Indraloka, or one of bliss in Brahmaloka.

Although the Buddha did not think that merit was accrued through a dutiful and virtuous social life, not long after his death, this very idea became plausible in Buddhist philosophy. In the *Milinda Panha* or Questions of Milinda (c. 100 BCE–200 CE), when king Milinda enquires about this conundrum, the sage Nagasena replies, 'And all of those who were gods, O king, were laymen. They had not entered the order. So these—while they were yet laymen, living at home, enjoying the pleasure of sense—saw face to face (realised in themselves) the condition of peace, the supreme good, Nirvana.' But then, if one could get salvation while still being a householder, why should he let himself suffer the difficulties of the ascetic life? If a disease abates without medicine, what is the advantage of weakening the body through emetics or purges, asks the king justifiably. Nagasena's reply is weak and unconvincing. He says:

> There are, O king, these twenty-eight good qualities in the vows, virtues really inherent in them; and on account of these all the Buddhas alike have longed for them and held them dear. And what are the twenty-eight? The keeping of the vows, O king, implies a mode of livelihood without evil, it has a blissful calm as its fruit, it avoids blame, it works no harm to others, it is free from danger, it brings no trouble on others, it is certain to bring with it growth in goodness, it wastes not away, it deludes not, it is in itself a protection, it works the satisfaction of desires and the taming of all beings... (Rhys Davids 1894, 251).

So then, virtue can be found in the above qualities even without taking the ascetic vow. It would indeed be a higher achievement to realise them while involved in a situation of temptation and struggle, rather than an ascetic vacuum. Be that as it may, the more important point is that it is human nature to search for happiness, however it can be found—both through physical as well as non-physical means. The Lokayata were wrong, but only in having confined this urge within the physical domain. They could also be wrong in not maintaining the right balance between individual happiness and collective happiness. An individual's unsocialised happiness may in the long run prove his own undoing. That is why the idea of happiness is always understood in a social–ethical context. But the Shraman response to hedonistic–individualistic ethics was to go to the other extreme of disparaging pleasure in all forms. Yet, seeking an ethically conditioned happiness is part of our natural make-up. Then, the bliss of Brahmaloka, and not self-extinction, is the real ideal that man should pursue.

The Buddha was not entirely correct when he argued that '[i]f the mortification of the body here is religion, then the body's happiness is only irreligion' (Cowell, Müller and Takakusu 1894, 73). For, although it is true that religiosity implies self-control and, to a great extent, the suppression of one's desires and emotions, this is so not because the pursuit of one's personal happiness is itself bad but because an unrestrained pursuit of happiness, without considering the happiness of others, may eventually bring pain to everyone. Man, after all, is a social animal, and collective happiness requires mutual sacrifices as well as mutual empathy. Self-mortification is not a necessary requirement of religiosity; it is a constraint put upon man by his own nature. It is therefore unfair to argue that the search for pleasure in heaven is an irreligion that emerges from this-worldly instincts. The criticism, that sectarians with faith in the positive Brahmanic principle still make a religion out of self-mortification, is valid though. It may be unnatural to seek pain without necessity, but it is also unnatural to disparage happiness only because it pertains to the body.

The Buddha was not averse to self-mortification as such.

He says, 'It is not the effort itself which I blame—which flinging aside the base pursues a high path of its own; but the wise, by all this common toil, ought to attain that state in which nothing needs ever to be done again' (Cowell, Müller and Takakusu 1894, 73). Towards this end, the first step he prescribes is to cut ties with one's own near and dear ones. Social or filial relations are based on attachment, while divine individuality is attained only when these fetters are broken. Such a decision to break with all ties must be final and uncompromising. Here, Shramanic schools differed from their orthodox counterparts: while for the latter, the vow of renunciation was taken at a 'later' stage in life, when family and other social obligations had been fulfilled, for the former such a postponement was unnecessary. The Brahman practice of 'late renunciation' was also a later development. Originally one could adopt an austere life at any time. The Vedic rishis would, after completing their tapas, re-join the hustle and bustle of life. They shuttled between their hermitages and the mountains where they practised their austerities. And when they went to the mountains, they often had wives and children waiting for them back home. Sometimes even the penances were temporarily suspended to contract a marriage or to intervene in pressing matters, like politics.

The idea of ashramas or 'stages of life', in the later Vedic tradition, followed from the philosophical development that replaced God, a creative–active being, with a non-productive, passive divinity. Young men were too immature to dabble in the mysteries of the *brahman*. One who has not as yet achieved the required level of contentment, with strong and demanding physical faculties, could not realise his own non-presence. But for the Shramanist, who neither believed in Brahma nor in *brahman*, there was no reason to postpone the vow of renunciation. Insofar as social ties were a form of bondage, the earlier they were rid of, the better. The attitude is best summarised in the following conversation featured in the Jaina "Uttaradhyayana Sutra", between a father who wants to keep tradition and his sons, who have already made up their mind to leave the world for good.

'Seeing that the lot of man is transitory and precarious, and that his life lasts not long, we take no delight in domestic life; we bid you farewell: we shall turn monks.' In order to dissuade them from a life of austerities, the father replied to those (would-be) monks: 'Those versed in the Vedas say that there will be no better world for men without sons. My sons, after you have studied the Vedas, and fed the priests, after you have placed your own sons at the head of your house, and after you have enjoyed life together with your wives, then you may depart to the woods as praiseworthy sages' (Jacobi 1895, 62–3).

In the case of Siddhartha, the royal chaplain argues in a similar vein in Asvaghosa's *Buddhacharita*: 'This resolve of thine is an excellent counsel, not unfit in itself but only unfit at present time.' Rather, what was expected of him was to enjoy 'for a while the sovereignty of the earth' and then 'go to the forest at the time provided by sastras.' But the Buddha's reply was also firm and logical as he said. 'Since from the moment of leaving the womb death is a characteristic adjunct, why... hast thou called my departure to the forest ill-timed.' As for performing the role of royalty, the retort was: 'How can it be right for the wise man to enter royalty, the home of illusion, where are found anxiety, passion, and weariness, and the violation of all rights through another's service? The golden palace seems to me to be on fire; the daintiest viands seem mixed with poison (and) infested with crocodiles....' Going further, 'I have been wounded by the enjoyment of the world, and I have come out longing to obtain peace; I would not accept an empire free from all ill even in the third heaven, how much less amongst men?' (Cowell, Müller and Takakusu 1894, 93–4, 97, 98, 119).

There is a great deal of truth and sublimity in what the Buddha is saying. The flimsiness, transitoriness and superficiality of worldly objects, does make a reflective person feel the urge to withdraw. Even if they don't end up doing it, there is a certain attraction to this withdrawal. Mindless pursuit of wealth, indiscriminate gratification of sexual passion, and lust for power, are attitudes that are quite common in everyday life. Pursuing such passions inevitably elicits a sense of insufficiency and self-defeat. 'A king is unfortunate, if he places his trust in his royalty which is apt to desert and loves crooked turns; and on the other hand, if he does not trust in it then what can be happiness of the king?' (Cowell, Müller and Takakusu 1894, 118). Wealth is also unworthy—the more one is wealthy the more one realises this fact. As is often said, while greed is unlimited, the need of a man is always limited. '[A]fter even conquering the whole earth, one city only can serve as a dwelling place, and even there only one house can be inhabited' (Cowell, Müller and Takakusu 1894, 118).

This psychology of withdrawal, however, acquires malignancy if not tempered with the ethics of responsive and responsible involvement. Not only is the pursuit of wealth and power an adjunct of man's socio-cultural life, his sanity and morality is dependent on it. A praxis of absolute self-abnegation and complete non-indulgence creates its own distortions in the psyche, which puts the very religiosity of man in peril. An impoverished man longs for money more than one who already has it in abundance; to withdraw from this power struggle is to throw oneself into a condition of slavery and self-degradation. Poverty or sexual abstinence, even when voluntary, are hardly conducive to religiosity; they lead to a psychological backlash, keeping the mind in distress and discontent. Of course, this discontent is also present in the involved life, but there, the struggle is for the fulfilment and not for the non-fulfilment of human urges. The critical difference between a sociologically involved ethics and the ethics of asceticism is that, though in both cases, man puts himself through struggle, in the former he aspires to spiritually satisfy himself while still being socially responsible, and in the latter, extreme ego-centricity takes hold of man as a complement to his excessive egolessness.

Life, by its very nature, cannot allow a complete rejection of itself. The internal elan of life forces it to live, to grow and to enrich itself. Even suffering is taken by life to be an aid in its natural self-development. Suffering and pain, in fact, play a greater role in bringing man closer to his authentic self-existence than a prolonged state of raw pleasure. Growth and progress everywhere are brought about through effort and struggle; pain is a logical accompaniment of this process. In a way, this principle was accepted in the spiritual praxis of self-mortification. But this acceptance was quite convoluted, because while a life was regarded as an unmitigated evil, an artificially induced pain was taken as the panacea and the source of deliverance.

While it is true that pain and struggle are a necessary condition of human life, it is also true that man always desires deliverance from pain and wants to emerge victorious in this struggle. Man always seeks happiness, though the quality and content of this happiness may differ in different cases. Further, while a certain kind of detachment from the world is necessary for religiosity, there is also no reason to shun life, at either personal or interpersonal levels. No man can live in a psycho-spiritual cocoon of confinement. The urge for friendship, fellowship and filial relationship is ingrained in human nature. The Shramanic doctrine could not kill this essential sociality: it conceived the idea of a 'sangha' or 'order', where renunciates joined together in spiritual pursuits. The 'brothers' and 'sisters' of this collective formed a hierarchy of religious officialdom, at the top of which was the 'teacher', the high priest who looked after the physical needs of his wards and maintained the discipline of his fiats. This was, by all accounts, an artificial situation, more distracting and more injurious to one's spiritual health than life in a community which was man's natural home. The Buddha calls one to 'wander alone like a rhinoceros' (Fausböll 1881, 6)—in the "Khaggavisana Sutta" or the Rhinoceros Sutra, one of the earliest texts in the Pali Buddhist canon—but leaving aside all filial affections was as unnatural as it was impossible. It was also as detrimental to one's spirituality as was its opposite of being lost into the mass of a collective.

A positive view of religiosity, grounded in the recognition of the twin principles of creativity and sociality, is inevitably a basis for an ethical praxis of a constructive and responsible life. The irony is that Shramanists accept the validity of this proposition and yet urge to go beyond it. In the "Sigalovada

Suttanta" of the *Digha Nikaya*, a 'young householder' is told
how 'the Ariyan disciple protects the six quarters [of social
relationships]'. Herein the 'following should be looked upon
as the six quarters:— parents as the east, teachers as the
south, wife and children as the west, friends and companions
as the north, servants and work people as the nadir, religious
teachers and brahmins as the zenith' (Rhys Davids 1921,
180). The Buddha holds that the servants at the nadir, the
Shudra position, must rise before the master, go to sleep after
him, take only what is given, perform their duties well, and
uphold their master's good name. In the ensuing details, the
different rights and responsibilities of these 'quarters' are
finely delineated, presenting a picture of a healthy and sane
mode of interpersonal life based on mutual commitment.
But when it comes to the ethics of a recluse, the insistence
is again on negative virtues of non-lying, non-injury, non-
stealing, non-possession and sexual abstinence.

Surely, there is a world of difference between just having
the virtue of non-lying and having the courage to speak the
truth even at the risk of one's life. In a society where the ruler
is oppressive or unjust, it is much easier to sit back in the
confines of a cave or a hermitage with one's piety of non-
lying and non-injury, than to resist the oppressor either by
speaking the truth or through violent means. In fact, not
to speak or act when injustice is perpetrated, by insisting
on the virtues of non-injury and non-action, in abetting
the oppressor, becomes a great act of impiety. It may also,
similarly, be a good commandment to not covet another's
possession; but a better one would be to earn one's livelihood
through honest and fair means. The Buddha did not deny
the idea of an honourable livelihood. But for him the best

option was to beg for one's sustenance: work was more of a positive vice. Not the positivity of action but the negativity of non-action and withdrawal was the ideal in the morality of the Shramans.

The apogee of this negative ethic is its exhortation, 'hate not'. This is, however, preceded by the corresponding rule, 'love not'. A recluse was to be like a 'beast unbound in the forest' which 'goes feeding at pleasure'. He was not to have emotional attachments with his kith and kin, or compassion and kindness for his companions and friends. The reason, as stated in the "Khaggavisana Sutta", was that one 'who has compassion on his friends and confidential (companions) loses (his own) advantage, having a fettered mind' (Fausböll 1881, 7). And so the Buddha exhorts him to wander alone like a rhinoceros. But this was much too dehumanising; later, attempts were made to correct the imbalance. The Buddha's image of being a personification of pity and compassion was decidedly a later construction, not that the teacher lacked these attributes in his life. The fact of the matter is that no man can live without having a softer side to his personality; in truth, the ethics of pity, with all the virtues of its allied feelings, like kindness, compassion, sympathy, forgiveness and so on, is not something which any creed can entirely subdue or avoid to recognise.

That mainstream Shramanism came to be identified with these soft ethics was natural and understandable. What was unnatural was its rejection of the harder values of anger, revenge, hate, violence... Just as softer values are turned into disvalues when applied in a wrong situation—showing compassion or forgiveness to an oppressive ruler—this latter set of hard values is not bad in itself when applied intelligently for the purposes of justice and peace. In the *Dhammapada*, the Buddha says that 'hatred does not cease by hatred at any time: hatred ceases by love' (Müller 1881, 5). But this was at best a partial truth. Hatred may and may not cease by love. An oppressive ruler, a wicked neighbour, a nasty friend, may, in the end, suffer a sense of remorse and mend their past behaviour. But there is no psychological compulsion for them to act in this way and not otherwise. It is far more probable that when not resisted, they not only persist but are also encouraged in their evil ways. A praxis of appropriating only the softer package, and not balancing it with the hard set, is an invitation to personal slavery, and a perpetuation of evil and injustice at the collective level.

For sure, there may exist a higher conception of love, the logical opposite of hate, which neatly harmonises both the harder and softer sets of values. Man realises this love in all his mundane relationships as part of his quest for ultimate beauty, ultimate good and ultimate truth. This love represents man's total religiosity and is the basis of obtaining peace and justice in society. It opposes evil, and not only by 'peaceful' means. The survival of life involves violence, both at the collective level and at an individual one. Shramanism, by eliminating violence from its ethical scheme, puts both the individual and society in peril.

However, 'hatred' is too hard a sentiment to enter the heart of an ascetic: he was not even allowed to be angry. According to the "Uttaradhyayan Sutra", ascribed to Mahavira, a monk was expected to forbear insults heaped on him and accept with equanimity even a beating:

> If a layman abuses a monk, he should not grow angry against

him; because he would be like a child... A monk should not be angry if beaten, nor should he therefore entertain sinful thoughts; knowing patience to be the highest good, a monk should meditate on the Law. If somebody strikes a restrained, resigned Sramana somewhere, he should think: 'I have not lost my life' (Jacobi 1895, 12–3).

Similarly, the Buddha said in the *Dhammapada* that one who wants hatred to cease from his heart must not harbour the thought that 'someone has abused me, he beat me, he defeated me' (Müller 1881, 4). In practising this rule, he never gave himself to anger even when provoked in the gravest manner. A jataka story relates an incident in his earlier birth in a Brahmanical family, as Cuddabodhi, when he maintains his tranquillity when his wife is sought to be ravished by a wicked king before his own eyes. The king is surprised by the absence of any sign of disapproval or resistance on the part of the monk and questions him about it. The Boddhisatva then delivers a long homily on the manifold vices of being angry. Among these, one was of course that: 'An angry man though resplendent with ornaments, looks ugly; the fire of wrath has taken away the splendour of his beauty.' For him not the wicked king but anger was the real enemy and so instead of putting up a resistance to former, he did it with respect to the latter 'although it was struggling within me' (Speyer 2010, 247).

Further, the most distinctive part of Shramanic spiritual discipline was the emphasis on the virtues of non-possession and non-injury—taken to its extreme in Jainism, but with some moderation in the other two schools. Ordinary moral qualities, like truth-speaking, non-stealing and so on, were also emphasised, but other universally accepted virtues like cleanliness, decency, self-respect, chivalry, altruism, humanitarianism, fighting against oppression and exploitation, were either ignored or even disparaged. All this suggests its fundamental asocial character; collective life was either accidental to human life, or had no bearing on its salvation. A regulated social order, necessary for the physical survival and spiritual fulfilment of man, cannot be ensured by observing the tenets of non-violence or non-possession at the cost of such social values as mentioned above. Collective life requires the idea of social justice to be placed at the top of the hierarchy of normative values; something most conspicuous in its absence in the Indian spiritual scheme of things.

Organised social life requires the presence of Law—the Vedic 'rta' or the Upanishadic 'dharma'. But the Buddhist 'dhamma' pertained entirely to personal conduct, devoid of political content. A monk was not expected to meddle in political affairs, except of course in exhorting kings to be pious and sympathetic to the Buddhist church. Kings were even recommended the ideal of leaving their kingly duties and joining the order of monks. The underlying assumption was that there was something inherently bad about involving oneself in such mundane affairs, even if it was for the good of the society. This attitude of political disengagement was exemplified in the famous incident when the Buddha remained unruffled when he was informed about an uprising taking place against his father in the latter's fiefdom. The same theory is upheld in the following Jaina text in which Indra, representing the Vedic–Brahmanic ideal, enters into a persuasive dialogue with the ancient king Nami who, 'after having enjoyed, in the company of the beautiful ladies of seraglio, excellent pleasure' had become 'enlightened' and given up that life.

> To the royal Seer who had reached the excellent stage of Pravragya, Sakra in the guise of a Brahmana addressed the following words: [...] "This is fire and storm, your palace is on fire! Reverend sir, why do you not look after your seraglio?" Nami answered ... "Happy are we, happy live we who call nothing our own; when Mithila is on fire, nothing is burned that belongs to me" [...] Indra answered [...] "Punishing thieves and robbers, cut-purses and burglars, you should establish public safety; thus you will be a Kshattriya." Nami answered: "Men frequently apply punishment wrongly: the innocent are put in prison, and the perpetrator of crime is set at liberty" (Jacobi 1895, 36–8).

Such cynical negation of the power principle was, even in theory, an ideology of political emasculation and slavery. Interestingly, it was also perceived as such by later Brahmanical writers, who found it to be of great help in their rivalry against their Buddhist adversaries.[2] As for the Buddha, he saw no difference between royalty and slavery; 'a king does not always smile, nor is a slave always in pain' (Cowell, Müller and Takakusu 1894, 118). He claimed, 'Since to be a king involves a wider range of command, therefore the pains of a king are great; for a king is like a peg—he endures trouble for the sake of the world.' He therefore preferred the begging bowl of a mendicant over the luxury of a royal palace. In the *Buddhacharita*, he says: 'He who lives on alms, my good friend, is not to be pitied, having gained his end and being set on escaping the fear of old age and death, he has here the best happiness, perfect calm, and hereafter all pains are for him abolished' (Cowell, Müller and Takakusu 1894, 119).

This kind of glorification of mendicancy and beggary may now appear to be very strange, but at the time, it was considered not only consistent with, but also an essential demand of, the ascetic virtue of non-possession. Jainas, as is well known, went to the extreme of even casting off their clothes (some of them of course made a compromise), to both literally and symbolically represent their ideology. The Buddha, however, made the wearing of clothes necessary and allowed the possession of a few trifles as being harmless. But begging for food, clothes and other essentials he made compulsory. In his own lifetime, though, this practice took an ironic turn, as monks, instead of being insecure about their daily needs, became the most economically secure and self-contented class of society. The rich were as generous in spending as the Buddha was in accepting their charity. He indeed made no discrimination in acceptance of offers to be fed, whether it came from a poor metal worker like Chunda, a king like Bimbisara or a courtesan like Ambapali. Being host to a party of monks was a matter of great honour, and the wealthy vied with each other to have them visit their respective houses. For his part, the Buddha was always obliging, never forgetting to deliver a religious sermon at the end of each feast.

Since it was the wealthy who, as a rule, invited monks to their houses, the food was sumptuous and bountiful. This did not create any breach of conscience, since the Buddha had put no strict conditions on the kind of food to be received as alms. Moreover, he even acceded to the offer made by king Bimbisara to build a permanent shelter for his homeless monks, so that they could spend their time on religious meditation with a greater peace of mind. The tradition thus established by the Buddha himself became a permanent feature of the religion after him, where kings, queens, businessmen and other sections of society made endowments of land and cash to build such shelters for ever-increasing numbers of religious seekers. That the ranks of monks swelled was not entirely for bona fide reasons, as many joined with purely worldly motives. This was admitted by Nagasena who, in reply to a question from the king Milinda, said that 'some (came) harassed by debt, and some perhaps to gain a livelihood' (Rhys Davids 1890, 50).

What was for the monk–mendicant the virtue of alms-taking was for the lay follower the virtue of alms-giving. A growing number of religious seekers depended on the munificence of rich hearts. In later literature, charity, all of a sudden, became one of the most sought-after virtues, as stories after stories—especially featuring the Buddha—were weaved, to underscore its importance. The Buddha, in his earlier birth as a swan, immolates himself in a fire to quench a hungry wayfarer. On another occasion, as an elephant, he lets himself fall from a mountain so that a whole crowd of hungry people can feed on his body. As a munificent king, the Boddhisatva cuts his own limb to give it to a vulture who would not eat anything except fresh flesh. What is unique in these stories is that, though the beneficiaries are not necessarily religious mendicants, the 'moral' is always that Brahmans and Shramans should be shown reverence and given the charity they deserve. This is very much like the Brahmanical authors of later centuries, who wrote any number of stories with the same message and moral, but not being so generous as to consider the Shramans as deserving of this religious charity.

With such high merits attached to it, it is not surprising that men and women of wealth were always forthcoming in extending patronage to Shraman sanghas. Buddhist viharas, both in their internal institutional organisation and their commerce with lay followers, especially the royalty, became the distinctive figures of what has since come to be known as the Buddhist culture of India. For it was not in the life of the masses that the religion of the Buddha made any difference, nor had any pretence to do so, concerned as it was with the deliverance of those who had dared to leave that world behind. Thanks to the liberal support they received, the monasteries never suffered shortages of either provisions or even hard cash. Given their life of comparative ease and comfort, the monks, like their Vedic predecessors, turned into great civilisers. Philosophical and literary activity flourished and so did the fine arts of architecture and sculpture. But while the monasteries were centres of learning and culture, in time, they also became hotbeds of corruption. The Mahayana and Tantra influences turned them into laboratories of all kinds of occult sciences and black magic practices. The corruption, however, had occurred even earlier. The presence of the 'sisters' in the sangha was, as the Buddha feared, to be a source of 'distraction'. As *Cullavagga*, a Vinaya text, records, the Bhikkus 'threw dirty waters over Bhikkunis, thinking, perhaps, that they would fall in love with them.' They also 'uncovered their bodies, or their thighs, or their private parts, and showed them to the Bhikkunis, or addressed the Bhikkunis with wicked words.' The 'sisters' also in turn did the same thing towards their monk-brothers and, somewhat surprisingly, the punishment meted out in both cases was very mild, for instance, a guilty party would no longer be saluted respectfully by their peers (Rhys Davids and Oldenberg 1885, 335).

The cultural ascendency and the corrupt machinery of Buddhist monasteries represent the rise and fall of Buddhism as a cultural phenomenon perfectly. There is some dispute about this analogical picture; it is not clear to what extent the Mahayana and Vajrayana developments were integral to the original Buddhist creed. But there is no doubt that during its cultural peak in India, Buddhism was a priestly religion with a sharp division between the clergy and the laity. The congregants were expected and exhorted to lead a virtuous life, while also being reverent and generous towards the mendicants. The clerics, meanwhile, lived their 'ordered' life in the sangha, which had its officialdom, with a head priest as the leader. The head priest, while living a life of splendid isolation, had to maintain commercial ties with royalty and other upper crust families. In possessing the refinements of learning and sophistication, as also the psychic powers of 'iddhi' ('riddhi' in Sanskrit), he inspired fear and awe. Like his Brahman counterparts, he advised kings on matters pertaining to the state and gave moral support to their expeditions of war, especially when they sought to subject kings with heretical leanings.

The exuberant and politically involved lifestyles of Shraman priests were not seen as a breach of tradition. It was an extension of the same metaethical principle, that ordinary human beings must abide by ethical rules, while for the realised person these rules were redundant. In the "Samannaphala Sutta" of *Digha Nikaya*, an unconverted Purna Kashyapa provides an account of a religious seer who has reached the stage of non-action. He says, were the ascetic 'to go along the south bank of the Ganges striking and slaying, mutilating and having men mutilated, oppressing and having men oppressed, there would be no guilt thence resulting, no increase of guilt would ensue. Were he to go along the north of the Ganges giving alms, and ordering gifts to be given, offering sacrifices or causing them to be offered, there would be no merit thence resulting, no increase in merit' (Rhys Davids 1899, 70). It is incidental, and yet important, that it was this Purna Kashyapa who became, after his conversion, the main ideologue of the new creed, and was much respected by the Buddha himself. Though the Buddha is not known to have consciously subscribed to the above view, the very logic of supra-sociality that inhered in an arhant implied that he was also supra-ethical. But then, sometimes the Buddha seemed to circumvent this rule. To a disciple named Udayi, for example, he once said; 'Now there are several days, Udayi, on which I ate out this bowl when it was full to the brim, and ate even more...' Of this, Nagasena says in the *Milinda Panha*:

> Just, O king, as it is desirable that a sick man to whom an emetic, or a purge, or a clyster has been administered, should be treated with a tonic; just so, O king, should the man who is full of evil, and who has not perceived the Four Truths, adopt the practice of restraint in the matter of eating. But just, O king, as there is no necessity of polishing, and rubbing down, and purifying a diamond gem of great brilliancy, of the finest water, and of natural purity; just so, O king, is there no restraint as to what actions he should perform, on the Tathagata, on him who hath attained to perfection in all that lies within the scope of a Buddha (Rhys Davids 1894, 7).

But it was not only in the matter of eating that the Buddha went beyond the rules. Despite the strict rule, that under no circumstances could monks accept gold and silver as gifts, he accepted 'a pair of the robes of cloth of gold' from Pukkusa, the young Mallian, one of which he, however, gave to Ananda (Rhys Davids 1881, 80). Besides, when asked by Ananda what may be the most befitting way to honour the remains of the Tathagata, he replied that it must be like what is done in the case of a king of kings. Asked further to elaborate, he says:

> They wrap the body of a king of kings, Ananda, in a new cloth. When that is done they wrap it in carded cotton wool. When that is done they wrap it in a new cloth—and so on till they have wrapped the body in five hundred successive layers of both kinds. Then they place the body in an oil vessel of iron, and cover that close up with another oil vessel of iron. They then build a funeral pile of all kinds of perfumes, and burn the body of the king of kings. And then at the four cross roads they erect a dagaba to the king of kings... And whosoever shall there place garlands or perfumes or paint, or make salutation there, or become in its presence calm in heart—that shall long be to them for a profit and a joy (Rhys Davids 1881, 92–3).

Even if the Buddha did not instruct it, such ceremonial extravagance sanctioned by his immediate disciples bears testimony to the fact that lavish priestly tendencies manifested in the religion right at the start. This was not even an uncommon development: the same thing happened in the case of Jainism and other sects of similar nature. So there is no pressing need to hypothesise a Brahman takeover of Shramanism, though it is a fact that Brahmans were the main intellectual support of the Buddha. One, already mentioned, was Purna Kashyapa, the elderly ascetic who converted to Buddhism. Aside from him, the brothers, Sariputta and Moggallana, were the most trusted companions of the Buddha, while Mahakashyapa, another reputed saint, was the one whom the Buddha treated with highest respect. When the Buddha died, Mahakashyapa traveled for seven days, all the way from his place of dwelling, to preside over the funeral ceremony; it is also recorded that the dead body refused to burn (when people from Kusinagara attempted to light the pyre) until he arrived. Moreover, when various Kshatriya princes, among others, began making claims for the remains of the Buddha, it was again Dona the Brahman who acted as the arbiter. There were many others, like the Bharadwaja brothers, Ajita, Annata, Kodanna, Uttara, Udaya and so on—all important enough to find frequent mention in Buddhist literature. Truth is, the main reason why Buddhism flourished, while others declined and perished, was its ability to attract distinguished Brahmans, who provided the nascent movement the necessary support of their knowledge and organisational skills.

The transformation of the creed of the Buddha to a priest-driven enterprise was, in a way, natural and necessary. A prophet preaches his doctrine and persuades people to accept it through the strength of his personality. But once he is gone, the creed faces new challenges, of both a theoretical and practical nature, which need to be overcome for it to survive. Now, while people from all the classes joined the sangha, Brahmans alone, in the delicate post-Buddha situation, possessed the necessary qualifications to best the creed's existential challenges. Even Ananda, a kin of the Buddha and a staunch loyalist, does not appear to have had any intellectual capabilities to sustain and support the movement ideologically, even though he played a leading role in maintaining the organisational structure of the movement when it was experiencing rapid growth. Besides, Brahmanism was not essentially a hereditary idea: in its original form it too was generated by the same forces of asceticism and occult, in which Shramanic sects like Buddhism and Jainism excelled. A Brahman, in the original, priestly meaning of the term, was one who acquired technical expertise in sacred (and secular) lore, and was for that reason able to minister the religious (ritual) needs of lay followers. He was a source of inspiration and a guide to the novices and neophytes who entered the order with spiritual aspirations.

Shramanism could not exist without Brahmans, just as Brahmanism never existed without essential Shraman ideas in its background.

Shramanism was, therefore, by no account, a great novelty. It expected the laity to be moral and offered it nothing new, except perhaps a certain especial emphasis on non-violence and, to some extent, a certain deemphasis on casteism. But neither of these ideas were exclusive to Shramanists, nor could Shramanists really stick to them consistently, especially outside their sanghas. At the existential level, Shramanism was still a gyana marga (way of knowledge), with all its trappings, partialities and perils. The path of knowledge not only disparaged creative–cultural and socially responsible action, but also involved an emphatic rejection of life at objective levels, and though this, in time, generated a reaction against irrational emotionality.

The axiology of pity, charity and non-possession, as expounded by the different Shraman schools—in an extreme

form by Jainism, and with some moderation by Buddhism—
was only a part of the discipline recommended by them to
attain the goal of nibbana. The root cause of human suffering
and entanglement in the world was an ignorance about the
truth of the world. But one's ignorance could not be removed
just by being told the truth. One had to work hard and figure
out his own path to realise the stark reality hidden behind
the apparent glitter. The state of realisation is a state of
perfect mental equilibrium, where all mental activity ceases
and the body acquires peace and equipoise. The destruction
of the past and present karma results in the removal of the
veil that hinders the soul's access to the hidden mysteries
of the universe. Or so say Jaina and Samkhya thinkers. A
realised person (siddha) is, for them, a person with absolute
knowledge (kevalin), who, through his state of knowing, can
perform miracles, like flying or changing one's visage, and
so on...

While the philosophy of these two systems ends with
a 'positive' ascription, in Buddhism, the stage beyond
realisation is one of total loss of the self-consciousness of
the soul, which in a sense also means the destruction of the
soul. The Buddhist ideal of samadhi, as already seen, was
the unwavering, perfect state of being, an absolute non-
experience which implied a state of complete non-action.
Actions follow psychical motivations, and if the mind is
unstirred, actions will automatically cease. Of course, this
doesn't mean that one stops performing actions altogether;
that is practically impossible. The real import here is about
performing actions without motives—to let actions happen
to one without being controlled by preceding psychological
factors. This implied the creation of a community that

seemed human, and yet was devoid of all the human qualities of rationality, creativity and love. What was to be an ascendence from the human to the superhuman, was also a fall, to the subhuman. In the state of samadhi, it was not the physical or biological man who died, but 'man' as such. Man became a simple biological being, no longer his previous spiritual self.

Nevertheless, humanity has survived in India, despite this spiritual onslaught. But this could only happen because of the Shramanic compromise with its rival Brahmanic doctrine. And so the social collective came to be divided into the laity and the clergy. Common folk were expected to follow ordinary Brahmanical ethics of Vedic theism, while the monks were encouraged to transcend these worldly niggles. The laity could gain the benefit of a noble, and even the salvation of heaven in some cases. Whereas the monks could access ultimate deliverance or nibbana. Brahmanical ideas had permeated so much in nascent Buddhism that it too began giving off the impression of an acceptance of caste ideology. For them, Kshatriya pedigree was the most superior, while Brahmans were by all accounts considered inferior and degraded. This caste hierarchy, with Kshatriyas at the top, was accepted as a given, and caste segregation and untouchability were scarcely condemned. A Shudra could however shed his social disabilities by joining the order of monks, in which case he could be even better than a Brahman who remained uninitiated.

It could be disputed whether what is known as the Buddhist culture or the Buddhist phase of Indian history was built on the original Buddhist principles. The Buddhist religion, even in the early stages of its growth, admitted tendencies which were in contradiction with the original ideals of its founder. For one thing, the gyana marga, with its emphatic rejection of life at the affective level, generated a reaction against emotionality. Love, according to the Buddha, was a worldly tether, and he would not allow even his own death to be mourned or lamented out of love for him. He even forbade people from 'following' him as a teacher—that too was a form of bondage. In the search of truth, rather, each person was to be his own light, he said:

> What, then, Ananda? Does the order expect that of me? I have preached the truth without making any distinction between exoteric and esoteric doctrine: for in respect of the truths, Ananda, the Tathagata has no such thing as the closed fist of a teacher, who keeps some things back. Surely, Ananda, should there be any one who harbours the thought, "It is I who will lead the brotherhood," or, "The order is dependent upon me," it is he who should lay down instructions in any matter concerning the order. Now the Tathagata, Ananda, thinks not that it is he who should lead the brotherhood, or that the order is dependent upon him. Why then should he leave instructions in any matter concerning the order? I too, O Ananda, am now grown old, and full of years, my journey is drawing to its close [...] / Therefore, O Ananda, be ye lamps unto yourselves. Be ye a refuge to yourselves. Betake yourselves to no external refuge. Hold fast to the truth as a lamp. Hold fast as a refuge to the truth. Look not for refuge to any one besides yourselves... (Rhys Davids 1881, 36–8).

These dying words of the Buddha can easily be compared to the later developments of the religion, especially its Mahayana version, which was a religion of esotericism and occultism par excellence. In this school, the historic persona of the Buddha was considered incidental, and in his place the concept of 'Buddha', as an all-pervading occult reality was mooted. This Buddha was not a preacher of a new creed but a metaphysical presence which was to be worshipped and realised through certain magical practices. There was a good deal of philosophising involved in this school of thought, which was once again something the teacher had vehemently sought to discourage. But even at a non-philosophical level, Buddha worship commenced pretty early in the history of the religion, in the form of relic and mound worship, reference to which can be found in the "Mahaparinibbana Sutta" (Rhys Davids 1881).

The transformation of Buddhism from a strictly credal religion to the religion of teacher-worship can be explained through the usual relapses many religions suffered from— when the creed *of* a teacher becomes a creed *about* that teacher. In this particular case, it generated some tension between the Mahayana and the Theravada, or Hinayana, traditions: the latter claimed to stick to the orthodox teachings of the Buddha. In the case of Jainism, on the other hand, religious worship and teacher worship were both upheld as parts of the doctrine. The idea was that the teacher (an arhant or a siddha or a tirthankara) was the soul in its original and realised state of omniscience, and hence, an attachment to it did not amount to an attachment with external reality, like in the case of the idea of a creator-preserver God in other religions. Since this teacher–soul is by definition unattached, its worship is nothing but the acquiring, for one's own self, the same qualities of non-attachment. Even if, due to psychological failings of worshippers, some attachment is aroused, incurring sin, it will be far too little compared to the immense benefits that would otherwise accrue from the act.

Teacher worship was not the only kind of worship practiced in Jainism. In the absence of a proper theology, the religion developed a most promiscuous kind of demonolatry, in which all kinds of natural or supernatural beings, like goblins, ghosts, serpents, trees, were sought to be appeased and worshipped. Among the interesting deities of the Jaina pantheon, there are, for instance, Shashan devtas and Shashan devis—lay men or women elevated to the status of gods on account of their devotion to a certain tirthankara. The queen Padmavati became a deity after she helped save the life of Parshvanath (an important Jaina tirthankara) from the assaults of his opponents. Similarly, Ambika, the wife of a Brahman, served food to a Jaina monk and was for that reason abandoned by her family. She left for the forests, and wherever she went, miracles occurred; her in-laws, in turn, were struck by disaster. In the end, her husband repented and came looking for her. But not knowing his real intentions and suspecting danger, she committed suicide. Her tragic sacrifice and her piety were accordingly eulogised and she too was hypostatised as a goddess. As Shashan devi, she came to be attached to the tirthankara, Nemi. Devi Chakreshvari is the Shashan devi of the Jaina tirthankara, Rishabh, in much the same way.

These goddesses were also sought by Jaina culture to be identified with popular Hindu mother-goddesses like Kali, Chandi and Durga. While at a theoretical level, these figures served the purpose of being occult objects of worship for initiates, on the popular front they performed the ordinary function of giving boons to devotees or saving them from impending danger. In this respect, the religion was not all that different from Hinduism. But one tricky problem arose: some of these goddesses, like Kali and Chandi, partook in meat, which was anathema for creeds preaching strict non-violence. To overcome this difficulty, ingenious solutions were found. In one story, Sachchiya, a Jaina goddess, usually identified with the Hindu Mahishasurmardini, was once hungry when she came upon a famous monk. He offered her some sweets, but being unaccustomed to such diet, she refused. This led the monk to launch into a lecture on vegetarianism, which ended in Sachchiya's conversion to the diet.

It is somewhat ironic that all the Shramanic traditions mentioned earlier began by rejecting the idea of a personal God, only to gradually develop a theology not very different from later Hinduism. The realised soul of the tirthankara became pretty much a god worthy of worship, as did the disincarnate Buddha. They were omniscient, omnipotent, omnipresent and eternal. For Samkhya with its Vedic–Brahmanic background, the transition to theism was even easier. But, in none of these schools was God a cosmological principle responsible for the creation of the world. Matter was independent of spirit(s), and together the two constituted the world of our experience. Even when God, as a supreme object of devotion, was admitted, it was still not considered to be an object of realisation. In the theistic yoga of Pantanjali, Ishwara was merely an aid in reaching the stage of samadhi, which was the soul's state of perfect stillness, having nothing to do with God.

Whatever the original intentions and ideas of their

teachers, Shraman cultural tradition was a curious admixture of highly speculative scholastic philosophy and crude pagan belief—much like how the Upanishadic sages speculated on the *brahman* while also retaining the worship of Vedic nature gods. Heterodox spiritual philosophy was nature worship in a different form. In Samkhya, prakriti, or nature, as the embodiment of existence (sattva), movement (rajas) and darkness (tamas), was the active reality which generated all being in the universe, while Purusha, or selves, experienced and enjoyed this natural world, even as they were passive beings with no role in the functioning of the world. It was nature, matter, which held power, shakti. This power was represented by the goddess Kali, who was worshipped both by the masses as also in the exclusive circle of mystics. Purusha was represented by Shiva, who, in the same religious imagery, lay sleeping on the ground, half dead, with his member erect, on which sat the naked Kali, in all her frightening and fearsome glory.

This idea of reality as the union of the male and female principles had its corresponding conception in Buddhism, where the sexual meeting of prajna and upaya was considered as the basic cosmic truth. The difference however was that in Buddhism, this meeting was more conservative, with the male principle, upaya, representing activity, and the female principle, prajna, being passive and docile. Prajna was the void of consciousness (shunnyata), the nothingness which was the fundamental truth of the world and the self, while upaya was the great compassion (mahakaruna), which breathed life into appearances, enlivening and activating them, so that they could proceed towards their ultimate goal of complete dissolution. Prajna was, again, personified in deities like

Tara, Varahi, Bhagwati, in whose worship one realised their underlying principle. Upaya was the Bodhisatva, the Buddha disincarnate, again a god to whom obeisance was due. The meeting of prajna and upaya generated absolute pleasure (mahasukha) which, in turn, ensured one's release from the cycles of birth and death.

This was the philosophy of Yogachara or Tantra, a shared heritage of nearly all the sects and subsects presently under discussion. But crucially, it was as much a matter of praxis as it was a matter of philosophy. In fact, the practice was ancient, and the theories later rationalisations. In it, the initiate emulated cosmic sexual activity with a young female partner, who represented prajna. The body took precedence over the spirit, because mahasukha essentially was the bodily pleasure that led to mental quietude and spiritual release. Tantricism was very much tied to human anatomy and physiology. In this cult, the body was the seat of the ultimate truth, its different parts having deep spiritual significance. Ordinary sexual pleasure is of limited and fleeting worth, but when it is freed from these limitations, it is transformed into a state of infinite bliss, the *summum bonum* of spiritual path. The Tantric sexual–yogic practice consisted in arresting the downward flow of semen in the act of sexual intercourse and instead forcing it to move upwards. The outflow of the semen once checked, led it to move upwards through various regions in the body, called chakras, finally reaching the head where ultimate bliss was produced.

In orthodox Tantra, this is called the arousal of the kundalini, which enables the yogin to acquire enormous power over the forces of nature, even though this is not the intended aim of the activity. Magic, sorcery and superstition, therefore, remained essential ingredients of this system. Tantra was also marked by a culture of metaethicalism, as was the case with the Upanishadic–Brahmanic mysticism; here too, once the yogin entered the site of the ritual, he was freed from the constraints of ordinary morality. He was like the Upanishadic Indra, beyond the taints of sin. The sexual partner could be any woman, of any family, of any age, of any relation to him, though some sects observed some scruples in the final regard in deference to social taboos.

Besides, the esotericism inherent in the doctrine implied the indispensability of the teacher to initiate and train a novice into the theory and practice of the ritual, which resulted in the elevation of his status to the position of a god. So, again, Tantra too was a culture of priests, with all their pretensions and exuberance. Their saints were quite often men of great learning and piety, greatly respected by different sections of society, including the rulers. They received liberal financial patronage from the rich and the royal. Personages like Nagarjuna, Asvaghosa and Patanjali built great philosophical systems and wielded political authority in the manner of Vedic priests. Among the masses, the religion was a pagan worship of demons and demonesses with implications in everyday life. It was also a religion of organised beggary and debauchery. While mendicancy was a usual hallmark of religiosity, it is naïve to think that the monks and nuns in monasteries, contented themselves by merely visualising and carving all those erotic figures found in Jaina temples and Buddhist caves. Finally, it was a religion in which political authority was, in theory, divorced from religious authority, although in practice the two mingled frequently, to much mutual benefit.

Another distinct priestly trait of this whole culture was the attitude of extreme laxity in matters of belief and practice. Contradictory ideas were made to intermingle, both at the cost of coherence and without concern for consistency. Samkhya thinkers conceived of prakriti after the model of the Upanishadic *brahman*, and Patanjali again injected the idea of supreme God into the naturalistic system of Samkhya. The later Mahayana conception of the supreme soul of the Bodhisatva was built entirely on the Upanishadic *brahman*. So on and so forth. Jaina thinkers even developed their famous theories of syadavada and anekantavada to justify this pluralistic approach to truth. This was obviously in opposition to the original views of their teachers who would have insisted on the objectivity and finality of their own theories in solving the riddle of life. The Buddha, for example, is reported to have emphasised:

> In whatsoever doctrine and discipline, Subhadda, the noble eightfold path is not found, neither in it is found a man of true saintliness of the first or the second or of the third or of the fourth degree. And in whatsoever doctrine and discipline, Subhadda, the noble eightfold path is found, is found the man of true saintliness of the first and the second and the third and the fourth degree. Now in this doctrine and discipline, Subhadda, is found the noble eightfold path, and in it alone, Subhadda, is the man of true saintliness. Void are the systems of other teachers— void of true saints. And in this one, Subhadda, may the brethren live the life that is right, so that the world be not bereft of Arhats (Rhys Davids 1881, 106–7).

This was the objective, rationalistic approach of the Buddha, which stood against the synthetic methodology adopted by the priests of any religion. That Buddhism and Jainism underwent a priestly transformation is admitted by all, and there also appears to be some substance in the observation that it was the traditional priestly class of Brahmans who effected most of these changes to serve their interests. What however remains moot is to what extent the later Mahayana doctrine, especially the Tantra practices, could be integrated with the original Buddhist creed. The changes were radical and indicated the tendency of Indian culture to traverse a dialectical path. The spiritual cults of the Buddha, Mahavira and Samkhya were supposedly reactions to the ritualist excesses and pretences of Brahman priests, but they ended up giving rise to the very tendency they initially opposed. Tantra was undeniably a doctrine of the elect, but its concrete manifestations were visible in popular religion too. And the way it promoted a bodily culture was in sharp contrast to the cult of spirituality propounded by founding teachers. The body, which was supposed to be the real trap and the ultimate source of bondage, now became the seat of truth. Women, who were earlier seductresses and demonesses (rakshasi), now became embodiments of shakti and prajna. Asceticism and abstinence remained the central precepts, but their highest realisation was to be found in the praxis of promiscuous sexual activity attended with drinking alcohol and eating meat (panch makar). It was indeed a drama of ironies.

There was therefore a clearly felt need for a middle course which would avoid excesses and extremes. This need was in fact felt by none other than the Buddha himself who thought that his own creed was such a middle path:

> There are two extremes, O Bhikkhus, which the man who has
> given up the world ought not to follow—the habitual practice,
> on the one hand, of those things whose attraction depends upon
> the passions, and especially of sensuality—a low pagan way (of
> seeking satisfaction) unworthy, unprofitable, and fit only for the
> worldly minded—and the habitual practice, on the other hand,
> of asceticism (or self-mortification), which is painful, unworthy,
> and unprofitable. / There is a middle path, O Bhikkhus, avoiding
> these two extremes, discovered by the Tathagata—a path which
> opens the eyes, and bestows understanding, which leads to
> peace of mind, to the higher wisdom, to full enlightenment, to
> Nirvana (Rhys Davids 1881, 146–7).

The Buddha had a personal reason to disapprove of the practice of hard penance and self-mortification to attain enlightenment. Since the beginning of his spiritual quest, he attempted self-mortification, even going to the farthest limit of starving himself for such long periods that he nearly died. But the promised realisation did not come. Being thus thwarted in his endeavour, he concluded that this method was futile, abandoning it altogether, and inviting even the charge of being a renegade. The enlightenment that eventually came was through a moral self-discipline without the rigours of orthodox methods. Moderation was therefore his point of departure, and he appropriately called his creed the middle path (madhyama marga).

Among the many important departures he made from existent practices, the most positive one was his clear and emphatic rejection of the idea of religious suicide and self-torture. Besides, he generally disapproved of miracle-mongering and denounced the absurdist antics of the ascetics. 'Kora the Khattiya who, on all fours, sprawled on earth, taking up his food, whether hard or soft, with his mouth.' He also saw no religiosity in either being naked or doing things in unclean, indecent or abnormal way. 'Not nakedness, not platted hair, not dirt, not fasting, or lying on the earth, not rubbing with dust, not sitting motionless, can purify a mortal who has not overcome desires' (Fausböll 1881, 38–9). In his view, even if 'dressed in fine apparel', when one exercises tranquillity and is quiet and restrained, he can attain the state of realisation. The Buddha was indeed so emphatic about moderation that when Devadatta, out of malice no doubt, tried to make an issue of it, he refused to be either defensive or apologetic. In matters of clothing, dwelling, sleeping and eating, he preferred the monks to have some freedom within the monastic framework rather than subjecting them to extreme austerities.

Especially in the matter of food, he showed a liberality which was certainly, from the existent ascetic standards, very unconventional, if not scandalous. He not only allowed the eating of meat and fish, with some conditions, but also permitted the use of various types of drinks and juices. Asvaghosa reports what the Buddha was thinking when he found himself utterly at a loss when he didn't attain realisation even after going to the last limit of an austere diet:

'But that cannot be attained by one who has lost his strength,'— so resuming his care for his body, he next pondered thus, how best to increase his bodily vigour: / 'Wearied with hunger, thirst, and fatigue, with his mind no longer self-possessed through fatigue, how should one who is not absolutely calm reach the end which is to be attained by his mind? / 'True calm is properly obtained by the constant satisfaction of the senses; the mind's self-possession is only obtained by the senses being perfectly satisfied. / 'True meditation is produced in him whose mind is self-possessed and at rest,—to him whose thoughts are engaged in meditation the exercise of perfect contemplation begins at once (Cowell, Müller and Takakusu 1894, 134).

Now these could indeed be regarded as real 'reforms', given the strict adherence to the principles of non-injury and non-possession accepted by all other schools of asceticism and mysticism popular in India in those times. But does this then mean that the Buddha really followed a moderate path as he claimed? The suggestion as given above would indicate that he was looking for some positive possibilities in matters of religious discipline. But his general negative attitude towards life, especially his complete rejection of sexuality, was something which kept him firmly within the ambit of asceticism. Even after discovering his 'middle path', not only did he not return to his wife and children, he even asked others to take the oath of celibacy as a necessary condition for the attainment of salvation. When Ananda asked for his permission to marry his girlfriend, the Buddha reluctantly acquiesced, but on the condition that the marriage not be consummated. Clearly, for him, though companionship did not hinder the path to realisation, sexuality did. 'So long as the desire of man towards the woman, even the smallest, is not destroyed, so long is his mind in bondage...' (Fausböll 1881, 69).

One can ask here that if 'true calm' can only be obtained by 'the senses being perfectly satisfied', does not the gratification of sexual urges do the same, because it is as necessary as the gratification of other instincts like hunger and thirst? Can one's mind be 'self-possessed' and 'at rest' while this commanding urge of the body is still unsatisfied? The Buddha does not address this question as he also takes a general view of condescension and contempt towards women (Rhys Davids 1881, 91). When Ananda asks him how to conduct oneself with womankind, his answer is a brutal 'Don't see them' and 'Abstain from speech'. He also warns that one must 'keep wide awake' against the dangers coming from women. It was probably for this reason that he was so reluctant to allow women to enter the sangha, although, against the Brahmanical view, he believed in their soul's emancipation. When, after being pressed by Ananda, he agreed to it, he added a condition that '[a] Bhikkuni, even if of a hundred years standing, shall make salutation to, shall rise up in the presence of, shall bow down before, and shall perform all proper duties towards a Bhikkhu, if only just initiated.' And while making this concession, his heart trembled as he became full of premonitions: 'If Ananda, women had not received permission to [...] enter the homeless state [...] then would the pure religion, Ananda, have lasted long, the good law have stood fast for a thousand years. But ... [it] will now stand fast for only five hundred years...' (Rhys Davids and Oldenberg 1885, 322–3, 325).

The question remains, what is the precise meaning of 'moderation', what are requirements of a 'middle path'? The answer would depend on even larger questions about whether spirit is opposed to matter or is it the case that though functionally different the two are only facets of a single self-same reality. One also requires the knowledge of whether life is a positive presence or a negative accident. Then, there is the question of whether the self is a stranger adrift in the universe by the contingency of birth, an isolated entity lost in the multitude; or if personality is fused with interpersonality and society is the natural home of man.

The Buddha certainly refused to approach these questions of life and world in a positive spirit and held fast to prevalent parameters. In the Buddha's scheme of things, spirit remained a prisoner of the body and insulated from the influence of its existential neighbours. Accordingly, he continued to think of worldly involvement as an unmitigated evil and of social action as inevitably binding. But to think the ideal of the self in terms of inaction and non-involvement, and yet to talk of a 'middle path,' was not quite consistent. If the Buddha's attitude towards life was what it was, the extremist sectarians were much more logical than him. For if the body is the seat of evil and the world a source of misery then these must be shunned in their entirety rather than making a halfway house between indulgence and abstinence. The Buddha's continued espousal of beggary and celibacy as the chief marks of his discipline placed him in the same category of uncultural monkism against which he seemed to revolt. He did not replace the immorality of indulgence with an ethical scheme of constructive involvement, but condemned the latter as the cause of life's misery and suffering. He did bring a reform of sorts by relaxing the rigours of certain extreme rules, but there was no attempt to change the rules of the game as such.

3

Waiting for Kalki

Among the many reasons why Buddhism survived, thrived even, while most other creeds perished, one was its policy of moderation, and another its Mahayana (Greater Vehicle) transformation, which lent it its popular character. The historically moot question about the extent to which the Mahayana doctrine was a deviation from the original Buddhist teachings is not difficult to answer in retrospect. Though Buddhism contained an ascetic excess, it also began to get permeated by the opposite excess of priestly exuberance. As we have already argued, a pagan creed, while having a cultural foundations, can assume a culturally overindulgent form out of necessity. The Buddha himself discouraged personal fidelity. He disliked philosophical speculation and would have disapproved of literary or artistic proclivities among his followers. Had the later adherents of his doctrine strictly stuck to his precepts, what came to be known as 'Buddhist culture' would not have emerged. Not only did the Mahayana priests (Brahmans?) develop an intricate system of logic, speculating on matters of life and world, they also brought the religion closer to society by doing commerce with the royal court and by creating visible markers—idols, mounds, columns, monasteries and shrines, concrete testimonies to a living and thriving Buddhist culture—that the laity could identify with religiously. In contrast, the first Shaivite and Vishnuite temples only appeared much later, by the sixth century CE.

We should not consider this as an unexpected anomaly or an embarrassing deviation. Even the egoless Buddha would eat hearty meals, receive precious gifts from the rich and was given to quick temper. He often conducted his ascetic discourse in an explicitly political vocabulary, as if he was the king of kings, a chakravartin. That the later Mahayana priests coveted positions of power and privilege is not a great breach of tradition, as some suspect. Having become a priestly religion, the principle of destruction was inherent in Buddhism. In the latter-day development of Buddhist culture, priests dabbled in occult practices of magic and sorcery, and the Buddha himself was considered a great magician, unshrinkingly indulgent in drinking and the company of women. For instance, prince Siddhartha is depicted enjoying the cliched rich-male preserves like wine and women in an Ishkvaku-era (third century CE) sculptural panel on display in the National Museum in New Delhi.

Over time, Buddhist culture suffered an ethical–political decline. It was replaced by the creed of the *Gita*, which, as a response to the ascetic doctrine of Buddhism, emphasised the indispensability of positive action and an involved life. In the third chapter on the karma yoga, the *Bhagavad Gita* emphatically declared:

> Not by abstention from work does a man attain freedom from action; nor by mere renunciation does he attain to his perfection. … For no one can remain even for a moment without doing work; every one is made to act helplessly by the impulses born of nature. … Do thou thy allotted work, for action is better than

inaction; even the maintenance of thy physical life cannot be effected without action (Radhakrishnan 1960, 108–10).

Not that the path of renunciation was altogether abandoned or even disapproved of by the *Gita*. In fact, its essential principles were retained consistently, especially its ideals of sthit-prajna (stable intellect) and samadhi. Renunciation was even recognised as one of the possible ways of attaining enlightenment. But now, the emphasis was more on an ascetic ideal achieved through the path of action. This point was emphasised in several verses:

> But he who controls the senses by the mind, O Arjuna, and without attachment engages the organs of action in the path of work, he is superior (Radhakrishnan 1960, 110). [...] The renunciation of works and their unselfish performance both lead to the soul's salvation. But of the two, the unselfish performance of works is better than their renunciation (Radhakrishnan 1960, 143). [...] But renunciation, O Mighty-armed (Arjuna), is difficult to attain without yoga ; the sage who is earnest in yoga (the way of works) attains soon to the Absolute (Radhakrishnan 1960, 145). [...] Work is said to be the means of the sage who wishes to attain to yoga; when he has attained to yoga, serenity is said to be the means (Radhakrishnan 1960, 152).

There were several reasons to live a life of action—one being that God himself was a great performer of actions. *Bhagavad Gita*'s God, as we shall see, was a 'personal' God and therefore an active one, as opposed to the 'impersonal' God of the Upanishads, who was more of a thinking-being. Both schools, however, held on to the idea that if one acted selflessly or unselfishly, in other words, if one's actions were detached or 'disinterested' (nishkama), the soul would remain untarnished, as the actions would not produce any effect on its status.

> Having abandoned attachment to the fruit of works, ever content, without any kind of dependence, he does nothing though he is ever engaged in work. [...] Having no desires, with his heart and self under control, giving up all possessions, performing action by the body alone, he commits no wrong. [...] He who is satisfied with whatever comes by chance, who has passed beyond the dualities (of pleasure and pain), who is free from jealousy, who remains the same in success and failure, even when he acts, he is not bound (Radhakrishnan 1960, 135–6).

This was the *Gita's* celebrated theory of 'nishkama karma'. As if to emphasise the political implications of this theory, the authors of the *Gita* appropriately placed it in the scene of an epic conflict. Arjuna, the war hero of *Mahabharata*, wavers just as the battle is about to begin. The god Krishna, in the form of a chariot driver, then persuades him to fight, by performing a long philosophical discourse. He makes many arguments, one being that as long as man is alive, action is inevitable and indispensable. One has only to take care that his actions are not motivated by desires and that he performs his caste duty (dharma or swa-dharma) for its own sake. The immediate concern of an individual, then, is to perform their duty and leave aside the question of consequences to God. Hence the plea of Krishna to Arjuna to kill his near and dear ones for the sake of his kingdom, insofar as that is the demand of his Kshatriya dharma.

As such, this was the first clear and articulate theistic

voice to emerge after a long spell of pagan demonolatry and occult atheism in Indian tradition. Before we discuss this aspect of the *Gita*'s credo, a few things need to be said about the theory of nishkama karma. To start, as against popular impression, the idea was more in the nature of being a sedimented articulation of some of the notions already inherent in the previously existing tradition, than being an original achievement of the *Gita*. Buddhism was an immediate inspiration; the new doctrine wasn't altogether dissonant with the earlier orthodox tradition either, its roots can even be traced back to these earlier sources. Even a Buddha or a Jina, after attaining salvation, did not become totally actionless. They lived lives that appeared entirely normal, except with the qualitative difference that normal psychic motivations ceased to apply to their bodily actions. An enlightened person may still love or hate, be angry or pleased, may even have fears and hopes (besides doing all the other ordinary activities like walking, talking, eating, sleeping...), but in his case they become, in some sense, 'unmotivated' or 'detached'. As detached actions, they do not produce the 'effects' which would otherwise bind the soul to the body, leading to its repeated rebirths.

While in Buddhism this could happen only after man had renounced his social bonds and entered the hermetic life, according to the *Gita*, the ideal could be realised in ordinary work-a-day life itself. Logically, if actions could be motiveless and 'unproductive' after the ascetic vow was taken, they could be so before that also. If man could eat and drink without motive, he could also have sex and do similar things under the same psychological condition. This possibility was amply admitted in the Tantra sects of both Buddhist and orthodox variety. But the authors of the *Gita*, while finally not being averse to this Tantric position, were, nevertheless, canny enough to adopt and advocate the idea in a more socially acceptable manner. Brahmans saw themselves as civilisers and upholders of public order and morality. It was therefore part of their job to act against the anti-social tendencies of all kinds. Since both Buddhist amorality and Tantric immorality were perilous to the collective, their negative response to them was natural. In their own way, therefore, they worked out a theory of moral praxis which was socially responsive and at the same time not lacking in religiosity.

The *Gita*, in other words, integrated Vedic actionism and Buddhist–Shramanic renunciation. While on the surface, this seems like a socially wholesome approach, it worked in an altogether different way for the Brahmans. They escaped the consequences of their immoral activities precisely by justifying their actions and their life of involvement through these principles. Despite being ascetics, Vedic rishis gave the impression of being arrogant, amorous and cruel, besides being much married and politically active. Obviously, these two contrary positions could be reconciled only through a doctrine wherein actions were 'detached' from motives— when actions become disinterested. Having sacrificed the Purusha and forsaken the ethical praxis connected with him, the idea of detached action was a handy excuse to explain away all the contradictions of their beliefs and behaviours. Such a logic was already implicitly present in the aether, to which the *Gita* gave a new formulation and emphasis.

As a matter of further degeneration, this new idea was also linked to dharma. While in ordinary usage, this word signifies work-a-day morality or 'duty', in the specific Brahmanical context, it is always understood as the adherence to one's class or caste duties. It was presumed that the performance of one's caste duties was self-justified and so not subject to any type of censorship. So, for Arjuna, a Kshatriya, it was imperative to fight, regardless of the consequences of his actions and irrespective of whether his cause was noble or ignoble. As long as his actions were disinterested, and he was doing his duty for duty's own sake, he deserved all merit. In fact, at some level, it was also thought that actions would lose their purity if tainted by ordinary ethical considerations. Ordinary ethical rules did not apply to an ascetic, a yogin; his actions had to be amoral, and hence detached.

The *Bhagavad Gita*, as a work of the priestly class, has a clear conception of a supreme creative God, but again, characteristically, it is impatient about the matter. It did not make a clear break with polytheistic vulgarity or mystical jugglery, and yet, there is a clear disapproval of such crudities in certain parts of the text.

> But those whose minds are distorted by desires resort to other gods, observing various rites, constrained by their own natures. [...] Whatever form any devotee with faith wishes to worship, I make that faith of his steady. [...] Endowed with that faith, he seeks the propitiation of such a one and from him he obtains his desires, the benefits being decreed by Me alone. [...] But temporary is the fruit gained by these men of small minds. The worshippers of the gods go to the gods but My devotees come to Me. [...] Men of no understanding think of Me, the unmanifest, as having manifestation, not knowing My higher nature, changeless and supreme (Radhakrishnan 1960, 173–4).

The *Gita*'s emphatic assertion of monotheism was significant not only because of the prevailing ascetic atheology, but also in the context of the older Vedic–theistic tradition, in which Prajapati Brahma, the creator of the universe, was believed in but not worshipped. Despite the *Gita*'s assertions of monotheism, it often prevaricated on this belief. Prevarication and ambivalence are in fact the characteristics which still mystify lay readers of the text. Not only was Vedic polytheism accepted in certain parts, but so was the authority of the Vedas. Then, in other parts, they were ridiculed and rejected.[1] The idea of a transcendental supreme God was affirmed categorically, but the text is also credited to have introduced, for the first time, the idea of an 'avatar'—God's incarnation in a human body.[2] Similarly, the path of renunciation was disapproved of at one place, while at another place it was presented as a genuine method to realise the *brahman*, and at yet another place, a new path of devotion (bhakti marga) was held to be superior.

It would appear that the authors of the *Gita*, while having the full ability to hit at the truth, were, nevertheless, unwilling to forgo the privileges which they probably considered their birth right. This comes out most clearly in their strident advocacy of sacrifices (Radhakrishnan 1960, 111–2) and also in their reaffirmation of the system of four varnas, despite admitting, in theory, to the equality of all human beings.[3] This fact becomes all the more evident through the authors' complete fidelity to the notion of 'dharma', understood as one's sense of caste or class duty. Krishna exhorts his protege to fight against his kin as a part of his duty as a Kshatriya, and not to establish righteousness or justice, though this may have been an implicit assumption, since the opposition is represented by evil men. After all, the war in question was being waged to reclaim a throne that had been usurped by none other than the cousins, which is quite a common occurrence in monarchical autocracies. For the most part, Krishna does not invoke the concept of social justice, a cause which is often used to justify wars. Instead, he inspires Arjuna by appealing to his caste pride, to his fear of social censor and ignominy, and, above all, to his sense of caste duty.

In addition to its distinct priestly traits, there is a palpable Buddhist influence on the *Gita*—especially on Krishna's conception as a quasi-personal god, to be worshipped almost in an atheistic manner. In spite of the Buddha's own atheism and his rejection of personality cult, the sectarian development of his ideology was entirely on theological lines. Like Indra before him, the Buddha too was elevated to the status of a personal god. His spiritual accomplishments led him to be regarded as divine, as someone to whom devotion was due. This image of the Buddha was then transplanted wholesale into the orthodox Brahmanical lore after suitable modifications. Thus Krishna too became god incarnate, but not so much because of his self-mortification (tapas) as due to God's (Vishnu's) own decision to descend into a human body. Such a divine descent occurred several times in the Buddha's case, when he reincarnated multiple times as a Bodhisatva. Yet, the Buddha's deemphasis of caste prejudices was not reflected in the Vishnuite case. The latter's reincarnations invariably served to reinforce caste order (dharma, which is varna-dharma).

Other than these manifest factors, deeper forces of history were also at work, of which some of the former were mere external symptoms. The refusal of the priestly class to worship the figure of Purusha and their subsequent replacement of him, at first by the forces of nature, and then by an impersonal, unconscious *brahman,* created a kind of desubjectivised culture which could not satisfy the personal and emotional dimensions of human, and even priestly, life. Even Shiva as an embodiment of pure bliss was more a representation of forgetfulness than of sober happiness and enjoyment. As an ascetic and mystic, he too was more impersonal than personal. The same also applied to the Buddha and the Jina arhants, who stressed the cognitive aspects of human personality at the expense of its conative and affective sides. Mysticism in general disparages sentimentality and is also opposed to volitional and creative expressions of life. As a religious–ethical creed, it usually tends to theorise an incomplete personhood, that is reflective and contemplative, but not active or creative.

Now, by preaching the idea of devotion to and worship of a creative and productive personal God, the *Gita* sought to correct the serious imbalances created by the earlier mystical tradition. However, because of their impatience with this personal God, the authors of the new doctrine soon corrupted it by incorporating the idea of incarnation in the ontology of the new god. A personal Purusha became a human purusha, subject to the cycle of births and rebirths. Instead of being a source of righteousness and justice—real dharma—he became the establisher of Brahmanic 'dharma'. As a further irony, this god in flesh and blood, became synonymous with the *brahman* itself. At the end of his discourse in the *Bhagavad Gita,* Krishna discloses, to an as yet unconvinced Arjuna, his true *brahman* form. The movement of ideas comes full circle as 'monotheism' relapses again into monism and mysticism.

Such adherence to traditional prejudices apart, the *Bhagavad Gita* truly does represent a landmark and a turning point in the Indian history of ideas. Its chief achievement lies in confronting squarely the most basic issue of authentic living, which is something all cultures confront at a certain stage of their civilisational development, when older modes of living begin to look irrelevant and harmful, and the search for new principles becomes imperative. The *Gita* exposed the inadequacies of atheism and asceticism, and attempted, in its own way, to strike a balance between the extremities of renunciation and indulgence. Essentially, it was trying to reconcile the irreconcilable. It was one thing to say that actions per se could not be binding and that what counted in a virtuous life was one's attitude. If the mind was detached, action ceased to be harmful. However, the *Gita* also went on to recognise the autonomy of the two paths of action and knowledge, and then synthesising them by saying that one led to the other or, alternatively, that one was merely a preparation for the other. Now, if one accepts that eventually one has to reach the stage of psychic immobility through the control of one's senses, the question arises, why delay the decision to become immobile? Conversely, if disinterestedness eviscerates an action of its effects, why should such a law be abandoned in the later stages of life and not be upheld all through. Besides, it can also be seen that by upholding the idea of stages of life, the *Gita* went back to a scheme of life as envisaged by Upanishadic seers.

What the authors of the *Gita* seem to have failed to realise was that the two paths of action and knowledge are rooted in two different sets of cosmological premises, and entail two different kinds of ethico-eschatological consequences. The path of detached and responsible action is more consistent with the belief in a personal transcendental God, while the path of renunciation better suits a pagan–pantheistic or atheistic system of beliefs. This is because action requires the *will* to act, and unless the believed-in God himself has this attribute as a part of his nature, he cannot be a source of an actionist ethics. Correspondingly, it is because the pantheistic God, the *brahman,* is denied this quality and made to be only a thinking-being, that he produces the same qualities in those who worship him. So, two different conceptions of God generate two different kinds of lifestyles which are incompatible with each other. In addition, the former usually leads to the idea of an egalitarian social order while the latter promotes the concept of a society with class distinction and class hierarchy. It is quite curious that, in the *Gita,* ideas of social justice and equality are discussed in the parts where the realisation of a personal God is emphasised, while those parts which state traditional beliefs (Radhakrishnan 1960, 145–51), uphold sacrifices and also the caste system (Radhakrishnan 1960, 126–32). Besides, transcendental theism also implies objectivity and inviolability of moral rules, whereas ascetic theory inevitably gives rise to amorality, if not immorality. The *Gita* at one place, for instance, reiterates the old Upanishadic idea of an ascetic's immunity to moral censor.

> Even if thou shouldst be the most sinful of all sinners, thou shalt cross over all evil by the boat of wisdom alone. [...] As the fire which is kindled turns its fuel to ashes, O Arjuna, even so does the fire of wisdom turn to ashes all work (Radhakrishnan 1960, 141).

This was, to be sure, a kind of retrogression, which renders all the claims of the *Gita* being an original or a revolutionary message appear questionable. The story of the *Gita* is indeed the story of an aborted revolution. It started with the promise and potential of engendering drastic reforms in outmoded Indian thought, but ended up reiterating the precepts of extant mystical–priestly culture. Historically, it heralded the end of what is known as the Buddhist era of Indian history, but instead of being the harbinger of a new egalitarian social life, it ushered in a revival of Brahmanical priesthood.

The new priestly order was not definitively Krishnite or Vishnuite–Krishnite, as envisaged by the *Gita*. Despite Krishna's attempt to identify himself with the *brahman*, he still appeared to be too personal to appeal to the priests. Occultism and mysticism were still the dominant modes of thinking, of which the old cult figure of Shiva was an unshakeable representative. However, under the influence of the *Gita*'s 'bhakti marga', there were now new expectations of the figure of God: he had to be a personal God who could be loved and worshipped by devotees; he had to be the creator and sustainer of the universe. Traditional conceptions of Shiva were either of him being a super-mystic or, as in the *Svetasvatara Upanishad*, of him as a substitute for the *brahman*: in both these systems he had no cosmological function to perform. Shiva, as an ascetic, lived a life of abstinence, shunning all physical involvement, especially sexual–creative activity. The latter in any case was a task ascribed to Prajapati Brahma.

With Brahma being out of favour, it became necessary to bring about certain changes in the concept and character of Shiva, so that he could perform the role of a personal creator

God, while also remaining an object of mystical pursuit. So now, the principle of creative, natural activity, enunciated in Samkhya and accepted also in the *Gita*, had to be integrated with the character of Shiva. Usually this was done by distributing opposing principles between male and female counterparts. In the present instance, the actionist part had to be retained in the figure of Shiva. Yet, in Shaivite legend, it is Parvati, the goddess of nature, who pursues a reluctant Shiva for marriage. Shiva eventually consents and the wedding takes place after a lot of opposition from Parvati's father, Daksha Prajapati, the original creator of the world.

Shiva's renunciation of asceticism was a dangerous signal to Brahma. A sexually active Shiva would usurp his exclusive creative and procreative rights. Hence, Brahma's reluctance to let Parvati marry him. This was a losing battle for him. According to a famous myth, Daksha does not invite Shiva for a sacrificial ceremony saying that the latter's unorthodox lifestyle is inappropriate. An irked Shiva disturbs the ceremony leading ultimately to Daksha's surrender and acceptance of his supremacy.[4] In a slightly different version of the story, Brahma himself contrives to make Shiva productive by marrying him off to Durga, also known as Shakti, whom he arranges to be born as his own daughter. Clearly, as times changed, Brahma was made to lose even that residual resistance which he formerly had, and made into a voluntary participant in the glorification of Shiva.

The transfer of creative activity from Brahma to Shiva— whether by force or voluntarily—marked the beginning of a new cult of worship of Shiva, as a non-absolute, non-mystical personal God. Though this change from one religion to another was more or less smooth, a kind of uneasiness continued to be felt for some time among the more orthodox sections about the changing of roles of the two deities. Thus, in another story, a few Vedic rishis decide to visit Shiva and are horrified to find him in sport with his spouse in the open. Shiva, uncaringly, and even mockingly, continues with the act. The rishis, infuriated by the indecency and disrespect shown to them, hurl a curse in the direction of the couple, and end up rending Parvati's body into pieces. In another version, instead of Parvati, they attack Shiva's phallus. Clearly, the attempt here is to return Shiva to his original uncreative position by castrating him, or by depriving him of his sexual partner, who was the actual shakti motivating and enabling him to be a creative agent. In yet another story, the gods, jealous of Shiva's immense productive powers, try to prevent him once again. They send Agni, in the form of a bird, who perches itself on the window of the room in which Shiva was copulating with his wife. Shiva recognises the bird and, true to his character, cares little. But Parvati is embarrassed and withdraws herself though still unsatiated. Shiva, angry at being disturbed, forces the bird to receive his semen in its mouth. This was, again, clearly an attempt to combine the new Shaivite theogony with older Aryan theology, though not without meaning some disparagement to the latter.

The whole idea of Shiva originally being an absolute, attribute-less God, and his subsequent transformation into a theistic, creator deity has been described in typical mythological form in various Shaivite Puranas, especially the *Shiva Purana*, which is the bible of this sect. Its first section, the "Rudra Samhita" describes, first briefly and then at length, what actually transpired in the passing over of the job of creation from Brahma Prajapati, lord of sacrifices, to a reluctant, mystically oriented and impotent ascetic deity, Shiva. In the text, Brahma relates the story to Narada in detail. This begins with the admission that Shiva is primarily an absolute God. The second chapter in this section states:

> Originally when Siva was separated from Sakti and was pure consciousness alone, He was attributeless, free from alternatives, devoid of forms and beyond the existent and non-existent (Shastri 1970, 279).

Shiva changes his character once united with Shakti, the female principle of nature, named variously as Durga, Uma, Satti, Parvati... This union of Shiva and Shakti is brought about by Brahma, who finds himself incapable of further creation. He is also driven by the need to take sweet revenge upon Shiva, who had mocked him for being in 'love' with his own daughter, Sandhya (Saraswati or Vac).[5] Brahma, thinking that 'unless the primordial Being Siva indulges in sexual sport, the creation would continue to be mediocre' (Shastri 1970, 306), first requests the God of love, Kama, and his wife Rati, to inflict him with their arrows, thereby arousing desire in him. Failing in it, he beseeches Durga to do the job saying, '[e]xcepting you none will be able to capture His mind' (Shastri 1970, 322). He then asks her to be born as the daughter of his son Daksha and then marry Shiva. Durga, though at first nonplussed by the idea, eventually agrees to it, realising herself that 'if Siva does not take a wife unto Himself, the creation cannot continue long' (Shastri 1970, 323). Durga then, of course, is reborn as Sati, a daughter of Daksha, and marries a reluctant Shiva, much against the wishes of her father. When Daksha does not invite Shiva to a sacrificial ceremony, she immolates herself in the fire. She is then reborn as Parvati, and marries Shiva once again. It is this marriage that Shiva properly consummates, leading to his creating the universe.

The story, as can be gathered, reflects in a most amusing way, the partly forced and partly voluntary surrender of the original Vedic cult (represented by Brahma) to the 'new' Agamic school, of which Shiva was the presiding deity. The 'marriage' of Shiva and Parvati is a contrived method whereby Shaivism was made to appear as an orthodox cult synthesisable to Vedic religion, albeit with the admission of some tension between the two, as reflected in Daksha's initial rejection of Shiva because he was a representative of the mystical ascetic movement, as against the school of action and sacrifice represented by Brahma and Daksha. That Daksha ultimately surrenders to Shiva expresses the historical fact that, increasingly, Shaivism had a greater claim at representing the orthodoxy than the Vedic religion.[6]

Personal ethos and impersonal absolutism were only two of the many aspects that went into the making of the whole Shiva complex. He was, in any case, considered as the most colourful deity with roots that went back to the pre-Vedic past. Even in the Vedic–Upanishadic times, he had an active career, first as Rudra and then as Shiva. He gained ascendency and especial relevance when he became the Brahmanic substitute for Buddhism and Jainism. Shaivite doctrine even shared an ideological kinship with Jainism, so much so that, had Shiva not adapted himself to Vedic practices, he could well have been proclaimed as one of the tirthankaras, if not the founder of the sect itself. This despite the long and bitter feuds between the two sects. Shaivism ended up replacing Jainism in its southern strongholds. It did the same with Buddhism in the northern parts of India, although large parts of the Mahayana doctrine were assimilated into later Shaiva theology. Besides, Shaivism also learnt idolatry from the two heterodox rivals. Temple culture, which became an essential characteristic of the Shiva-cult, was a legacy inherited from Buddhism and Jainism.

Shaivism also shared a relationship of consanguinity with mother-goddess cults, and through them to the Tantra sects that were dominant across the length and breadth of the subcontinent. It was also claimed that Shiva was the founder of yoga (he's known as the mahayogi), a practice with decidedly non-Vedic origins, which remained an abiding current in all schools of Indian philosophy whether orthodox or heterodox. As a deity, Shiva was equally revered by the Suras (Devas) and Asuras, and he, in turn, favoured both parties with his boons when duly praised and worshipped. In fact, he was worshipped by almost all classes of religious seekers, be they the most pious mystics of the Upanishadic tradition or the most degraded of them, like the Aghoris, who dwell in charnel grounds and worshipped him in his Aghor form (literally 'to whom nothing is horrible'). Moreover, while for orthodox Shaivites, he was an active agent of cosmic creation, in the Tantra, he was a passive spectator of events, too passive to even be crushed by his own consort Kali—Tantric paintings show Kali standing on the chest of Shiva's corpse.

Above all, what made Shiva a darling of generations of Aryanised Brahmans was his metamorphosis from his earlier role as the destroyer of sacrifice to someone who is unconcerned about, or even a partaker in, these ceremonies.

In the *Linga Purana*, for example, Brahma says: 'Perfect knowledge, teaching of the Vedas, offerings to the gods, meditation, sacrifices, penance, charitable gifts, study of the Vedas, all these undoubtedly contribute to the devotion of Lord Siva' (Shastri 1960, 45). Besides, Shiva's multiplicitous nature especially suited the proclivities of priests, giving them an opportunity to adapt to ideologically conflicting situations. Shaivic mysticism was occultism in disguise, and the possession of occult powers, or even a pretension of it, facilitated the priests in playing the game of power effectively and in maintaining their stranglehold over both their new Kshatriya patrons and the public at large.

There is also an ethical dimension to this Shiva complex which needs mention. Earlier, Shiva was seen either as a malevolent demon or a wandering ascetic, not much given to observing the ordinary rules of domestic life. In his new incarnation, his behaviour was much more civilised, partly as a result of his Aryanisation, symbolised in the myth of his marriage to Parvati. This was, in a way, a sign of changing times. The growing acculturation of Indian society resulting from an imperial polity which fuelled the process of urbanisation, somewhat affected social thought. Occultism was still prevalent, but due to the excesses of the earlier (Buddhist?) era, it was falling into disrepute. An indication of this trend is discernible in the *Gita*, which is refreshingly free from any references to magic and sorcery. The same tendency was also seen in the emergent Shiva concept, where the job of the deity was largely confined to giving boons to his devotees. It still contained a strong element of occult, but it was more positive and constructive. This, however, does not mean that Shiva entirely sheds his earlier personality. He retains much of it, albeit by supplementing it with what has come to be called as his auspicious self. It goes without saying that in this double image of Shiva, the priests found a rationalisation for their occasional immoralities while retaining the sanctity of ordinary rules in the rest of their lives.

With its elaborate rituals and intricate theology, Shaivism, in both its obverse and inverse (Tantric) versions, was already an institutionalised religion, strengthened further by a burgeoning temple culture. Hindu temples, as we find them today, made a comparatively late appearance in India and were in all likelihood an offshoot of the Buddhist architectural works commissioned by the royalty in earlier centuries. The Buddhist and Jaina monasteries, where relics or symbolic representations (to be later replaced by idols of the founders) were worshipped, were also a probable source of inspiration for burgeoning temple architecture. In Shaivism too, symbol-worship was the initial form of ritual. The worship of the images of Shiva, his consort and his various progenies, was only a later development.

But a temple was not simply an 'abode' of a god where devotees came to pay their offerings. A lot of intricate planning, in accordance with certain fixed rules and rituals, went into the making of a temple-structure. In fact, the philosophical ramparts of the creed were sought to be translated and given concrete expression through the physical elements that comprised a given structure. Since the chief idea in Shaivite philosophical theology was divine creative activity in the image of human sexuality, worship was directed through the physical representations of male and female sexual organs, as signifying two sides of said activity. Shaivism, however, was not simply limited to the worship of the phallus and the womb (linga and yoni). All the elements and characters of its mythology were visually depicted on stones. The exteriors of the temples were plastered with exquisitely carved images of nude young girls and couples in erotic poses. In the interior, it was more of the same.

This was a familiar fusion of eroticism and spiritualism, characteristic of priestly religions all over the world. Nude sculpture being a conspicuous feature of temples of antiquity, it was not accidental that Shaivate architecture carried this motif, and yet it wasn't merely a decorative choice. This style was an essential part of religious architecture, to the extent that a building without such figures was not worth visiting for devotees and was also useless from the point of view of fulfilling pious desires. A place without love-images (kamakala) was considered base and forsaken, resembling a dark abyss, to be shunned like the den of death, or so declared a medieval Sanskrit text on temple architecture.[7]

It was further stressed in the system that divine love-play must also be imitated by a religious seeker to attain fulfilment. This obviously required the presence of female devotees who would cooperate with their male counterparts in rehearsing religious activity. To fulfil this need, young girls were ceremonially married off to the phallic deity, and the priest then deflowered them on behalf of the idol and kept them as mistresses. The girls who were presented as offering were always of a tender age and they were without exception from non-Brahman lower castes. Once they entered the temples, these 'slaves of gods' (devadasis) were treated as temple property and given rigorous training in music and dance. They were expected to do the cleaning and other daily chores of the temple; they bathed the idols and entertained the priests, royalty and other members of the nobility with their performances, for which separate dancing halls were built within the temple, adjacent to the sanctum sanctorum.

As big temples came to be fabulously wealthy, with a stockpile of gold, silver and jewellery, the girls too were, sometimes, allowed a position of respect, a share in the wealth, and were even considered holy and auspicious. They were, however, public property and anybody with sufficient means (excepting the untouchables) could avail their services.

This was the Indian system of religious sex work, erected on the foundation of a mystical philosophy and a philosophical cosmogony. It generated, what in modern times have come to be known as, the greatest symbols of Indian culture. The music and dance currently popularised as the great heritage of Indian tradition had their source either in the totemistic culture of tribals or the temple culture of medieval and pre-medieval times. The dance system presently known as Bharatnatyam was, for example, originally called Dasiattam (the dance of the devadasis), and it contained erotic motifs signifying divine sexual duality.

The devadasi tradition was most prominent in South India, while the worship of the stone representations of the male and female members was a feature present in most Shiva temples across the country. Many of the rituals connected with this worship had implicit sexual meanings. In Bengal, an image of a goddess was not made without using earth taken from a devadasi's house. Sex workers were considered auspicious, and had Kartikeya, a progeny of Shiva, as their presiding deity.

Temples were also symbols of Brahman wrath and

their self-degradation. Insofar as they perpetuated the worship of Shiva in his non-absolute creative form, a kind of corruption of the original Shiva doctrine, the cultus was always regarded by a section of Brahmans as inferior. They disparaged idolatry for its association with Buddhism and other heretical sects. The 'higher' (Aryanised) Brahmans considered associating with this whole business of image-worship in temples to be beneath their dignity for a long time. For them, temples had come into existence as a result of the distortion of the Shiva concept, which they disapproved of and even fought against, without success. In the story of Shiva's sporting with his wife in public, to the anger of rishis, Shiva's phallus was cut into pieces. Shiva temples are said to have emerged at the places where the pieces of his dismembered member landed. The temples dedicated to mother goddesses also have a similar lore of origination. So the idol-worship of Shiva and its patronisation by certain Brahman sections was an undesirable development from the Brahman's own point of view. But they tolerated it because, given the circumstances, it was the most potent means to perpetuate their ideology over the minds of the people, besides being a source of wealth and respect.

Shaivism, even in its multiplicity, was a true priestly creed which combined theism with pantheism, and in which mysticism coexisted with ritualism. It also combined asceticism with eroticism, and spirituality with sensuality. It advocated a personal ethics of absolute passivity and non-violence, even as, on a collective level, it promoted the dharma of power. While the priests of the cult pretended to live a detached life engaged in the peaceful pursuit of spiritual enlightenment or artistic accomplishment, at the same time they coaxed their patron kings to extend their territories by waging wars against their neighbours, to fulfil their Kshatriya dharma. The ascetic ideal was sought to be realised not only by the control of the senses and mind, but also by making oneself totally incapable of performing sexual activity, an emulation of the hermaphrodite characteristic of one of Shiva's forms (known as ardhnarishwara, the half-man-half-woman deity). Whatever knowledge they acquired through these practices, they utilised it to get closer to the seats of power. Brahmans mostly served as ministers and chaplains to the royalty, and the latter too, in its turn, would never shrink from patronising them with riches and respect.

As always, even as the Brahmans and Kshatriyas, as the two upper classes, collaborated to perpetuate their domination over the masses, there emerged undercurrents of tension and mutual jealousies. This is seen in the famous Puranic story in which the haughty Kshatriya princess, Sharmishta, chides Devyani, the daughter of a Brahman priest, for making a claim of superiority. She argues how Brahmans couldn't be superior since, even for their subsistence, they depended on Kshatriya charity and munificence. In a similar story, a Kshatriya king named Kshup and a Brahman named Dadheech, a descendent of Chyavana muni, who were once bosom friends, fall out over the same question. They first argue about their respective claims of superiority and then indulge in a violent quarrel, in which, ultimately, the king is defeated. This was different from the result in the former case, where the princess pushes the poor Brahman girl into a ditch causing her to die.

In more historical terms, the Brahman–Kshatriya conflict is evident from the famous incident of Mahapadma Nanda, the Buddhist ruler of Pataliputra, who heaped insult upon Chanakya, a rustic Brahman. The latter then strategised to bring about the downfall of his tormentor. As it happened, Chandragupta Maurya, whom Chanakya championed, and who overthrew the Nanda king, himself became a follower of Jainism, and renounced his throne and the world. In this, he was also followed by his son Samudragupta. Bindusara, who succeeded Maurya, was a Buddhist sympathiser and his illustrious son, Ashoka, is well known to have been an active propagandist of Buddhism. All this meant that the rulers, in spite of their dependence upon Brahmans, had, in general, no love lost for Brahmanic ideals or institutions. For the Brahmans themselves, this meant that despite their best efforts, power remained slippery in their hands. In one instance, however, they were able to turn the table on their Kshatriya detractors. This was when king Brahadratha was overthrown by his Brahman military commander, Pushyamitra Shunga (who ruled c. 185–c. 149 BCE), in a bloody coup d'état.

One way to distinguish themselves from the Brahmans was for the Kshatriyas to pursue a different ideological line, and this was what they did earlier, when princes like Mahavira and Gautama Buddha formed their own ascetic sects, in opposition to the Vedic religion of sacrificial mysticism. But this religion of asceticism and renunciation, having proved itself to be inadequate as state enterprise and for communal life in general, was not expected to be favoured by the Sungas (second century BCE) and the Guptas (third to sixth century CE). These new ruling dynasties therefore chose to patronise the cult of Vishnu in place of Shiva, who remained pre-eminently a Brahman favourite.

Vishnu had faint origins in the *Rig Veda*, where he is presented as a sun god who encroaches upon the wide following of Indra (to which Indrani, Indra's wife, draws the attention of her husband). However, through the successive centuries that followed the Vedic era, he remained an obscure deity, never getting the kind of prominence that other gods like Shiva enjoyed. This was until the writers of the epics *Ramayana* and *Mahabharata*, for their own reasons, brought him into the limelight by presenting him as a rival of Shiva. The new ruling tribes, like the Yadus, being descendants of Mongoloid stock, opted for Vishnu as their deity since they already had a cult of sun worship prevalent amongst them. Besides, Vishnu, unlike Shiva, who was highly mystical and occult-centric, was a more concrete and relatable deity, taking avatar forms in both human and animal bodies. Also, imagining themselves as having a divine pedigree helped Kshatriyas counter the ever-present Brahman claim of nobler birth. That Vishnu was originally a Kshatriya-favouring deity is brought out clearly in the earlier-mentioned quarrel of Dadheech and King Kshup, in which the latter, finding himself incapable of countering the magical attacks hurled by the Brahman (who was a Shiva devotee), seeks the protection of Vishnu. Vishnu does come to his succour but is unable to achieve victory over Shiva.

Brahmans, for their own part, did not mind the emergence of Vishnu as a Kshatriya god, and in time, a section of them even adopted him as their own. One reason for this was that Vishnu did not have the kind of mystical aura that surrounded Shiva, which meant that the magical power emanating from the occult worship of Shiva remained with the Brahmans. Besides, in the theoretical development of the Vishnu concept, which was entirely handled by the Brahmans, he was made to be a subordinate and inferior deity in comparison to Shiva. Thus both as a nature (sun) god and in his later form as a creator of the natural world, he was a non-absolute, finite idea who could hardly match in stature with the absolute, infinite Shiva. As a matter of further degeneration, his conception was anthropomorphised and he was said to manifest himself through human incarnations. This was by all accounts a novel idea not to be found in the previous Vedic or Shaivite theology. The Brahmans even floated a theory which claimed that all the Vishnuite incarnations were because of a curse that was put on him for a sin he committed. So the story goes that during the war between the gods and the anti-gods (Devas and Asuras), on one occasion the Asuras were left without protection due to the absence of the sage, Sukra, who was their leader and guide. Indra, seizing upon the opportunity, launched a massive assault on his enemies. The Asuras, realising their imminent defeat, went to the mother of the sage, who also possessed some magical powers, which she then successfully used to humble the army of Indra. Thus thwarted, Indra, fearing for his life, beseeched the help of Vishnu. Vishnu did come to the succour of Indra and succeeded in killing the stubborn woman. But slaying of women was considered a heinous crime, and when Sukra learnt what had happened, he cursed Vishnu to be born several times in baser forms. Hence the incarnations.

Even as the Brahmans conceded some divine ground to the Kshatriyas, they also took care that the latter didn't develop a self-image more exalted than was their due. A conscious attempt was made to make these Vishnuite incarnations appear as upholders of Brahmanic ideals and interests. Thus, Krishna, the most distinguished among the incarnations of Vishnu, upholds, in the *Gita*, the four-fold division of society and also the Vedic theory of karma marga—these two institutions had been somewhat eclipsed due to Buddhist and Jaina developments. In the *Mahabharata*, Krishna and his brother-incarnation, Balarama, oversee the destruction of Kshatriyas by siding with opposing factions. Rama, another important incarnation, was a virtual slave of priests, owing to the latter all the weaknesses of his personality. The third Rama, the Rama-with-the-axe (Parashu Rama), again an avatar of Vishnu, waged twenty-one wars against the Kshatriyas, and wiped out their race so that not a single male survived and the females were taken by Brahmans for cohabitation. Besides, Vishnu, as a man-lion (Narasimha) killed the king, Hiranyakashyapu, who was a sworn enemy of the gods. In the form of Vamana (dwarf), Vishnu conspired to the effect that the mighty and pious king Bali was not only forced to abdicate from his throne but was also banished from his kingdom. In some incarnations, Vishnu performs feats that relate to the creation and sustenance of world: these include his incarnations as a fish, a tortoise and a boar. As a fish, he heralds the new birth of humanity after the great deluge; as a tortoise, he retrieves whatever was left of value in that deluge; and as a boar, he helps rescue the earth which was thrown into a sea by the demon, Hiranyaksha.

A more problematic case is the claim that the Buddha was one of the incarnations of Vishnu. While this indicates the convoluted logic so typical of priests wanting to kill an idea by making it part of their system, in the final analysis, the difficulty remained that the Buddha, with all his anti-

Vedic and anti-priestly posturing could not be fitted into the kind of subordinate role performed by other incarnations mentioned above. The authors of Puranas, however, had a more ingenious idea to overcome this difficulty. Reflecting over the nature of this incarnation, they proposed the following theory in the *Bhagvata Purana*:

> Thereupon the glorious God incarnated Himself as Buddha, and with a view to bring about confusion of their understanding and to create avarice in them taught them many false religions in the guise of a Pashanda (Sanyal 1929, 145).

With the decline and fall of the Gupta empire, most of the subcontinent suffered political disintegration and aggression from alien races. In the realm of ideas, while no revolution took place and no great movement emerged, the period nevertheless witnessed a consolidation of various sectarian ideologies that had been burgeoning in earlier centuries. There was a proliferation of sects and subsects with divergent, even antagonistic, philosophical or philosophico–theological views, all competing with each other for supremacy. Jainism, having originated in the east, travelled westward and southward, enjoying patronage from a number of small and big kingdoms. Buddhism too survived its persecution at the hands of the Sungas, and was intellectually robust enough to keep winning lay, as well as elite, converts. Among the orthodox sects, both the Shaiva–Shakta and the Vaishnava cults were maintaining their sway. Competing with them were also the left-hand Tantric sects, like Pashupatas, Ganapatyas, Kapalikas, with their strange beliefs and unconventional religious rituals.

The whole subcontinent, at this time, was steeped in the lore of magic and sorcery. The original Vedic orthodoxy was still alive, but its leading exponents, like Kumarila Bhatta and Mandan Mishra, of the seventh and eighth centuries CE, identified it solely with the sacrificial karma marga, ignoring its Upanishadic–mystical interpretation. During this time, a wholly new school emerged, the Mimamsakas, founded by Jaimini, who went as far as to deny the existence of God, propounding the theory that rituals by themselves were capable of giving the rewards desired by a devotee. The Vedic tradition was thus identified with ritualism, and mystical–spiritual praxis became the exclusive domain of non-Vedic Agamic schools. So far as the latter enjoyed acceptance and popularity among the masses as well as the more elite sections of society, and also since the former was viewed as an exclusive doctrine of Brahmans, the need of the hour was to make the Vedas a popular ideology by integrating it with the Agamic religion, thereby making it attractive for the masses.

This was, to be sure, a gigantic task and the man who proved equal to it was the great Shankaracharya, an eighth century genius and, arguably, the real founder of Hinduism.

Shankara is rightly celebrated for his theory of non-dualism, but from the point of view of socio-religious history, his greater contribution lies in synthesising the divergent trends of Indian religions and making them appear as parts of a single whole. The two, however, were related tasks. It was precisely his adherence to a pantheistic ideology that allowed him to systematically accommodate the beliefs and practices of a pagan, polytheistic religion and the heterodoxies of Jainism and Buddhism, and even (though partly) of left extremism. (Tantrism had a 'left-handed' aspect known as vamachara, involving practices regarded as crooked, reverse, contrary, opposite, yet considered beautiful and charming, as opposed to dakshinachara regarded as straightforward, honest, impartial, amiable, compliant and submissive.) Whether or not this was done at the expense of logical consistency, the fact remains that Vedic ritualism, Upanishadic mysticism and left-hand spiritism all coexisted in perfect harmony in Shankaracharya's Vedantic system.

While Shankara may have had predecessors who upheld a strict theory of ontological non-dualism, it is to him that India owes its first religious systematisation. The theory, as formulated by him, consists of four claims: (i) the *brahman* alone is real, (ii) the world is illusion, (iii) the soul or self in itself is unreal, and (iv) the true self (atman) cannot be different from the *brahman*. Philosophically, Shankara's starting point was the same as any idealist: he began with the recognition of the truth of the immediate self-revealed presence of our consciousness. Consciousness, then, is not something other than the self but identical with it—what is revealed to us is the consciousness of consciousness itself, and not of any extraneous subject inhering in the objects of thought. The objects of thought, the so-called external world, can also not be extraneous to the subject, insofar as its presence is contingent upon its being a part of consciousness. The world in this sense could, at best, have an epistemic and not an ontic presence. But Shankara denies even this, arguing that objects have a very fleeting presence and the effects they produce ephemeral. They come into being only to immediately perish. For their origination, they require a cause and their dissolution means their submergence in the substance from which they originate. This causal substance which is the source and end of all things is the absolute or the *brahman*, the eternally existent consciousness.

The world, though ultimately unreal, still has a kind of psychological presence. It is not absolutely non-existent, in the sense that the horns of a donkey or the sons of a barren woman are non-existent. The best way to understand the world's status is to compare it with the objects and events of our dreams. The 'reality' of the events in our dreams lasts till the dream does; it evaporates as soon as one is awake. The physical world too is revealed as non-existent when one is awakened to the fact of the *brahman's* ultimate reality. The unreality of the phenomenal world, of course, includes our individualised selves, their assertion being equally dependent upon our convoluted ways of seeing things. All assertions about realities other than the *brahman* are results of false consciousness or ignorance, true knowledge being the knowledge of the *brahman* itself.

Shankara's was a recondite system of philosophy which he built by employing all kinds of arguments—scriptural, logical, analogical, linguistic and even circuitous and tautological—against his possible or actual opponents, whether orthodox or heterodox. The range of ideas and arguments was so wide as to render any aspiring critic speechless. This was probably one of the reasons (besides a number of truths contained in the system) why it had the kind of impact it did on the future generations of Indian thinkers. Shankara attempted a reconciliation of what was seemingly irreconcilable. The belief in an absolute impersonal *brahman*, for instance, would disallow the worship of a personal God. But Ishwara, or a God with qualities (saguna), had his due place in Shankara's scheme, both as the creator of the universe and as an object worthy of love and worship. For him, it was the *brahman* itself which, to our imperfect minds, presents itself as a personalised being to be loved and worshipped. However, he says that, just as a Brahman acting as a Kshatriya king on stage does not alter his actual status of being a Brahman, the absolute appearing as non-absolute cannot actually become non-absolute for that reason. Nor can actions that are performed on stage be equal in value to the real events of which they are imitations. The appearances of the phenomenal world, for this reason, cannot be of any ontological or epistemological significance. In his *Brahma-Sutra-Bhasya*, Shankara holds that the *brahman*, in any case, is the substance of all that exists and just as 'it is seen that though all the seeds grow on the same soil, there is a great variety in their leaves, flowers, fruits, odour, tastes, etc. ...so it is justifiable even for the non-dual Brahman to have such distinctions as becoming the embodied soul and God, and the different products (like earth etc.)' (Gambhiranand 1965, 350).

As for the admissibility of belief in multiple gods within the pantheistic framework, the following explanation was offered by Shankara:

Starting with the (question of Sakalya), "How many gods are there?" (Br. III. ix. 1), the number of gods is determined (by Yajnavalkya) to be "three hundred and three, and three thousand and three". And when the question is put, "Which are those?", the Upanisad states, (through Yajnavalkya), "These are but the manifestations of them; but there are only thirty-three gods" (Br. III. ix. 2), by which statement the Upanisad shows that each god can have many forms simultaneously. Similarly the thirty-three are shown to be included in six; and so it goes on till to the question, "Which is the one God?" the answer is given, "The Vital Force (Hiranyagarbha)" (Br. III. ix. 9). By showing here the identity of all the gods with Hiranyagarbha, the Upanisad reveals that Hiranyagarbha Himself has multiple forms simultaneously (Gambhiranand 1965, 206–7).

As is evident, the argument here is based on scriptural authority and not a rational explanation of how an absolute unmanifestable *brahman* can divide itself into multiple gods with corporeal bodies and at least be partly subject to the laws of nature.

In this context, it also needs to be remembered that Shankara was born in a Vaishnava family, and Krishna remained his favoured deity throughout his life. On the other hand, Shiva was the god he invoked for mystical ends, since the Upanishadic *brahman* was too philosophical an idea to be of any great practical worth. Shankara was also an ardent worshipper of various mother goddesses, and is credited to have had some accomplishments in Tantra discipline (though he abhorred and opposed its more excessive forms). This in effect meant that sectarian differences within the mainstream of Hindu tradition did not carry any meaning for him. The targets of his attack were anti-Vedic sects like Jainism and Buddhism, and also the extremist left-hand schools who ridiculed Vedic practices openly. The left-hand or vamachara school replaced the traditional five elements (tattvas) of the Hindu cosmos, with what are called the five Ms: mamsa (flesh, meat), matsya (fish), madya (fermented grapes, wine), mudra (frumentum, cereal, parched grain, or gestures), and maithuna (sexual union). All these schools

practiced mysticism and asceticism of different shades, and
Shankara claimed that mysticism as such had a Vedic legacy,
finding its fuller expression in the Upanishads.

After the *Gita*, Hinduism came to regard the path of
action as a necessary stage of life, before one scaled greater
spiritual heights. Smiritikaras had accordingly prescribed an
active social life to be necessary before one could take up
renunciation and meditation. Shankara, although himself a
great admirer of the *Gita*, refused to subscribe to this theory
and, instead, adopted the line of his Jaina and Buddhist
opponents, who considered an early resolution to renounce
a better policy. Shankara also rejected the *Gita*'s claim that
both, the path of action and the path of knowledge, equally
led to spiritual perfection. For him, the former led to the
world of the gods and heaven, and the latter to the *brahman*
and release. In his famous commentary on the *Gita*, when
confronted by passages juxtaposing the two paths, he makes
no effort to explain them away in the light of his own
standpoint. Parenthetically, he states his own position with
all the emphasis he can command:

> Pure self-knowledge alone is the means to the Highest Bliss; for,
> as removing the notion of variety, it culminates in liberation
> (kaivalya). Avidya is the perception of variety involving actions,
> factors of action, and the ends of actions. It is always present in
> the Self. "Mine is action: I am the agent; I do this act for such and
> such a result" in this form avidya has been active in time without
> a beginning. The remover of this avidya is the knowledge of the
> Self... Since, moreover, the Highest Bliss is not an effect to be
> accomplished by action, works cannot be the means to it (Sastri
> 1947, 500–1).

It is again one of the great ironies of Indian history that the one who preached renunciation in such emphatic terms, and himself renounced the world at the tender age of eight (it is said that he almost coerced his mother into giving her assent for this purpose), lived a life of most intense activity and accomplished such goals which few could achieve even if given many lives. In a short life of thirty-two years, a peripatetic Shankara engaged in reading, writing, learning, teaching, meeting all kinds of people, performing miracles, establishing orders, resuscitating old temples, building new ones, holding polemics against his opponents and converting them to his doctrine. In his last years, he even set out for what, in biographical parlance, can be called as his 'journey for conquest'—an exercise aimed at winning over the kings and heads of heterodox sects to his own creed, an end in which he was accompanied by, besides his own followers and disciples, a royal army headed by a king.

The reason why a life lived in such a great frenzy should not be considered as the most telling argument against his own life-philosophy of monkism and resignation, will forever remain obscure for any of his critical admirers. But there were other failures too.

Among the more interesting incidents in his life, one relates to his encounter with a famous Mimamsa follower of his time, Mandana Mishra of the Mithila region in present-day Bihar, whom Shankara defeated in a polemic. While Mandana was defeated, his wife, Ubhaya Bharati, who was equally learned and wise, also challenged Shankara. Though reluctantly, Shankara nevertheless agreed to it. Now, the shrewd woman, knowing that it was impossible to defeat the great teacher in religious sciences, decided to ask him questions relating to the 'science of sex' (kama shastra). The celibate Shankara was nonplussed and timidly asked for a few months to prepare himself to answer her questions. He spent time searching for answers, and once, while he was flying across the sky, he happened to see the lifeless body of a deceased king. Seeing this it occurred to him that if he could enter into the king's body, he would be able to live with the queens, and learn what he could not as a renunciate. As one adept in occult powers, the task was not difficult for him and he proposed the idea before his disciples. The disciples were dismayed; they protested and advised him against such a venture, that would violate his vow of celibacy besides being undignified and immoral. Shankara was adamant and asked the pupils not to be too prickly. His own argument for justifying this proposed action was the following. Replying to his chief disciple Sanandan, he said:

> Your statement is well intentioned but you have seen only the external side of the issue and have not entered into its interior. Don't you know that it is one's will which is at the base of all his intentions. One who looks down on the world, if he does any action it would matter nothing. For one who has realised the whole world to be illusory and unreal, the world cannot put him into bondage. Actions produce effects only in the case of those whose egos are involved in the actions. When the ego is destroyed by knowledge the doer does not get any fruits of his actions. Even if he kills a Brahman, no sin is incurred. And even if he performs thousand horse-sacrifices, no reward is given. Don't you remember the episode as mentioned in Rig Veda where the will-free *brahman*-knowing Indra killed Trishiras [three-headed] Vishwarupa, the son of Twashta, and threw the munis before the wolves to eat them.

But no harm was done to him.... (Shankara Digvijaya, 9.95).

A similar incident happened on the occasion of his mother's death. According to the scriptures, only the eldest son of a deceased could light their pyre; and Shankara, being present, was supposed to do it. But there was a difficulty. Shankara was a renunciate, and as a renunciate, he was disallowed from performing the ritual. This was a real dilemma for the saint. On the one hand was his intense love for his mother and the desire for the release of her soul, and on the other hand was his own resolve to shun action. While some schools of Vedic jurisprudence permitted a departure from the rule in extreme situations or prescribed some expiatory rites to neutralise the effects of a violation, Shankara himself insisted that a violation of rules was inexpiable. Despite such a harsh view, it was the love for his mother which triumphed and Shankara decided to perform the ritual. Another difficulty arose when his relatives and neighbours began to oppose such a violation and refused to carry the old woman's corpse to the cremation ground. Shankara was then forced to cremate her in his own yard. In his anger, he cursed the villagers that in future all the dead in Kalady would be similarly burnt in front of their own houses. It is said that from then on, it has remained an ordinary practice in the village.

From the point of view of the law, the breach committed by Shankara would have destroyed the labour of his whole life, though from a human point of view, what he did was quite normal. A humane and humanistic perspective on life would also have obviated for him the need to take recourse to the subterfuge of mystical metaethics to explain away his deviant behaviour in the Mandana Mishra episode. The lapses of Shankara were, however, not only his personal failures, but failures of his system too. The disparagement of sexuality, and seeing love as a form of bondage, could be great philosophy, but it was not an answer to the needs of human existence. What sustains human life's internal urge for survival, both at the personal and interpersonal levels, are emotions and desires which produce actions. Life cannot self-immolate except by way of an aberration; nor can it be wished away as an illusion. A life-denying philosophy therefore could not be an authentic route for the goal of the ultimate contentment of the self.

While Shankara's revivification of the mystical lore of the Upanishads may have been prompted by his own mental predilections, it was also an effort to save the religion of the Vedas from becoming extinct. This was so because the religion was closely associated with the cult of sacrifice, which was increasingly seen as an anachronism in that time. Besides, while the metaethics of the Vedanta provided a theoretical justification for priestly immoralities, its actual contentlessness made it an omnibus ideology, which could carry any idea or ideal without creating tension in the system, and could even absorb heterodox elements. Above all, its essential Brahmanism also reinforced the declining institutions of orthodox teachers who possessed esoteric knowledge and could, for that reason, claim a superiority over all beings, including gods. No one outside this esoteric community would have the right to share in this knowledge and hence the hierarchy of caste would continue. Shankara himself was rather an extremist and is famous for his excessive-seeming proclamation that molten lead should be poured into the ears of a Shudra who is careless enough to listen to a sacred Vedic hymn (the injunction originally appeared in the *Gautama Dharma Sutra*). This was by no means an emotional outburst; it was, instead, a well-considered idea, an inseparable part of the system:

> *Vedantin:* Faced with this, we say: The Sudra has no competence, since he cannot study the Vedas; for one becomes competent for things spoken of in the Vedas, after one has studied the Vedas and known these things from them. But there can be no reading of the Vedas by a Sudra, for Vedic study presupposes the investiture with the sacred thread, which ceremony is confined to the three castes. As for aspiration, it cannot qualify anyone unless one has the ability. Mere ability in the ordinary sense also cannot qualify anyone; for scriptural ability is needed in a scriptural matter. But this scriptural ability is denied by the prohibition of the right to study (Gambhiranand 1965, 230).

This is a pretty circuitous argument. A Shudra cannot have the knowledge of Vedas because he has no competence for it, and he has no competence for it because he cannot study the Vedas. He may of course have the aptitude, ability and aspiration, but insofar as he has not undergone the investiture ceremony, these qualities would make no difference. Shankara, further, invokes the authority of scriptures to buttress his point. In a candid paragraph, he states:

> This is another reason why the Sudra has no right: by the Smrti he is debarred from hearing, studying, and acquiring the meaning of the Vedas. The Smrti mentions that a Sudra has no right to hear the Vedas, no right to study the Vedas, and no right to acquire the meaning of the Vedas (and perform the rites). As for prohibition of hearing, we have the text, "Then should he happen to hear the Vedas, the expiation consists in his ears being

filled with lead and lac", and "He who is a Sudra is a walking crematorium. Hence one should not read in the neighbourhood of a Sudra". From this follows the prohibition about study. How can one study the Vedas when they are not to be recited within his hearing? Then there is the chopping off of his tongue if he should utter the Vedas and the cutting of the body to pieces if he should commit it to memory ... This position is confirmed by the Smrti text, "One should read out to the four castes (keeping the Brahmana in front)", which declares the competence for all the four castes for the acquisition of the anecdotes and mythologies. But the conclusion stands that a Sudra has no right to knowledge through Vedas (Gambhiranand 1965,233–4).

Brahmans indeed wrote the Puranas to impart the Shudras with the knowledge of 'anecdotes and mythologies'. This greatly strengthened their caste domination, since, the Brahmans, as the repository of 'real' science, remained in the possession of occult powers, while the masses (Shudras) were opiated by creating for them a world of fantasies. The Puranic stories had the running theme of perpetual warfare between the party of gods, as represented by Brahmans, and the party of anti-gods comprising the native unconverted masses. In this, the former always emerged victorious. For his part, Shankara did not confine himself with providing a theoretical reinforcement to the system of caste hierarchy. Among his many achievements, one was the establishment of four monasteries in the four corners of the subcontinent, each representing one Veda (Puri in the east for *Rig Veda*, Sringeri in the south for *Yajur*, Dwaraka in the west for *Sama*, and one near Badrinath for *Atharva*) which were each headed by an arch-priest whose chief duty was to protect and preserve the institution of varna-dharma or caste duties.

These priests were also asked to maintain a high standard of life, much like kings, in accordance with the grandeur and glory of their high status.

It becomes quite clear that, in Shankara, we encounter a personality in which the principle of the unity of mystical experience and the institution of priesthood found its perfect expression. This is just one aspect of the matter. The other, and philosophically more important, aspect is the implicit belief that, at the base of social gradation, lies the essential spiritual inequality of man. So then, social inequality reflected the underlying spiritual inferiority or superiority of an individual, occasioned by the effects of their actions in previous birth(s). From this it followed that, except for a few Brahmans (males), all the rest including the majority of Brahmans themselves, males and females, were spiritually ill-equipped to attain the highest stage of realisation. Accordingly, they had to follow different spiritual disciplines and worship different sets of deities in order to attain their goals in life. For a traveller on the path of knowledge, for the one who has renounced the world and lives a life of monkhood, such practices had no meaning. Instead, he was supposed to shun all work, good or bad, especially avoiding the performance of rituals, and control his desires and emotions.

This was, however, a theoretical position, and, in practice, was humanly as difficult as it could be. The *Gita* had already declared that a complete withdrawal from the world and avoidance of action was impossible. And Shankara himself, despite being a sanyasin (monk) and one who had realised the *brahman*, could not overcome filial emotion for his mother and even lay a curse out of anger on those whose objection to his performing the funeral rite was unexceptionable. Besides, he worshipped all kinds of deities, like Krishna, Vishnu, Shiva and various mother-goddesses. In his own life, then, his theories failed to find a good realisation. Moreover, his standpoint contradicted with the stance of the *Gita*, which had clearly advocated the possibility of even a Shudra attaining release through what the scripture called the path of devotion or worship (bhakti). In fact, Shankara himself is said to have encountered Mahadeva (Shiva) in the guise of a Chandala (Pottan Teyyam). Apparently, without realising who he is, Shankara asks him to move out of his way.

> Sankara runs into Pottan, who carried a child at his waist and a pot of toddy on his head, and asks him to get out of the way to avoid distance pollution... Pottan Teyyam employs the very weapon of advaita—non-duality, the oneness of being—against the proponent of that philosophical system (Saktidharan 2019, 120–21).

The outcaste Chandala asks Shankara how he could foreclose the door of salvation to the Shudras when he believed all reality as being united in the *brahman*. At this, Shankara was reportedly dumbstruck and conveniently concludes that the Chandala is Shiva, but the truth is he probably could not persuade himself to believe in the rational idea of the spiritual equality of all men and women.

Shankara's defence of the idea of hierarchical spirituality could indeed be a well deliberated priestly attempt to defend an institution which was under attack from all sides. Both the heterodox systems of Jainism and Buddhism and orthodox Shaivism, in its right-hand and left-hand versions, which were at the time holding sway over the masses (especially in South India), had firmly rejected the Brahmanical notions of hierarchy and had thereby made themselves more attractive to the populace than the Vedic religion. Vishnuite theology, having its origin in the non-Aryan races, also preached the same doctrine through its twin scriptures of the *Bhagvata Purana* and the *Gita*. Shankara, though himself a Vishnuite, could perceive the dangers from these various schools and devised his own method of warding them off, by introducing the theory of graded truths which in juxtaposition excluded each other.

It is not exactly known what kind of impact Shankara's view made in this particular area of theoretical praxis. What is known is that he succeeded in converting quite a few kings and queens away from their earlier commitment to Jainism or Buddhism. What creates doubt in believing that his successes were lasting is the fact that not long after his time, many of the kingdoms he influenced were found to be sympathising again with the same old heterodox religions, some even going to the extent of persecuting rival neo-Vedic sects. In this period, the Shankarite Vedic–Shaivic orthodoxy was seen as an oppressive doctrine, its chief upholders, the Brahmans being taken as an epitome of snobbery, cruelty and bigotry. There was again a real threat to the Brahmanical institution, its central thrust being considered to be anti-people both in a spiritual and a social sense. At this juncture, a movement of reaction within the orthodox circles was expected to emerge. And it was not until about three hundred years later that the non-dualist philosophy of Shankara found its nemesis in the system of another great seer—Ramanuja of Sriperumbudur in today's

northern Tamil Nadu—who matched his predecessor in
intellectual profundity, missionary fervour and dynamism.
Like Shankara, Ramanuja too wrote commentaries on
Brahma Sutras, the *Gita* and various Upanishads, to combat
what he considered to be a philosophically puerile theory of
an attribute-lacking *brahman*.

The philosophical system of 'qualified' non-dualism
or Vishishta–Advaitavada, which Ramanuja developed
was as recondite and abstruse a system as that of non-
dualism propounded by Shankara. Unlike the latter who
depended mostly on scriptures and institutional dogmatism,
Ramanuja's forte was his logical acumen and his proclivity
to uphold man's faculty of critical experience. As he argued,
one can only believe in the scriptures and their supposed
infallibility by listening to them, which is itself a form of
sense perception. Moreover, if one thinks that the scriptures
command a superior authority over perceptions, which are
liable to error, then again it is perceptual cognition which
enables one to realise the superiority of the former and the
inferiority of the latter. It is true that perceptions are often
deceptive, as for example when a rope is mistaken for a snake
in the dark; but such errors are often detected and corrected
by subsequent perceptions and not through any extra-
perceptual faculty. This again shows the indispensability of
this mode of cognition. If one 'knows' that seeing a snake
instead of a rope is an illusion, then this knowledge is itself a
result of one's having seen the rope which appears to another
person as a snake. To regard sight as an illusion would mean
that both the perceivers—the one seeing it as rope and the
other seeing it as snake—are harbouring an illusion equally.[8]

On such and other arguments, Ramanuja establishes

the essential credibility of perceptual knowledge, which in turn makes the task of defending a belief in the material world easier. In the first place, he argues, it can be seen that all cognitive events inevitably contain both subjective and objective elements, and neither of these can be reduced to or assimilated into the other. For example, in the case of sight, an occurrence takes the form 'I saw this' where the term 'this' stands for the objective reality which enters into the subjectivity of 'I', thus creating knowledge: This 'this' can also not be an undifferentiated, non-particular entity, for inasmuch as it is seen, it is seen to be an individualised thing. Perception of a thing means the perception of the generic and other properties of that thing, and although these properties are shared possessions of all things of the world, their different configurations make them into different and differentiated things. Therefore, to deny the qualified things and admitting in their place only an attributeless thing-in-itself, as the idealists or followers of Advaita do, would not be in keeping with the ordinarily accepted criterion of truth. Scriptural arguments can also not be invoked to buttress the latter position insofar as they contain words and sentences which become meaningful only by relating themselves to each other. This fact also suggests that, in their individual capacities, they are independent and differentiated. Even indefinite perceptions, like dreams, swoons and such, have the same quality of being particularised events, for, dreams do bring changes in our body like how sometimes the mere suspicion of being poisoned or being bitten by a snake can cause death or at least some lower-order physiological effect. They cannot therefore be completely disregarded as unreal.

It can be seen that the controversy between the exponents of Advaita and Ramanuja is essentially a controversy between traditional idealism and realism. Ramanuja, representing the latter school, uses common-sense logic to 'set at naught' the view 'that experience itself is existence'. (Remember here Berkeley's famous dictum: *esse est percipi*.) By using the same tools of criticism, he proceeds further to demolish the reverse fallacy of reducing the self to what may be called the physical–psychological ego, and which the Advaita philosophy regarded as an unreality or 'maya'. On this, he points to the fact that, in any case of 'I experience this', 'I' and 'experience' are cognised as separate terms which together make possible the event of that cognition. Here, 'experience' is a qualifying attribute of the self, just like how a stick qualifies a man when he is holding it. This would mean that 'I' is an independent reality and should not be mistaken for our contrived physical egoity (ahankara) as the Advaitists claimed. If egoity is physical, it cannot display the properties of luminosity and consciousness which only a spiritual being can possess. As part of the material body, it belongs to the realm of non-selfhood and therefore is an object of consciousness, not its subject. 'Just as the quality of being consciousness is not admissible in relation to the principle of egoity, which is the object of that (consciousness), so also the quality of being the knower cannot be admitted in relation to what constitutes the object of (knowledge) itself' (Rangacharya and Varadacharya 1899, 86).

Consciousness though not a property of egoity, however, is conjoined with it, giving it its particularity. It is through this internal organ that our spiritual self performs various cognitive activities like perceiving, remembering, projecting etc. Being thus conditioned by a physical principle and having always this or that thing as its object, consciousness is not a pure, undifferentiated entity. The 'self' is therefore separate from the *brahman* in being itself a qualified, conditioned and originated thing—as against the latter, which is unoriginated, unconditioned and unqualified. Though unqualified, the *brahman* is not attributeless. On the contrary, it is the bearer of all fine qualities. According to Ramanuja, the scriptures which deny the *brahman* any attributes, are mostly referring to those attributes which are specific to the material world or to those which are generally not considered auspicious. Unlike Shankara's *brahman*, Ramanuja's conception of it is that of a creator, preserver, destroyer, besides also being existence and consciousness, as Shankara admitted. Thus he says:

What has been urged by the purvapakshins to the effect that Vedanta passages such as "Existence alone my dear child, that was in the beginning" (Chhand. Up. VI. 2.1) and the like are intended to establish that thing alone which is devoid of attributes and is of the uniform nature of intelligence, this (view also) is incorrect; because in the way of providing the proposition that, by knowing a certain one thing, all things become known, it is declared that the highest Brahman, which is denoted by the word *Sat* (or existence), is the material cause of the world, is the efficient cause of the world, is omniscient, omnipotent, wills the truth, pervades all, supports all, controls all, and is characterised by innumerable other auspicious qualities, and that the whole has that (Brahman) for its soul... the evil qualities appertaining to matter (or prakriti) are first negative (in relation to the Brahman); and then it is declared that the highest Brahman possesses innumerably auspicious qualities such as eternity, omnipresence, subtlety, all-pervasiveness, in-destructibility, the quality of being the source of all, omniscience, and so on (Thibaut 1904).

Ramanuja's exposition of a philosophical theology with a personal God at its centre, was undoubtedly a watershed moment in the history of Indian religious thought. For, while it formally marked the end of the Vedic cult of sacrifices (although Ramanuja himself did not disbelieve in it), Shaivism too, which was hitherto mostly a religion of mystic occultism, came to be practiced as a creed of theistic devotion. Here onwards, Vishnuism became the dominant religion, splitting into various subsects in time.

The thinkers who closely followed Ramanuja reinforced the theistic tendencies of his system by upping their fierce attacks on the doctrines of illusionism and pantheism. Nimbarka, of the thirteenth century, from the Telugu-speaking community, who was Ramanuja's junior contemporary, propounded the theory of 'unity-in-difference' (bhedabheda), in which he stressed the soul's essential difference with the world on the one hand, and with the *brahman* on the other—though he did not mean that they were *absolutely* separate entities. Madhva, of the thirteenth century, from the Kannada-speaking region, another great Vaishnavite activist, came down heavily on Shankara's illusionism and rejected even Ramanuja's approach of treating the soul and the world as intrinsic to the 'body' of God. He even dispensed Vedantic jargon, reverting to the old theology of the Vedas, which was, for all practical purposes, abandoned in favour of the Upanishads and Brahmasutras. These latter texts were not literally rejected but, instead, their content was given a new meaning consistent with the non-pantheistic attitude of the Vedas. Madhva personally regarded the *brahman* (identified with Vishnu) to be an absolutely transcendental being who created and supervised the world without being, in any way, attached to it. For him, the human soul was also multiplicitous, existing in its own right, though dependent for its origination on God.

In view of these changes that the notions of God and reality underwent, it was natural that the authors of the new doctrine revised existing eschatological theories, especially their answers to that most controversial question: what is the most effective way to attain liberation. The illusionist theory had quite naturally led to a non-activist view of life; it held the realisation of God or the *brahman* as its principal goal. Earlier, the *Gita* had rejected this position, and as part of its general theistic outlook, had elevated the path of action to a respectable status, treating it as the first step towards the attainment of knowledge. As against Shankara, therefore, these theists rehabilitated the *Gita's* doctrine, and once again action without attachment became a viable path to salvation. Both Ramanuja and Madhva are therefore found to advocate the view that a life lived according to the rules and norms of morality, while observing prescribed rituals, was enough for the purification of the soul, making it a receptacle of God's knowledge. The knowledge of God, again, in this context, did not mean a realisation of the identity of God with soul or reality. Rather, it was like being in the presence of God, in sharing his attributes of power, bliss, knowledge, and so on. This end could be achieved both by renouncing or without renouncing the world. What was, however, essentially required in either case was that one should cultivate love and devotion towards God. The path of devotion was not taken to be an independent path, but as a frame of mind in which God's majesty is steadily kept in view and his company and grace continually sought. Accompanying this was a theory of self-surrender (prapatti), something that was entirely absent in the earlier pantheistic orthodoxy. Though this idea was, in some ways, different from the concept of 'bhakti', nevertheless the two fitted well in the new framework.

The changed perspective on the eschatological question also brought in its wake some significant changes on the issue of whether or not Shudras were entitled to final emancipation. The *Gita* can be interpreted as having taken a bold stand in declaring them, along with the other sections of 'sinful birth' (papa-yonayah)—women and Vaishyas—to be able enough to reach the goal of spiritual realisation (Radhakrishnan 1960, 190). But this was too revolutionary an idea to find favour with the traditionalists, especially those represented by the Mimamsakas and Advaitists. We find therefore that an embarrassed Shankara just skips over the relevant verses without making any comment in his commentary on the *Gita* (Sastri 1947, 257). In his commentary on the Brahmasutras also he was faced with a similar problem. In Brahmasutra literature, one finds the mention of several names like Janasruti, Satyakama Jabala, Dharmakjadha, Vidura, and so on, who attained ultimate knowledge despite being low-born. Shankara tries to explain away all these cases through subterfuge. He says that Janasruti was actually a Kshatriya and not a Shudra; Satyakama too was, in fact, a Brahman, as he told the truth (about his illegitimate birth) to the sage, Gautama. In the cases of Dharmakjadha and Vidura, he says they were those 'to whom knowledge dawns as a result of (good) tendencies acquired in the past lives' (Gambhiranand 1965, 234).

However, for Ramanuja, Madhva and all the others

of the bhakti school, the stand taken by the *Gita* was unassailable. Ramanuja, therefore, while commenting on the aforementioned verse, does not make any excuse, nor does he try to give an interpretation different from the natural one (as he does in the case of many other inconvenient verses). He is in fact credited to have followed the idea most sincerely, both in belief and in practice. It is claimed that he once took a Shudra as a teacher, and that, in another instance, he recited some of the most sacred mantras before a lay audience. Even more daring was his open hobnobbing with Chandalas and advocating their right to worship Brahmanical deities (he even held ceremonies to invest the sacred thread on Shudras and Panchamas, as the outcastes came to be called). Though he was a revolutionary of sorts in these respects, one can still find evidence of his reluctance to adopt the idea whole-heartedly. He does not deny that the ultimate knowledge of the *brahman* will remain a privilege of the three upper varnas, and that the fourth one, was dependent on divine grace to be able to make worthwhile progress in their spiritual journey.

Given the long-held prejudices, the idea of a Shudra attaining salvation could not be expected to be easily palatable for even the most liberal-hearted Brahmans. Therefore, in principle, though not denying the injunctions of the *Gita*, later theists often prevaricated on this issue. Some devised ingenious methods to get around this difficulty. The authors of Vishnu-centric Puranas, for example, took the position that there were different degrees of salvation, and a Shudra's attainment of final release was different from that of a yogin (mystic) or even an ordinary Brahman. In the *Kurma Purana* it is written:

The abode of Brahmanas who regularly perform the righteous duties prescribed for them, is the region of Prajapati. The abode of Kshatriyas who do not run away from the battlefield is the region of Indra. The abode of Vaishyas who observe their duties, is the region of Maruts (The wind gods). / The abode of the Sudras who maintain themselves by serving (the three upper castes) is the Gandharva region... / The abode of Yogins is the immortal region called *Vyoman*—the greatest, imperishable, eternal, and blissful abode of Isvara. It is the highest point, the Supreme goal to be achieved (Tagare 1981, 29).[9]

Despite its admittance of a certain level of spiritual equality, the new theology was far from being an ideology of social revolution. Social gradation based on the condition of one's birth was systematically retained. It was the *Gita* itself which left this possibility open when it emphatically declared that, for an individual, perfection consisted only in the performance of one's dharma (caste duties). To perform the dharma of a class other than one's own, even if meritorious, was dangerous and abominable (XI, 45–6). The *Bhagvata Purana*, the bible of Vishnuite sectarians, holds that: "A person performing his duties and following the special profession prescribed for his order, gradually attains to the nature of Supreme Spirit, and is set free by him from the miseries of the bonds of affections" (Sanyal 1973, 674). Different castes are obviously expected to perform different professions and duties depending on their 'aptitudes' and 'characteristics'. Among these, those peculiar to Shudras, as described by this text (Sanyal 1973, 427), are:

To serve the Brahmanas without any hypocrisy, and to the kine and the deities, and to be satisfied with whatever is acquired thereby constitute the characteristics of Sudras.

This was of course so, under the universal condition that:

> The nature of the people born in various orders and conditions
> was after their place of birth. Those born in the high places were
> high, and those born in low places were low.

The term 'Shudra', it must be remembered, applied to those people who though considered low-born, were, nevertheless, 'caste' people, comprising largely of agriculturists, artisans, performing skilled and unskilled labour; quite different from the Shudras was the class of 'out-castes' or untouchables, comprising the Chandalas, Nishadas (fishermen), atheists and heretics, children of inter-caste marriages and such. For this group the *Bhagvata* pronounced: 'Impurity, falsehood, stealing, atheism, picking quarrels for nothing, lust and anger are the characteristic of the very low caste people who disappear in the end' (Sanyal 1973, 427). The 'disappearance in the end' of course implied that they were to live a subhuman of existence in this world and could not aspire for any spiritual position in the afterlife either. So it is clear that Vishnuite eschatology of the *Gita*, though liberal enough to accede spiritual status to the Shudras, still excluded from its ambit a section of human beings of a considerable size, whom it considered to be doomed forever. The question of untouchables' souls was completely unaddressed, and socially their very sight was considered polluting. In such circumstances, Ramanuja's occasional mingling with the Chandalas would appear to be more due to his personal predilections, and his example was not followed by any of his orthodox successors, either in principle or in practice.

While there is no denying that the bhakti-centric revolt against Shankarite orthodoxy was basically motivated by genuine philosophical convictions, there were also extraneous factors which played their own role in shaping the mental outlook of these seers. For one, there may have been a kind of intra-caste hostility against the Namboodris, to which caste Shankara belonged and who considered the rest of the Brahmans to be far inferior to them. Coming as they did from the families of lower order Brahmans, the bhakti seers would have naturally disliked the latter's airs of superiority. Then there was also the desire to wean the Shudras away from the more attractive creeds of Jainism and Buddhism, which, though at the time had been wiped out from the northern regions of the subcontinent, were still dominant in the South, enjoying patronage from a number of royal kingdoms. The Shankarite assault had no doubt challenged the stranglehold of these religions, but eventually its oppressive character would have again led various sections of people to rally around the creeds which though not exactly a panacea for liberation were still of a far less exploitative character. As was pointed out in an earlier context, it was not as though the Vaishnava Brahmans were against the conversion of Shudras to heretical sects; they would indeed have welcomed it, had it not led to a diminished flow of gifts and an erosion of their authority. Vishnuism therefore was just another attempt by the priests to strengthen the institution of four-fold caste division by opening a window to accommodate the spiritual aspirations of common masses without in any way affecting their own ecclesiastical privileges in religious and politico-economic spheres.

That, despite having a reformist face, the bhakti school remained a priestly institution is also evident from its synthetic character. Shankara had struck a compromise with rival heretic creeds by incorporating their negativist and pessimistic ideas in his system. Bhakti-centric Brahmans, for their part, restored the theistic purity of the original Vedic doctrine while downplaying the importance of sacrificial ceremonies, especially those parts which contained violence and sexual latitude. The Buddha was made to be an incarnation of Vishnu, though his basic status was of one who demoralised and misled the Kshatriyas by preaching a false doctrine. Other than the Buddha, the recognition of Parashurama as an incarnation of Vishnu suggested that a reconciliation with the Shaivite cult was also sought. In fact, not just Shiva, but all the different gods and goddesses were given due recognition, though their place was subordinated to the supreme position of Vishnu.

Moreover, the idea of bhakti or devotion to a supreme God, with its attendant notion of equality of all men, was already, at this time, a well-established idea in South India, popularised by the Vaishnavite Alvars and the Saivite Nayanmars. It was fast emerging as a parallel creed, accepted on a large scale by the Shudra masses as a spiritually and socially liberating creed. Ramanuja and Madhva's attempt to make this idea an essential part of their creed could, therefore, well have been an example of familiar priestly exercise to take into account emergent trends and accommodate them into their system, after suitable modifications. The two seers also had to take note of the growing impact of Islam as a religion of devotion and equality for the masses, as well as the elite, as exemplified in the emergence of the Virasaiva sect, which resembled

Islam in important ways. This sect was once very popular in present-day Karnataka and still nominally survives in the Brahmanical community of Lingayatas, though, with the passage of time, it too has suffered relapse and has now been absorbed into Hinduism proper.

Both Ramanuja and Madhva sought to reject Shankara's gnosticism along with his doctrine of an impersonal God. But as far as the former question was concerned, they could not consistently stick to it, since the *Gita*, which they held dear, upheld gnostic ideas. Both tried to identify somehow the notion of knowledge with the idea of devotion, saying that anyone who pursued God with full sincerity of mind and heart would eventually succeed in attaining the *brahman*. He would of course realise not the non-difference of his self with God but a kind of 'community of characteristics' with him. The path of devotion included, besides doing one's duties without a desire for benefits, the incessant meditation on the reality of the *brahman*. Such devotion and worship, at its purest level, would reveal to the devotee, the knowledge of Vishnu in his most transcendental (para) form. And this is normally not expected to be attained, except by those who are entitled to the knowledge of Vedas—the three upper varnas but more specifically the Brahmans.

Ramanuja, especially here, took the position that the attainment of self-realisation does not mean the termination of a life of action and that one should continue with the performance of prescribed rituals, except when one is in a state of mystical ecstasy. Madhva, on the other hand, admitted to the possibility of exclusively pursuing the path of knowledge, though he too considered a detached, active life with a sincere devotion to God as the most reliable way of achieving salvation. Madhva was a renunciate and so were Ramanuja, Vallabha, Chaitanya and all others of this school. This practice of renunciation being taken as a necessary concomitant of the spiritual quest, in the context of these seers' lives, indicates that they put a premium on it in their common outlook on life's end. This, together with the earlier factors of God being considered as having transcendental as well as non-transcendental dimensions, in addition to their belief that only a few elects had access to the transcendental aspect of God, suggested that in the new theology there was a place for mysticism and esoterism.

Once an esoteric element is introduced in a religious system, the practice of teacher worship automatically follows, as it did in the case of these theistic philosophers. A devotee's access to God was no longer a direct one, but rather mediated by a 'knowledgeable' person or a teacher (guru). This teacher is not a mere path-giver or an instructor of spiritual discipline; he brings about a mysterious intervention between a devotee and God. In the bhakti school too, therefore, this institution of teacher worship was a substantial presence. The teacher was a god, an incarnation of God and sometimes even higher than God. He was to be addressed as 'lord' and nothing he did, however much it contradicted the ordinary understanding of ethics, was to be assailed or not complied with. This belief in the mediated attainment of the knowledge of the supra-transcendent aspect of God, had also its corresponding idea of the necessity of a mediator to approach God in his lowest manifestation: his image or idol (archa-swarup). Idolatry and temple worship thus became an essential part of religiosity in these theistic orders, which in effect meant that like Shaivism, Vaishnavism too sustained an identical system of priestly institution despite its claims of being a monotheistic creed. Apart from being a para—meaning supreme, as in para-brahman, the supreme *brahman*—and archa or idol, Vishnu also appeared in 'flesh and blood', in a human body. That God assumed a physical form meant that love for him also had to take on a physical dimension. It was thus that the child Krishna was loved for his pranks, as vouched in the much remembered poetry of Surdas, and in his youth he was everyone's prince charming, a Mohana, who is pursued by the devotee with all the zeal of a lover (Mirabai). The twelfth century poet, Jayadeva, an early devotee of Krishna, similarly sang (divine) songs of erotic quality, of the God's lusty dalliances with milk-maids, especially with his favourite, Radha, another man's wife.[10] All this had its basis in the scripture, *Bhagvata Purana* or *Srimad Bhagatvam*, where, again, a curious admixture of spirituality and eroticism is found.

> The auspicious Sukadeva continued:—O king! Having heard these piteous words of the *Gopees,* Krishna, the foremost of those, versed in the *Yoga,* smiled and was pleased with them. Though always delighting in his own self, he still joined in dalliances with them. Freely mingling in the company of these damsels... [he put] forth his arms embracing the damsels touching their hands, curling locks, thighs, breasts, scratching them with his fingernails, indulging in laughs, jokes and with repartees, piercing them with his glance, and with other amorous tricks, he (Krishna) delighted the *Gopees* bringing them under the spell of Cupid (The God of love) (Sanyal 1973, 124).

The sheer physicality of the divine love play could, however, have confounded any ordinary listener of the story. This happened to be the case with king Parikshit, to whom it was presently being related. Dismayed at the great irony involved in the situation, he asked:

O Brahman! the Almighty Lord of the universe did incarnate himself by a portion only for the propagation of the true religion and for the suppression of vile ones. He is the Creator, Expounder, as well as the Upholder of the dignity of piety. O Brahman! How did he then act in direct contravention to all systems of religion, by having intimate love-play with the wives of others? The Lord of the Jadus had attained the fruition of all his desires; with what end in view, he then perpetrated this, shameful act (Sanyal 1973, 137–8)?

In fact, Krishna himself understood that his acts were a breach of propriety and ordinary ethical rules, and he often tried to persuade the women, who rushed to tryst with him on hearing the sound of his flute, to return. Chiding them severely, he says:

The supreme duties of women are to serve their husbands with a sincere heart, to look after the well-being of the friends of their husbands and to rear and support their children. Women desirous of attaining the region where their husbands go after death, should not desert their husbands, even if they be of bad character, unfortunate, old, imbecile, invalid and poor, but not morally fallen. The prostitution carried on by private women is hateful all the more, and is attended with more danger. It breeds misery and infamy and is a hindrance to the attainment of heaven. So it ought to be totally and emphatically condemned (Sanyal 1973, 121).

Why then did he not comply with the rules he himself set

out? It was partly of course in deference to the sentiment of pure devotion on the part of the women. More importantly, at higher mystical levels, morality no longer remains binding, and one's flights to divine realms make him part of a celestial reality where worldly rules and codes cease to be of significance. Thus, in reply to the above query raised by the king, the narrator gives the following explanation:

> The auspicious Sukadeva replies, — "O King! Even the lords of people (such as Brahma, Indra, etc.) deviate from the path of virtue and become guilty of improper acts. But these acts do not bring any sin on the powerful and dispassionate ones (who perpetrate them), even as fire is not to be blamed for burning all things. But those who are not masters of their passions should not commit such an act even in their minds. If they do these acts of foolishness, they are sure to meet with destruction, even as persons, except Rudra, meet with destruction having drunk poison. The words of the guardians of people are true. But their actions are scarcely true.... No religious merit accrues to those people, who are free from egoism, when they perform an act of piety; neither doth any sin hang on them, when they commit an improper act. What wonder then, that the lord of all created beings [...] will have nothing to do with pious and impious acts; that is, there is not piety or impiety with respect to the Almighty Supreme Lord (Krishna) (Sanyal 1973, 138).

This was a way to explain away the immoral conduct of a divine personage, much in the same way as in Shankara's case, when he was defended for copulating with the wives of a dead king. So, on one level, Vishnuite doctrine seemed to run parallel to its rival doctrine of Shaivism. In fact, as the former evolved over time, many other ideas which were hitherto considered degenerate, left-hand worship, also became characteristic of this sect. Of comparative importance, for example, was the emergence of a cult of the worship of Radha, the lady-love of Krishna, who was believed to have completely merged herself in her lord through her pure and sincere devotion to him. Naturally, those who entertained similar desires in their hearts were motivated to imitate her in her various forms. The followers of the Vallabha sects, therefore, often wore women's garments, danced, sang and acted like cowherdesses, and some of them even pretended to menstruate every month. As the cult was already characterised by a preponderance of the feminine element, its followers would often undergo a sort of mental self-castration (in order to fully realise the ideal of a dependent and passive devotee of the lord), as was done in some Shaivite sectaries, imitating the ascetic and impotent persona of Shiva. Radha was considered as Krishna's Shakti, created by him, eternally united with him as his consort. Krishna was also believed to have contained within himself the female principle, and thus becoming a Vishnuite version of the 'ardhanarishwara' (the half-man, half-woman conception of Shiva). Moreover, like Shiva, who was called mahayogi, Krishna is also referred to as 'lord of ascetics', 'source of yoga', 'soul of yoga', and so on, in various Puranas.

Although the Vaishnava cult could never equal the debauchery of the left-hand extremism of the Shiva cult, presumably because of the presence of a monotheistic element in it, there did develop a culture which was thoroughly mystical and priestly. The fact of the matter is that despite the efforts of reformers like Ramanuja and

Madhva, Vishnuite theology, as against its philosophy, came to acquire a pantheistic content and set the same occult goals for its adherents as was the case with Shaiva sects. The *Bhagvata Purana*, the ideological mainstay of this school, is replete with illusionistic and pantheistic ideas, which were also partly adumbrated in the *Gita* itself. In the latter text, Krishna reveals to a doubting Arjuna (unconvinced about killing his cousins to fulfil his Kshatriya dharma) his all-encompassing form; he shows himself to be identical with the universe, where all notions of birth and death, joy and sorrow, time and space, action and inaction, are found to be sheer illusions (see chapters X and XI of the *Gita*). In the *Bhagvata* also, Krishna is described as one 'being stationed as the governor through thy illusive power, thou dost by three-fold qualities of Maya (illusion), create, preserve and destroy in thee this universe which is beyond all conceptions'. At another place in the same *Bhagvata Purana* it is said:

> Consider this world which is being perceived by your mind, words, eyes and ears as mental, illusory and transitory. A man without a knowledge about the distinction between Prakriti and Purusha is liable to view the objects of the world as essentially distinct from one another ... He who is above both good and bad... [s]uch persons, the friend of all creatures of quiescent minds firm about knowledge and discriminative knowledge, behold the Universe as identical with me and never come to grief (Sanyal 1973, 165–6).

And yet, it was certainly not a philosophy of complete identity or non-dualism of the Shankara type. Instead, it was something close to Nimbarka's 'identity in difference', or even Ramanuja's theory of the universe being the 'body' of the *brahman*. All was in God, all was his manifestation; the world's apparent diversity was merely a deception and its origin was in God. Perfection (siddhi) therefore consisted in reaching a state of realisation through a devotion to this conception of God. One who knows reality does not discriminate between good and bad or right and wrong, for God is above all these distinctions. In him reside both gods and demons, honesty and dishonesty, Brahmans and Chandala, and so on:

> O the most enlightened one! that man who, by the light of knowledge, beholds all creatures to be like unto my own personality, and serves them as such is a wise one. It is that man also, who makes no distinction between a regenerate person and a *chandala*... between individuals giving wealth unto the Brahmana, or stealing away what is possessed by him, between the sun and a spark and between the deceitful and the honest (Sanyal 1973, 259).

This attitude of non-differentiation between the evil and the ugly, and the good and the auspicious, should not to be taken as an exercise in pure cynicism. The above were more in the realm of metaphysics than ethics. For the same reason, it is also not indicative of any great altruism and egalitarianism on the part of its writers. A Chandala or a thief may be served (worshipped) as being part of the cosmic reality, but he will not be granted spiritual merit or social approbation on the same grounds. In fact, passages from the same text have already been cited that show that though the Shudras do have some hope for their eventual release from the bondage of karma, this does not correspond to their social status, and the fate of a Pariah is sealed on both counts. The present Vishnuite position is much like Shankara's doctrine, where a Chandala, although a part of the *brahman,* was still reviled and shunned as the plague of humanity (a 'walking crematorium'). The Vishnuites of course could not go to the same extreme of denigrating the Chandala figure of Pottan Teyyam as Shankara did, partly because of the less hieratic origins of the sect and partly because of the theistic backdrop of the doctrine. All said and done, Vaishnavism remained a hieratic ideology, with Brahmans at its centre and the rest of humanity occupying the periphery, either as slaves or as enemies.

In Vishnuite literature, though Krishna is not a Brahman, but a king, he is an inveterate enemy of the ruling class. He kills, either by deceit or by his own physical prowess, a number of kings belonging to non-Aryan tribes, and presides over the destruction of the Aryan families of Kuru and Panchala kings. By the end of his career, which was already full of bloody episodes, he proceeds to destroy his own tribe of Yadus, which was dominant at the time in the region adjacent to Indraprastha (present-day Delhi). This he does to fulfil the desires of Brahmans, who had cursed the tribe for some reason. Before their destruction, the Yadus are described as debauched drunkards, constantly quarrelling among themselves. Fed up with their depraved behaviour, Krishna advises them to leave the accursed land of Dwarka and migrate to a place where better conditions prevailed:

Let the women, the boys, and the old men go to the Sankhydhara; and let us go to Provasha, where the holy Sarswati river flows by towards the west. There we would bathe in that holy river; and by strict fasting we would make ourselves sanctified. There also we would pour forth water upon the gods, and anoint and worship them with a restrained heart. Moreover, there we would propitiate the magnanimous regenerate persons; as also we would render immense services unto them by giving away kine, lands, gold, clothes, elephants, horses, cars and handsome buildings unto them. Do thou know that Destiny is thus the destroyer of all miseries, as well as it is the highest abode of all prosperity. The worship of twice-born persons and that of celestials and kine are only associated with persons of respectable parentage (Sanyal 1973, 264–5).

Once again, we see a fully Brahman-centric worldview being espoused. The above is an exhortation to the people to subserve the priest and also to be generous to them in giving valuable gifts. It was, therefore, a fresh attempt on the part of a new generation of priests to rejuvenate the idea of priestly privileges, after the system of Vedic sacrifices had become an anachronism and Shaivite orthodoxy had turned crude, corrupt and socially oppressive. In the new dispensation, through idolatry and temple worship, a ritualistic religion was reborn for the masses, while higher knowledge was still the possession of Brahmans. Asceticism was meritorious, though it did not prevent the king of ascetics, Krishna, to espouse thousands of women through marital or extra-marital relationships. Like Shaivism, and also the earlier Vedic and Brahmanic–Upanishadic systems, here too mysticism coexisted with ritualism, and the ascetic ideal was recompensed with extreme eroticism. Above all, Vishnuite doctrine also turned anti-Kshatriya and anti-Shudra. Vishnu, in his many incarnations, often struck down the Kshatriyas whenever they became too strong. Similarly, in his final incarnation, as Kalki, it is believed he will give a similar blow to the Shudras. As the *Bhagvata Purana* says: 'Then in the *Kali Yuga,* incarnating himself as Kalki. He will slay the Sudra kings' (Sanyal 1973, 155).

The Shudras, for their part, had a parallel movement of bhakti, the hallmarks of which were in strict adherence to monotheism and in opposition to all forms of ritualism and religious formalism. Having realised that polytheistic nature worship and idolatry were at the root of the priestly–Brahmanical exploitation of the masses, the Shudra saints thought it advisable to wean people away from these practices. But, partly because of a lack of intellectual rigour, and partly because of the inability of its leaders to shake themselves completely off the juggernaut of tradition, the movement failed in achieving its objective. For one thing, the belief in the metempsychosis was scrupulously retained, and the God who was worshipped was quite often the one given to them by their oppressors: Vishnu either in the form of Rama, Krishna or someone else. Their ethics was also an ethics of love, the preeminent principle of self-imposed political emasculation and social withdrawal. The trend began in the pre-medieval era and continues up to our own times, where an ideology of resistance and struggle is being sought to be derived from the religion of non-resistance and resignation.

Epilogue

One of the indisputable things said about India's cultural tradition is that, at its heart lies spirituality, which, though in itself is a pretty vague idea, has a more or less definitive meaning in the Indian context. It is a complex idea, multi-faceted and multi-dimensional, with ramifications in the fields of metaphysics, epistemology, ethics, axiology and social and political economy. Despite this all-encompassing scope, it still has a certain unity, even simplicity, of meaning, that can be discussed in order to understand the essentials of the nation's civilisational ecosystem.

The ritualistic spirituality of the Vedas may, at one level, appear to be radically different from the philosophical slant of the Upanishads, and the latter might be taken to represent a kind of orthodoxy, that is so stubbornly contested by the heterodox schools of Buddhism and Jainism (of the Shramanic tradition). Again, these two sets of ideas may look rather divergent when compared with the Bhakti sects of later centuries, which in turn took varied forms across various times and regions in their historical evolution. The Shaivites, the Shaktas and the Vaishnavites were rivals for a long time, until some kind of a reconciliation was reached relatively recently, thanks to the efforts of Bengal's Ramakrishna and his illustrious disciple, Vivekananda.

Even as there was diversity in unity, there was unity in diversity and a continuity in change. The Upanishads were originally an inseparable part of Vedic literature, until, in modern times, they began to be published and studied separately. Similarly, while the Buddha and Mahavira espoused metaphysical doctrines in opposition to Upanishadic theories, and denounced the ritualism of the Vedas (which had an essential caste component), the overall approach of looking at life in the world remained the same, as was the eschatology of salvation and liberation, and the path of asceticism and mysticism, as a means of achieving the ideals. In these latter respects, even the Bhakti saints did not deviate much even though some of the earlier practices were abandoned in favour of new ones.

It can be safely said that while the branches were multiple, the roots (and even perhaps, the trunk) were one and the same. If the tree represented spirituality in general, the branches were the multiple sects and cults that emerged and flourished in different times and different regions. Only Islam and Christianity were different, and that was precisely because they were non-indigenous—products of a very different socio-religious milieu. Even in their cases, Christian spirituality corresponded with Indian developments in putting a premium on the idea of asceticism (at least for the clergy) and in its institution of priesthood. Indian spirituality also impacted Islam in its Sufi iteration, which was, and still remains, a strong current in the region.

This book has attempted to demonstrate that spiritualist *weltanschauung* has its own peculiar cosmology, theory of knowledge, systems of values and morals, and, most crucially, strong prescriptions for shaping the institutional order and structure of society. What centrally guides this ideology and what makes up its statics and dynamics, is a certain kind of 'logic', which is neither Aristotelian–Russellian nor Hegelian–Marxian. It is indeed a kind of bi-polar metalogic, with two excesses along with their corresponding deficiencies, which in their interplay lead to the notion of a 'middle', that is real in being productive and dynamic in its very unreachability. This is foregrounded by the ideas of transcendence and transgression that manifest in individual behaviours and social institutions whenever and wherever said metalogic plays itself out.

In the orthodox Upanishadic tradition, with Shankara supposedly as its most authentic representative, ultimate reality was a supra-material but not exactly the God of popular belief. The *brahman* was an impersonal, attributeless, absolute being that was too abstract and transcendental to be an object of worship. This absolute being was not to be worshipped or loved or obeyed, nor was it the source of succour in times of distress. Physical matter and human soul were, by extension, unreal and illusory—maya. In fact, the *brahman* itself was mistaken for these non-realities due to ignorance, avidya. This reality was not just transcendental but supra-transcendental, something beyond the beyond, something above conception and comprehension. Now this was an excess that carried with it an opposite excess in which unity broke into multiplicity (of gods and goddesses); the impersonal gave way to the anthropomorphic, abstraction gave way to physiolatry. The absolute was indeed seen to be identical with nature, which became the latter's manifestation or illusory unfoldment.

The Shramans, while recognising some amount of substantiality in matter, reduced the spiritual (*brahman* and atman), both to have either only a momentary (kshanika) existence or a non-existence, a void, a zeroness (shunnyata). But this atheology did not stop them from believing in quite a few of the older gods. They even went so far as to add many of their own. Their pantheon was much more animistic, and crowded, with 'spirits' than their Upanishadic predecessors.

There were thus excesses and deficiencies with no middle in sight. A similar act played out in the domain of knowledge, where rationality, which is supposed to define humanity, was overshot and a leap was taken into the realm of the supra-rational and the irrational.

It is indeed strange that reason, as a source of knowledge, is nearly unrecognised in Indian philosophical discourse. Logic was present, but used mostly for the purposes of sectarian polemics. There is also the mind, the manas, which is considered to be a part of the body, and therefore unreal. The *brahman* could not be realised through the senses or even the mind. 'Realisation' came by way of 'stabilising' the intellect: that is, by making all activities of intellect cease, so that no worldly thoughts or desires enter the mind to divert the yogin from the contemplation of the *brahman*. This was the state of 'stable intellect', or samadhi, as the *Gita* calls it—a kind of suprarational mystical experience (bordering, in some respects, on occult), that kept with it the deficiencies and irrationalities of superstitions, magic and miracle mongering. The presence of these crudities, in a climate suffused with mystical ideas and practices, had theoretical underpinnings in so far as the supra-rational wasn't knowledge in the positive sense, and this deficit could only be compensated for, by a belief in the extra-natural and the supernatural.

Superstitiousness and belief in the supernatural had critical implications for life in society, the most important of which was the emergence of a radical division between the priestly class and the class of their lay followers. The gods were under the control of priests, at their beck and call by virtue of their ability to correctly recite the mantras at sacrificial ceremonies, and on occasions of birth, marriage, death and other important events in man's life. Priests were of course 'mediators', who imposed their own will upon man, by calling it the will of gods. Through the power of mantras, they could bless or curse, build or ruin, the lives of men and women. They had the power of knowledge, which they used extensively and ruthlessly, to enslave, not only the masses, but also kings and their cohorts. They alone claimed the right to knowledge, denying it to the rest, prescribing extreme punishments for those who attempted to intrude in their exclusive territory. Knowledge was power, but, to clarify again, it wasn't secular power, and was rather the power of the occult knowledge of mantras, acquired through the practices of austerity (tapas) and asceticism, that made them powerful enough to have a free run even in the secular realm. Despite their claim to unworldliness, priests lived in the world, visited kings in their courts and palaces, and had unrestricted access even to royal harems. Priests also fought wars for (sometimes also against) kings. As for the common people, the Visha, the Shudra, they were out of sight, their reality taken for granted as controlled and enslaved subjects.

Ancient Indian political economy was centred around the Brahman priests rather than the Kshatriya kings, the latter playing mainly the role of co-opted associates, only occasionally rebelling against them. The fear of the gods was pervasive, and so also the fear of priests. The masses, as instruments of service, lived as they were supposed and asked to live, as a people of service. The limitations of the age did not allow them to even think or talk about the ideas of equality, liberty and justice. Inequality was ingrained as the natural result of the circumstances of one's birth; liberty, a privilege of the elite; and justice was simply another name for deep injustice, and the denial of equality and liberty. Varna, or the contingency of one's birth, was the dominant and all-encompassing idea, and any conceivable disturbance (in the forms of intermixing of castes) in this system (varna-sankara) was a personal tragedy and a collective disaster.

There is no such thing as 'spiritual equality' and varna is never determined by one's occupation, as some modern apologists claim. Spiritual equality comes when the same kind of soul is seen to be present in all humans, but here, the individual souls were non-existent in themselves, being only the false shadows of a non-substantial *brahman*, or a fleeting, unthinkable, untalkable non-reality (Buddhism). Pagan mystical philosophy does not admit to a flat view of the universe. Instead, it has a theory of ordered cosmology in which beings constitute a hierarchy from the lowest to highest forms. It is an ascending order, where the lowest has the least and the highest has the greatest quantity and quality of soul. From physical-material to plant to animal, and then, to human life, and within the human, from Shudra to Vaishya to Kshatriya to Brahman, the spirit becomes more and more refined.

The idea of the *brahman* as atman, while being so unitary and simple, was at the same time also complex (once again one excess leading to another). The theory here precludes the possibility of spiritual equality, and in fact, is the main reason behind the idea of varna. Varna was based on occupation, but one's occupation was determined by birth. Varna itself was determined by the karma performed according to swadharma in previous births. In fact, within the Brahmans, as also within all castes, there is the distinction of high and low, based presumably on the same principle of spiritual inequality. The non-Brahmans, however, could, notionally and potentially, attain equality but that would take ages. Any lapse may result in a fall down the ladder and the process of climbing starts all over again. In effect, both spiritual and social inequality will persist, since the scaffold of hierarchy remains in place.

Varna was also not a product of the accidents of history—something that happened 'later', as the apologists would like us to believe. It was there right at the beginning of history, in fact, from the time of the creation of the world as espoused in the "Purusha Sukta" of the *Rig Veda*. It was a part and parcel of the pagan-mystical worldview that prevailed in ancient and post-ancient India. There are, however, two mitigating factors that need recognition. Firstly, the distinction of high and low, of contemplative elites and servile masses (with the warrior class in between), has been a feature of the pagan thought-system in every culture. Plato adhered to it, as did the Zoroastrians of Iran, and so many others. Secondly, some kind of hierarchy is inevitable in any civilised society, whether based on birth, profession, or an individual's own proclivities. What however made the Indian system particularly oppressive and long-lasting was its iron-cast rigidity, its hereditary character and its philosophical validation and religious justification. Further, a priesthood founded on a principle of knowledge/power requires a class of dispossessed and disempowered masses to coexist with it. The idea of a privileged few intrinsically entails the counter-idea of the unprivileged, the under-privileged, the deprived and ignorant majority. Added to all this was a chandala mindset, a will to be subjugated and enslaved, a morbid urge to be in the service of the powerful. The priest's will to power always accompanied the will to pity, and self-pity.

The ascetic-priest, while being an epitome of the power principle, often presented himself as a man with the affectations of pity. (The idea of 'love' was not a part of the ethical or axiological vocabulary until much later, when the Bhakti saints began to use it probably under the influence of Muslim Sufis. But in their case, too, it was more a situation of love for God than love for man.) In the priestly Brahman retelling, Vishnu appeared in the guise of the Buddha, the embodiment of pity (again, not love). The purpose again was to disempower the Kshatriyas and, by extension, the rest of the populace. In the case of Buddhism, too, 'pity' (karuna) appears more as a metaphysical than ethical principle. Buddha was conceived in the Mahayana tradition not as a man of pity but himself a 'great pity' (mahakaruna), who, in the company of prajna (the void of consciousness), was the cause of the emergence of an everchanging, untethered world.

Even when the pity principle was practised as a moral precept, it took such extreme forms that it became distorted and deficient, to the extent that the whole effect was neutralised. For one thing, the will to pity was directed more towards animals than humans, as the reading of Jataka stories show. In the case of Jainism, pity exclusively meant being non-violent towards animals. In fact, the lower the form of animals, the higher the level of pity. (Even in the present day, the Jaina saints, while being extremely pitiful towards ants and insects, are in the forefront of giving moral, strategic and financial support to the forces of aggression and violence in the national polity).

Furthermore, the monk-priests also often made the strange claim that, while they had to strictly follow the principle of non-injury, being bound by their ascetic oath, the lay followers could injure and kill in the name of sectarian and 'national' interests. In taking this position, the adage 'guilt by association' does not come to their minds, nor does it appear to them that it completely reverses their position of absolute non-injury, with which they often distinguish themselves from the 'semitic' religions. Besides, this view borders on proclaiming a double-morality—one set of rules for the monks and another set for the laity. The people could still be violent even if such conduct incurs consequences.

The Shraman ethic, while emphasising non-aggression and non-violence, was also the ethics of non-resistance and surrender to the forces of oppression. The ascetic-priest preferred a conformity to the ideal of amoralism than moralism. This was because, while, to be rational and moral was to be human, the suprahuman idea required one to transcend morality itself. Prescriptive ethics, centred around the notion of dharma, was sought to be supplanted by the ideas of swa-dharma and swa-bhava, which in the present context meant caste-duty and the caste-nature of man. When there was a conflict between dharma and swa-dharma, it was the latter that was to be acted upon, as Krishna so emphatically and clearly counsels Arjuna in the *Gita*. The paradise, and the realisation of the *brahman*, is attained not so much by practicing dharma but by observing the dictates of one's swa-dharma or varna-dharma. Thus, the Pandavas who occasionally lapsed in thinking and talking in terms of dharma, had to go through the purgatory of hell, while Duryodhana went straight to heaven for observing his Kshatriya duty of fighting and dying in the battlefield.

The saint as being suprahuman was also supra-moral, i.e., beyond good and evil. For, once he had reached the stage of sthit-prajna, he was not the master of his own actions. Agency then belonged either to the *brahman* or to his own self/caste-nature. As suprahuman, he was beyond the restrictions of ordinary moral rules required for ordered living in society. He was neither good (as an ethical category) nor evil, and his actions were not his own. The transcendence, the supra-transcendence, implicated within itself the principle of transgression.

In sum, India's cultural tradition, as essentialised in its spiritual centre, and having the ascetic-priests as its gate-keepers, has survived the vicissitudes of time without losing its identity and continuity. The Shudras in this conspiratorial saga were the resources, 'the assets', to be used, abused, and then abandoned when they became of no use. They could even be eliminated if they turned 'rogue'—for resisting and being rebellious. The old gods faded but never disappeared, and the new gods that came on the scene were not totally new, and were just iterations of the old ones who stayed in the dark. In the present, a new supreme god has been invented/discovered which is not exactly native but an import from West. It has its rituals, its shrines and its priests, and it asks its believers to live and die for it. India has moved from the religion of nature worship to nation-worship and, as if not to admit a complete rupture, the latter is identified with the worship of mother goddesses like Durga and Kali. Both nature and nation are physical constructs, contingent realities, hypostatised in the minds of believers, but which a humanist will think of as in the service of man rather than the other way around.

India's story, even when not written out as a grand narrative, is still at a stage where the gods and goddesses, the saints and the priests, and kings and queens, play-act their respective roles and are themselves the spectators and cheering audiences. The Shudras, the ati-Shudras and neo-Shudras, as undeserving subhumans, are kept out, away from their sights. The cup of sacred wine in the yajna is to be rightfully offered only to the people of 'class', even as the masses, the Shudras, are supposed to be, deservedly, denied it.

Notes

Prologue

1 Note the different meanings of *brahman* and Brahman in this work. The italicised and lower-cased *brahman,* a category of knowledge, often used in relation to (or in conjunction with) atman, refers to the Advaita and Upanishadic concept of the fundamental reality encompassing all being. Brahman, on the other hand, refers to the caste. Brahmanas refer to the commentaries on the Vedas; italicised only when referring to specific texts such as *Satapata Brahmana.*

Chapter 1

1 For most of the citations from the *Rig Veda,* Ralph Griffith's translation (1896) has been followed.

2 'No evil spirits have impelled us, Indra, nor fiends, O Mightiest God, with their devices. Let our true God subdue the hostile rabble: let not the lewd approach our holy worship. (Griffith 1896; VII, 21.5) 'On most auspicious path he goes to battle he toiled to win heaven's light, full fain to gain it; He seized the hundred-gated castle's treasure by craft, unchecked, and slew the lustful demons' (Griffith 1896; X, 99.3).

3 'How unto the great Asura didst thou speak here? How, with shining manliness, unto the yellow (hari) father? Having given, O Varuna, a spotted [cow] as sacrificial fee, thou hast with the mind intended (? cikits) rebestowal (?). / Not at pleasure am I a

re-bestower; for examinations (?) do I drive home this spotted [cow]; by what poesy (kavya) now, O Atharvan, [art] thou [poet]? by what is produced (jata) art thou jatavedas?' (Whitney 1905; V, 11. 1–2). See also Ibid. VII, 104.

4   This from the Rig Veda: 'Who for ten milch-kine purchaseth from me this Indra who is mine? When he hath slain the Vrtras let the buyer give him back to me' (Griffith 1896; IV, 24.10).

5   'Sunk in the pit the Rsi Kutsa called, to aid, Indra the Vrtra-slayer, Lord of power and might. Even as a chariot from a difficult ravine, bountiful Vasus, rescue us from all distress (Griffith 1896; I, 106.6).

6   Griffith has, in his translation, omitted the relevant verses, perhaps finding it too obscene to translate.

7   '... and Indra is the Rishis' friend (muninam sakha)' (Griffith 1896; VIII, 18.14).

8   The image of Varuna, as depicted in these hymns, is in clear contrast with the image of Indra, who appears in the text, conspicuously enough, as a personification of unrestrained power and might, besides being a god who exults in consuming wine and fighting wars. The evidence for this is scattered across Vedic literature, and there is, therefore, no need to quote the verses here to substantiate the point. The following hymn from the Rig Veda may serve as a sample: 'Heroes with noble horses, fain for battle, selected warriors, call on me in combat. I Indra Maghavan, excite the conflict; I stir the dust, Lord of surpassing vigour. / All this I did. The Gods' own conquering power never impedeth me whom none opposeth... (Griffith 1896; IV, 42. 5–6). The clash between Varuna and Indra was essentially a clash between the forces of good and evil, which the two gods represented respectively. That Indra won the battle may have been a misfortune but it is a historical fact. One of its consequences was that the different priestly clans, who earlier owed allegiance to Varuna, came to the side of Indra after his victory. This victory is most lucidly

described in the following *Rig* hymn, where Agni (fire) finally decides to come to the side of Indra after deserting Varuna. 'I come a God foreseeing from the godless to immortality by secret pathways, While I, ungracious one, desert the gracious, leave mine own friends and seek the kin of strangers. / I, looking to the guest of other lineage, have founded many a rule of Law and Order. I bid farewell to the Great God, the Father, and, for neglect, obtain my share of worship. / I tarried many a year within this altar: I leave the Father, for my choice is Indra. Away pass Agni, Varuna and Soma. Rule ever changes: this I come to favour' (Griffith 1896; X, 124. 2–4). Having secured his victory, Indra even condescendingly offers Varuna a compromise, inviting him to share in the glory of the Aryans over the natives: 'These Asuras have lost their powers of magic. But thou, O Varuna, if thou dost love me, O King, discerning truth and right from falsehood, come and be Lord and Ruler of my kingdom. / Here is the light of heaven, here allis lovely; here there is radiance, here is air's wide region. Let us two slaughter Vrtra. Forth, O Soma! Thou art oblation: we therewith will serve thee' (Griffith 1896; X, 124. 5–6).

9   'Thy progeny will be distinguished by the characteristics of the Brahmana; for they will be ready to take gifts, thirsty after drinking (Soma), and hungry of eating food, and ready to roam about according to their pleasure... Thy offspring will be born with the characteristics of Vaishyas, paying taxes to another king, to be enjoyed by another; they will be oppressed according to the pleasure of the king... Thy progeny will have the characteristics of the Sudras, they are to serve another the three higher castes, to be expelled and beaten according to the pleasure (of their masters)' (Haug 1922, 332–3; 7.29).

10   '... He (Adhvaryu) walks round by the back of the hall, and placing one (of the cups) in the Vaisya's, or Raganya's hand, he says, 'with this I buy Him of thee' For the Soma is truth, prosperity, light; and the Sura is untruth, misery, darkness: he thus imbues the

sacrificer with the Truth, prosperity and light; and smites the Vaisya with untruth, misery, and darkness; Whatever benefit (or enjoyment) he desires, he obtains for himself by those (cups of Sura). But that cup of honey he presents to the Brahman, together with the golden vessel. In presenting it to the Brahman, he imbues himself with immortal life; for gold is immortal life; – and whatsoever benefit he desires that he thereby obtains for himself. / These eleven (kindling sticks) he puts on for one who is not either a noble, or a domestic chaplain (purohita); for incomplete are those eleven and incomplete is he who is not either a noble, or a domestic priest' (Eggeling 1882; 5, 1.28.11–2).

11 See for details Haq 1992, 317–19.

12 'Brahma arose as the first of the gods - The maker of all, the protector of the world. He told the knowledge of Brahma (Brahma-Vidya), the foundation of all knowledge; To Atharva (n), His eldest son. / What Brahma taught of Atharvan, Even that knowledge of Brahma, Atharavan told in ancient time to Angir, He told it to Bharadvaja Satyavaha; Bharadvaja, to Angiras - both the higher and the lower (knowledge)' (Hume 1877, 366; 1.1.1–2).

Chapter 2

1   This quote from the Jaina text, the *Kalpa Sutra*, which contains the biographies of the many tirthankaras: 'Mahavira has just become incarnate in the continent of Jambudvipa, in the region of Bharat Varsha, that part of Bharata which has in the south (of Meru), in the city of Kundagama, the Brahmanical division, in the womb of the Brahmani Devanandi, of the tribe of Jalandhra, the wife of the Brahman Rishabha Datta, of tribe of Kodola... After a little while, reflecting within himself on the subject before him, the following thoughts occurred to the mind of Sakra, prince and the king of the Gods; Surely such a thing as this never happened in past, happens

not in present, nor will happen in future time, that an Arhat, a chakravarti, a Baldeva, or a Vasudeva should be born in a low caste family, a servile family, a degraded family, a poor family, a mean family, a beggar's family or a Brahman's family; but, on the contrary, an Ikshavaku family as in the family of Ikshavaku, or the Harivansha family or some such of pure descent. The best thing that can be done is to withdraw the venerable and ascetic Mahavira from the womb of Devanandi and place him in that of Trisala, the Kshatnyam of the family of Vasistha, wife of Siddhartha the Kshatriya, of the family of Kashyapa, both of pure Kshatriya descent' (Stevenson 1972, 35–7).

2   That the creeds of Buddha, Jaina and such others were estimated as lowly by Brahmans is indicated in the following story in the *Bhagvata Purana*. King Prithu had organised a sacrificial ceremony conducted by Muni Atri. This is sought to be disturbed by Indra. The muni orders Indra to be killed. Indra flees but he is pursued by Prithu's son and, '[a]s Indra was quickly journeying through the sky along with the stolen horse Maharishi Atri again saw him so doing and he urged the Prince to kill Indra and to recover the horse... This time the prince did not chase Indra but in violent rage discharged a dreadful arrow at Indra. Thereupon, leaving off the stolen horse and his garb, Indra fled away... The forms of disguise left off by Indra at that time were all despicable ones and the persons of evil nature and weak understanding accepted them. All forms that Indra assumed for the purpose of stealing the sacrificial horse in disguised forms are therefore considered to be vile and generally adopted by persons known as Pashandas (impious ones). The guises so assumed and cast off by Indra for the purpose of stealing the horse with a view to thwarting the performance of Prithu's sacrifice have been the cause of unreligious creeds as professed by Jainas, Buddhas, and Kapalikas. Although such forms of faith differ widely from the true religion or truth, they attracted the attention of the people. Such creeds in

view of their intelligent arguments prove apparently charming to weak minds' (Sanyal 1973, 4).

Chapter 3

1 'The undiscerning who rejoice in the letter of the Veda, who contend that there is nothing else, whose nature is desire and who are intent on heaven, proclaim these flowery words that result in rebirth as the fruit of actions and (lay down) various specialised rites for the attainment of enjoyment and power' (Radhakrishnan 1960, 94).

2 'Though (I am) unborn, and My self (is) imperishable, though (I am) the lord of all creatures, yet establishing Myself in My own nature, I come into (empiric) being through My power (maya). [...] Whenever there is a decline of righteousness and rise of righteousness, O Bharata (Arjuna), then I send forth (create incarnate) Myself' (Radhakrishnan 1960, 126–7).

3 'Sages see with an equal eye, a learned and humble Brahmin, a cow, an elephant or even a dog or an outcast. [...] Even here (on earth) the created (world) is overcome by those whose mind is established in equality God is flawless and the same in all. Therefore are these (persons) established in God' (Radhakrishnan 1960, 148–9).

4 The story, as related in the *Shiva Purana* (Section II, Chapter 1), is as follows: 'Then Daksa the haughty, performed a sacrifice without Siva, although he had invited Visnu, me and all other devas. / Since he was in delusion he was very furious. So he did not invite Rudra and his own daughter Sati. He was greatly deluded by his own fate. [...] Though not invited by her haughty father she did go to her father's house securing the reluctant permission of Siva. / Seeing no share of Rudra set apart and being slighted by her father, she reproached all those who were present there and cast off her

body. / On hearing that, lord Siva became unbearably furious and pulling at his matted hair he created Virabhadra. / When he was created along with attendants he began asking "What shall I do?" The entire annihilation of Daksa's sacrifice and the disgrace of every one present there was the order issued by Siva. / The lord of the Ganas (Virabhadra) accompanied by his soldiers reached the place immediately after receiving the orders. / They worked a great havoc there. Virabhadra chastised everyone and spared none. / After defeating Vishnu and the Devas with strenuous effort, the chief of Ganas cut off the head of Daksa and consigned it to sacrificial fire' (Shastri 1970, 276–7).

5   This from the *Shiva Purana*: "Formerly on seeing my daughter Sandhya in the company of my sons I was afflicted by the arrows of cupid and much upset. / When remembered by Dharma, Rudra, the highest lord and greatest yogin came there. He reproached me as well as my sons and went back to His abode. [...] Under great delusion and goaded by the envious feelings towards the lord I conspired with my sons to find out ways and means to delude the lord Himself. Here again I was deluded by Siva's Maya. / O great sage, in Siva the great lord, all those ways and means pursued by me and my sons became ineffective. / When my strategy failed [...] I humbly served Sakti and when she was pleased I created her as the daughter of Daksa [...] This was my endeavour to make Hara (Shiva) enamoured of her. / The goddess Uma became Daksa's daughter [...] became Rudra's wife [...] Rudra became a householder and the, great lord performed divine sports' (Shastri 1970, 275–6).

6   In Section I, Chapter 8, of the *Shiva Purana*, a story goes that once Brahma and Vishnu had a chance meeting and introduced each other as the lord of the universe. A fierce clash followed, attracting the attention of other heavenly gods, who requested Shiva to intervene. Only too willing, Shiva came upon the scene of the battle and transformed himself into a column of radiant

light. The two disputing deities, surprised at the appearance of the strange entity, decided to resolve their dispute on the condition that the one who could scale the column and reach its top or bottom would be declared the winner. Vishnu couldn't succeed and admitted defeat. But Brahma, who also failed, played a trick. Pretending that he had reached the top, he presented the Ketaki flower as false evidence for his claim. Vishnu was duped but not Shiva, who had created the illusion. Appearing in person, he praised Vishnu for speaking the truth. For Brahma, the following punishment was meted:

> Mahadeva then created a wonderful person, Bhairava, from the middle of his brows to quell the pride of Brahma. / This Bhairava knelt before the lord in the battle-field and said—"O lord, what shall I do?..." / "Dear, here is Brahma, the first deity of the universe. Worship him with your sharp-pointed, quick moving sword." / With one of his hands he caught hold of the tuft of Brahma' s fifth head that was guilty of haughtily uttering a falsehood, and with the hands he furiously shook his sword in order to cut it off. / Your father trembled... and fell at the feet of Bhairava. ... [The lord then relented and turning the deceitful Brahma said:] "O Brahma, in order to extort honour from the people you assumed that role of the lord in a roguish manner. ./ Hence you shall not be honoured, nor shall you have your own temple or festival (Shastri 1970, 58).

It is indeed significant that of all the gods Brahma alone has no temple dedicated to him anywhere in India, except in one place in Rajasthan.

7   *Silpa Prakasa*, a medieval Sanskrit text from Orissa by Ramacandra Kaulacara, says: 'In connections with this, hear the descriptions of the *kama-bandha* which I am describing according to the Silpa doctrine (Silpavidya): / Love is the root of the universe. From love all beings are born. Primordial elements and all beings are reabsorbed again in love. / Without Siva and Sakti creation would

be nothing but mere imagination. Without Kama there would be no birth or death. / Siva himself is visibly manifested as the Mahalinga, and Sakti in the form of Bhaga (womb). By their union the whole universe comes into being. This is called the action of love (kama-kriya). / The science of kamakala (kamakalavidya) is an extensive subject in the Agamas. A place without love-images is known as a "place to be shunned". / In the tradition of the Kaulacara it is always a base, forsaken place, resembling a dark abyss, which is shunned like the den of Death. / Without offering puja to the kamakala-yantra, the Sakti puja and the sadhana become as useless as the bath of an elephant. / The shrine on which that yantra is standing is a Viramandira. Through this yantra all obstacles and fears are certainly destroyed. / Ghosts (bhutas), departed spirits (pretas), goblins (pisacas), fearful demons (kaunapas) and other hideous creatures will flee far away at the mere sight of the yantra. / Hear me, I am speaking about this carefully kept secret with should never be given to any one who is not an initiate of Kaulacara' (Boner and Sarma 1966, 327–9).

8   In his Sri Bhasya, Ramanuja says: 'This opinion of persons who are devoid of those special qualities which make one worthy of the choice of the Highest Person who is taught in the Upanishads—of those (persons) whose understanding is, in its entirety, tainted with the innate impression of beginninglessly ancient sins, and who are ignorant of the essential nature of words and sentences and their correct meanings, and (are ignorant) also of such sound logical process... [and] based upon perception and all other (well known) criteria of truth,—...this opinion of such persons... deserves to be disregarded by all those who are conversant with that knowledge of truth [and] are supported by logic' (Rangacharya and Varadacharya 1899, 53–4).

9   See also Vishnu Purana (V.1. 14) and (V. 37. 69-71).

10 A passage in the Gita Govind, whose songs are often used in devadasi traditions, and even in contemporary dance performances,

goes: 'So the encounter in love began, When the shuddering of
bodies hindered firm embrace; where the joy of complementing
one another with searching looks was interrupted by blinkings;
where the mutual sipping of the honey of each other's lips was
impeded by the utterances of small love cries. Yet even these
seeming hindrances enhanced the delight in love-play, / Though
entwined in her arms though crushed by the weight of her
breasts though smitten by her fingernails though bitten by her
small teeth though overwhelmed by the thrust of her thighs his
locks seized the nectar of her lips he drew immense pleasure from
such sweet torments. Strange indeed are the ways of love! / She
desired to triumph over her lover in the delirious encounter of
love and launched a bold offensive above him. But by this alone,
in a little while her lips were still her vine-like arms grew languid
her chest was heaving her eyes were closed. How does a women
succeed manly force? / Blessed is he, who drinks the honey of the
lips of the gazelle-eyed Radha embracing her breasts made firm
by her indrawn sigh, her cheeks quivering with delight her eyes
closing lagour her mouth half-open saying delirious words of love
the lustre of her pearly teeth illuminating of her lips her body
filled with serene delight' (Mukhopadhyay 1980).

References

Boner, Alice and Sadasiva Rath Sarma. 1966. *Silpa Prakasa of Ramacandra Mahapatra Kaula Bhattaraka*. Leiden: Leiden Publishing.

Bühler, Georg. 1882. *The Sacred Laws of the Aryas, Part II*. Oxford: The Clarendon Press.

Cowell, E. B., F. Max Müller and J. Takakusu. 1894. *Buddhist Mahayana Texts*. Oxford: The Clarendon Press.

Eggeling, Julius. 1882. *The Satapatha-Brahmana*. Oxford: The Clarendon Press.

Fausböll, V. 1881. *The Sutta-Nipata*. Oxford: The Clarendon Press.

Gambhiranand, Swami. 1965. *Brahma-Sutra-Bhasya of Sri Sankaracharya*. Calcutta: Advaita Ashram.

Ganguli, Kisari Mohan. 1883–1896. *The Mahabharata of Krishna-Dwaipayana Vyasa*. Calcutta: Bharata Press.

Griffith, Ralph T.H. 1896. *The Rig Veda*. Benares: E.J. Lazarus.

Haq, Jalalul. 1992. *Nation and Nation-Worship In India*. New Delhi: Genuine Publications.

Haug, Martin. 1922. *The Aitareya Brahmanam of the Rigveda*. Allahabad: Panini Office.

Hume, R.E. 1877. *The Thirteen Principal Upanishads*. Oxford: Oxford University Press.

Jacobi, Hermann. 1884. *Gaina Sutras: Part I—The Akaranga Sutra, The Kalpa Sutra*. Oxford: The Clarendon Press.

———. 1895. *Gaina Sutras, Part II—The Uttaradhyayana Sutra, The*

Sutrakritanga Sutra. Oxford: The Clarendon Press.

Joseph, Tony. 2018. *Early Indians: The Story of Our Ancestors and Where We Came From*. New Delhi: Juggernaut Books.

Mukhopadhyay, Durgadas. 1980. *In Praise of Krishna: Gita Govinda*. New Delhi: Manimax Pub.

Müller, F. Max. 1879. *The Upanishads, Part I*. Oxford: The Clarendon Press.

———. 1881. *The Dhammapada*. Oxford: The Clarendon Press.

Radhakrishnan, S. 1960. *The Bhagavadgita*. London: Unwin.

Rangacharya, M. and M.B. Varadacharya Aiyangar. 1899. *The Vedanta-Sutras with the Sri Bhasya of Ramanujacharya, Vol. I*. Madras: The Brahmanvadin Press.

Rhys Davids, T.W. 1881. *Buddhist Suttas*. Oxford : The Clarendon Press.

———. 1890. *The Questions of King Milinda*. London: Oxford University Press.

———. 1894. *The Questions of King Milinda, Part II*. London: Oxford University Press.

———. 1899. *Dialogues of the Buddha, Part I*. London: Oxford University Press.

———. 1899. *Brahma-Gala Sutta*. London: Oxford University Press.

———. 1921. *Dialogues of the Buddha, Part III*. London: Oxford University Press.

Rhys Davids, T.W. and Hermann Oldenberg. 1885. *Vinaya Texts, Part III: The Kullavagga, IV–XII*. Oxford: The Clarendon Press.

Saktidharan, A.V. 2019. *Antigod's Own Country: A Short History of Brahminical Colonisation of Kerala*. Delhi: Navayana.

Sanyal, J. M. 1929. *The Srimad-Bhagabatam of Krishna-Dwaipayana Vyasa, Vol. 1*. Bengal: Datta Bose and Co.

———. 1973. *The Srimad-Bhagabatam of Krishna-Dwaipayana Vyasa, Vol. 4*. Calcutta: Oriental Publishing.

———. 1973. *The Srimad-Bhagabatam of Krishna-Dwaipayana Vyasa, Vol. 5*. Calcutta: Oriental Publishing.

Sastri, A.M. 1947. *The Bhagavad Gita with the Commentary of Sri Sankaracharya*. Madras: Samata Books.

Shastri, J. L. 1960. *The Lingapurana, Part 1: Ancient Indian Tradition And Mythology, Vol. 5*. New Delhi: Motilal Banarsidass.

———. 1970. *The Siva-Purana, Vol. I*. New Delhi: Motilal Banarsidass.

Speyer, J.S. 2010. *Jatakamala or Garland of Birth-Stories by Aryasura*. Electronic Edition.

Stevenson, J. 1972. *The Kalpa Sutra*. Varanasi: D.D. Bharat-Bharati.

Tagare, G.V. 1981. *The Kurma-Purana–Part I*. New Delhi: Motilal Banarsidass.

Thibaut, George. 1904. *The Vedanta-Sutras with the Commentary by Ramanuja*. Oxford: The Clarendon Press.

Walshe, Maurice. 1995. *The Long Discourses of the Buddha*. Boston: Wisdom Publications.

Whitney, W.D. 1905. *Atharva-Veda Samhita*. Cambridge: Harvard University.

Index

absolute, 8–9, 93, 100, 104, 108–9, 165, 172, 183, 194–6, 202–3, 207, 211–4, 250: and *brahman*, 8–9, 93, 211–4, 250; and the Buddha, 108–9, 172; and the *Gita*, 183; and gradation, 104, 202–3; and Jaina, 165; and Krishna, 183; and Logos, 100; and mahasukha, 172; and non-absolute, 194, 203, 207, 213; and Radhakrishnan, 183; and Samkhya, 165; and Shankara, 211–4; and Shiva, 9, 194–6, 202–3, 207; and Vishnu, 9

Aditi, 61–3, 70, 75, 101: and Adityas, 70; and Tvashtra, 62–3

Aditya, 70, 75–6, 79, 99–100, 100–1: and Saraswati, 100–1; as the sun, 99–100

Advaita, 223, 225, 226–7, 231, 259n1: and idealism, 226–7; and non-duality, 223; and Ramanuja, 225, 226–7; and Shankara, 223, 225

Agastya, 57, 67, 69. *See also* rishi

Aghoris, 198. *See also* Shiva

Agni, 41, 54, 57–8, 59, 61–2, 69, 71, 73–4, 98, 100–1, 195, 260–1n8: and Angirases, 57–9; and fire in sacrifice; 57–8, 98; and munis, 41; and Varuna, 61–2, 260–1n8

Ajatasatru, 89, 95–6, 110: and atman, 89; and Brahmans, 95–6; and Gargya, 95–6

Ajivikas, 113, 121–2: and ascetics, 113; and Buddhism, 113, 121–2

Akbar, 20

Allah, 27, 96

Ambedkar, B.R., 16

Ananda, 162, 163–4, 167, 178–9: and questions of indulgence, 162, 178–9

anekantavada, 174

Angirases, 51, 57–9: Angiras, 67–8, 86, 134, 262n12: and Bhrigu, 57, 58–9; and fire, 59, 67–8; and Indra, 57–9; and indulgence, 134; and magic, 57–8; and rishis crossing sides, 51, 57–8; and sacrifice, 57–8

Apsaras, 53, 60, 69